SOCIAL BEHAVIOR and PERSONALITY

Acknowledgments

It is a pleasure for me to give credit to three people who helped considerably in the writing of this book. Stephen Finn read the entire manuscript and David Buss read several chapters; their comments were valuable. Laurie Durante typed the entire manuscript and saved me from many mistakes.

SOCIAL BEHAVIOR and PERSONALITY

Arnold H. Buss
University of Texas

 LAWRENCE ERLBAUM ASSOCIATES, PUBLISHERS
1986   Hillsdale, New Jersey   London

Lawrence Erlbaum Associates, Inc., Publishers
365 Broadway
Hillsdale, New Jersey 07642

Library of Congress Cataloging in Publication Data

Buss, Arnold H., 1924–
    Social behavior and personality.

    Bibliography: p.
    Includes indexes.
    1. Interpersonal relations. 2. Personality--Social
aspects. I. Title. [DNLM: 1. Personality. 2. Psychological Theory. 3. Social Behavior. BF 698 B981s]
HM132.B86   1986   155.2   85-29331
ISBN 0-89859-812-5

Printed in the United States of America
10 9 8 7 6 5 4 3 2 1

Contents

For Jared, Gannon,
and Ryan

SOCIAL BEHAVIOR and PERSONALITY

1 Introduction

The *Journal of Personality and Social Psychology* has separate sections devoted to social psychology and to personality psychology, a division that reflects the different goals and methods of the respective psychologists. Most of those who study social behavior focus on the processes assumed to underlie such behavior, and they tend to neglect the personality traits of their subjects. Most of those who study personality focus on the dimensions of individual differences and tend to neglect the social contexts and processes that are important determinants of behavior. There are exceptions, to be sure, but two adjacent areas of investigation are usually cut off from each other. The isolation may originate in the separate historical development of each field and in the way students are trained to specialize in particular areas of study. These reasons notwithstanding, social behavior is influenced by personality dispositions, and personality traits can emerge from enduring, oft-repeated social contexts, and so there must be value in considering the two fields together.

This book is not the first to make this attempt. Carson (1969) attempted to integrate a social psychological theory with two personality theories. The social psychological theory was the exchange theory of Thibaut and Kelley (1959), which assigns rewards and costs in dyadic relationships and attempts quantitative predictions about outcomes through the use of cost-benefit matrices. One personality conception was Sullivan's (1953) interpersonal approach to personality and abnormal behavior. The other was the taxonomy of interpersonal traits introduced by Leary (1957).

A recent book by Aronoff and Wilson (1985) is more ambitious and detailed in its specification of social behavior. It resembles Carson's book in using one major personality conception, that of Murray (1938), though the theories of Maslow, Freud, Fromm, Jung, and Erikson are also cited. The book also uses modern concepts and research on social perception, information processing, and attraction. In addition to dyadic behavior, it attempts to explain group processes.

Veroff and Veroff (1980) offer their own personality theory, using stages of development to integrate social motives (which they call incentives). Not all their motives are social in nature, but three of them are, and the flavor of their approach may be seen in the following quotations about these three. Concerning *attachment,* "The organism learns to enjoy attachment to certain others. The major reason this attachment incentive is generated is because familiar others anchor growing infants, who must often experience their burgeoning cognitive experiences as sea of overstimulation" (p. 23). Concerning *social relatedness,* "The major basis of reinforcement of this social incentive is the pleasure and approval of significant others . . . any time a person considers that his own actions will be evaluated by others, the person will have the potential for experiencing a social-relatedness incentive" (p. 25). Concerning *belongingness,* it arises from "the child's growing exploration of how he fits into the social system; where he belongs, who his reference groups are, what he is likely to achieve, how other people will react to him" (p. 25).

These three books do not exhaust the approaches that might be used to integrate personality with social behavior, nor do they exhaust the field of social behavior. Furthermore, it is assumed here that no single conception or pair of conceptions can adequately account for the variety of social behaviors and personality traits. It seems preferable to keep one's options open and to inquire about which theoretical conception is especially applicable to a particular domain of social behavior or personality. Of particular relevance are ideas about the origin of social behaviors and personality traits. Social psychological theories tend to be curiously silent about the origin of social behaviors or their developmental course, but an attempt to fill this gap would be beyond the scope of this book. Personality theories, however, do discuss the source of personality traits, usually in terms of development.

MODELS OF PERSONALITY

The term *models* is used deliberately, for none of the traditional theories of personality are discussed here. There is considerable debate about their importance beyond material for textbooks and courses on theories of personality. The traditional theories, although perhaps worthwhile as general theories of personality, are not oriented specifically to the study of social behavior. As a general background for what follows, however, two models of the origins of personality traits require discussion.

The *passive* model assumes that the environment acts directly on individuals to produce personality traits, and each person is an available vessel into which personality contents are poured. The psychological processes that mediate these environmental effects are classical conditioning, instrumental conditioning, observational learning, and cognitive learning. For social behavior, families presumably play a crucial role, and a large research effort has focused on how one family differs from the next. The net result of this research has been a consensus that differences among families contribute little to the development of personality traits, and the place to look may be within families (Buss & Plomin, 1984). Families are not the only source of environmental effects, and it is known from research on twins that the environment contributes substantially to personality traits (Loehlin & Nichols, 1976). These authors, however, after reviewing their own and others' research, concluded that, "in the personality domain we seem to see environmental effects that operate almost randomly with respect to the sorts of variables that psychologists (and other people) have traditionally deemed important in personality development" (p. 92).

Part of the problem may reside in the passive model, which is beguiling in its simplicity and its appeal to psychologists who tend to manipulate environmental variables. Few psychologists seriously doubt that the environment has an impact on personality, but it is becoming increasingly clear that the recipient of this impact is not an organism that will accommodate to just any environmental determinant.

The solution is to add the *active* model, which assumes that individuals are curious and manipulative, and they are major determiners of what happens to them. One origin of individual differences is genetic endowment, which can lead to personality traits not only directly but also through interaction with the environment (Buss & Plomin, 1984; Scarr & McCartney, 1983). Whatever the source of personality traits, once established they can modify and interact with the environment, especially the social environment, as follows.

Adults often select work environments, which can vary from the sociable atmosphere of sales work to the isolation of the starwatching of astronomers. They can decide whether to play group or individual sports and competitive or noncompetitive games. They can choose to attend parties or remain home alone with the television set. Students can study with classmates or alone. Although the options of children are more limited, they also can choose playmates, sports, games, and other avocations that vary in sociality, competition, skill, and excitement. Some people schedule their lives so that there is no free time and they are always under pressure, whereas others avoid taking on demanding tasks and therefore live in a more relaxed environment. This is not to say that there are unlimited choices but only that we at least partly determine the environments that can affect us.

Individuals are of course elements of the social environment and can therefore set the tone for social behavior. Consider two people in conversation about to be joined by a third person. The pair might be talking volubly and excitedly or hardly conversing at all; their faces might be contorted in anger or smiling in friendship. Thus, the ambience of the social situation that confronts the third person has been established by the personalities and interaction of the two participants. When there is a party, the guests often know in advance that it probably will be dull and lifeless or exciting and perhaps even dangerous. In many social contexts, then, the tone for social behavior often is set by the participants.

When in a social context, each of us reacts to the behavior of others, thereby affecting what they do presently and subsequently. Thus a humorist may find the jokes greeted by roaring laughter or silence and polite smiles. Attempts at conversation can result in eager responsivity or thinly disguised rejection. Each of us repeatedly rewards or punishes the social behavior of others, that is, provides an environment that has consequences for subsequent social encounters and perhaps even for personality.

The active model also implies that the impact of the environment will be modified by the personality of the recipient. If a sociable person is thrown in with a group of people and must interact with them, this environment matches the need established by the personality trait, and the person should be content, even happy. If an unsociable person is forced to be in such an environment, the mismatch may cause annoyance and strain. For some people, a safe job laden with routine fits their needs for order and security, whereas excitement seekers would find such a job tedious and boring.

Social interaction provides an especially important environment, and the parent–child dyad provides appropriate examples. Suppose a parent tends to dominate a child, demanding exact obedience. One child may agree with the parental demands, another may be coerced into submission, a third may respond with surly compliance, and a fourth may openly rebel. The impact of a consistently domineering parent is likely to depend on the child's prior personality, and the enduring outcome might range from abject submissiveness to aggressive rebelliousness. Similarly, a child might react to head-to-head competition as something to be feared because of likely failure or as a challenge that might establish superiority.

Thus the active model suggests several types in interactions between person and environment. The individual can select from an array of environments, set the tone for the social behavior of others, or become part of the environment by acting as a reinforcing agent. Any particular environment, especially social contexts, can affect people in divergent ways, which means that each person may modify the impact of the environment. These interactions are especially important for social behavior, which by definition occurs in a social environment.

WHAT THIS BOOK IS ABOUT

In this volume, social behaviors and contexts are analyzed, and distinctions are suggested. Social behaviors not previously seen as similar are linked. The conceptions of others are borrowed but typically applied to a narrower domain than heretofore. The emphasis, however, is on original formulations.

Not all social behavior is examined. The focus is on the interpersonal behavior that occurs in face-to-face interaction. Not all interpersonal behavior is appropriate for the task, and two criteria determine inclusion: The social behavior must be important in everyday life, and personality traits must be strongly involved. Presumably, the two criteria are correlated, for if a given social behavior is significant in everyday life, it is likely to be affected by personality traits.

A sketchy account of the various topics furnishes examples of the general approach. What are the truly social rewards, the ones that can be obtained only from others directly, in contrast to those that can be obtained impersonally as well? Two types of such rewards are suggested, together with an exposition of their dimensions, occurrence during development, and their linkage with relationships.

The primordial social relationship is the mother–infant bond. It has implications for the origin of self-esteem, and it shares features with adult attachments. Concerning dominance, there are four means of achieving it. Each has its own rewards, its own impact on others, and its own associated personality traits. Prosocial behavior is examined from the twin perspectives of social and cognitive maturity. Altruism is examined from several perspectives, and multiple parental roles are viewed in light of knowledge about altruism, dominance, and social rewards.

The self in social interaction can be observed, but there are also implicit private aspects of the self that are either kept from others or allowed to become public. The contingencies of social behavior may reinforce social manipulation, but we need to specify the individuals who tend to manage impressions or adhere closely to social rules, the details of these behaviors, and the conditions under which they are likely to occur.

Social anxiety, which is discomfort in social contexts, is an important aspect of social behavior, especially early in the acquaintance process. An examination of both infant and adolescent behavior reveals the presence of two kinds of shyness, one starting early in life and one starting later. The other major variety of social anxiety is speech anxiety, one of the most frequent fears in the population. These various issues converge on the concept of attention from others, which can be aversive for those who are socially anxious or rewarding for exhibitionists.

Most research and theory centers on the content of social behavior and the processes underlying it. The stylistic aspect of social behavior, the how of responses, plays an important role in our impact on others, including their perceptions of us. Two conceptions are offered, one for the physical elements of style and one for the psychological dimensions of style.

Ordinarily, each chapter would start with a review of previous work, followed by the particular contributions of this book. This sequence would not work here, however, because the reader would be lost in a review of literature presented prior to the integrating conceptions that would give the review coherence and meaning. Therefore, the usual sequence is reversed, and each chapter starts with and consists mainly of original conceptions or the integration (or reformulation) of past conceptions. Previous work that is highly relevant is summarized at the end of each chapter in a section called Notes.

When personality traits are mentioned in published work on social behavior, the traits are usually named and the trait measure is cited, but the reader rarely knows precisely what was assessed. The items in a self-report questionnaire may not reflect its name, or the scale may contain several different kinds of items, leaving a reader to wonder what the trait really is. One solution is to present sufficient details of the trait measure for the reader to see exactly what is being assessed, and that is done here. The first time a personality trait is mentioned, the personality scale is presented. Thereafter, whenever the trait is mentioned, there is only a literature citation, but all the trait measures mentioned in the book also appear in an alphabetical appendix.

This solution imposes two limitations on the selection of measures of personality traits. The first is that they can be published here, which excludes omnibus personality inventories and some other questionnaires as well. The second is that virtually all the measures are self-report questionnaires, not because they dominate the field but because they provide the reader with a reasonable idea of the content of the trait. Projective techniques, for instance, require complex scoring or coding, and copyright laws prevent displaying the stimulus materials. When there are several self-report measures of the same trait, these criteria are used to select one: use of standard psychometric procedures and appropriateness to the social behavior with which the personality trait is linked.

Finally, there are two kinds of personality traits discussed: inputs and outputs. The major emphasis is on traits that affect interpersonal behavior (inputs), but also included are personality traits likely to emerge from social interactions that occur over months and years (outputs).

NOTES

Theories of Social (Interpersonal) Behavior

Two theories derive from sociology. The first is role theory, which uses the analogue of stage performance. People in everyday life play social and vocational roles in a manner analogous to an actor playing a stage role: "Individuals in society occupy positions, and their role performance in these positions is determined by social norms, demands, and rules; by the role performances of others in their respective positions; by those who observe and react to the performance; and by the individual's particular capabilities and personality" (Thomas & Biddle, 1966, p. 4). There are societal expectations for social roles, and one of the major determinants of how closely role performance approximates expectations is the personality of the person who plays the role.

The stage metaphor is also involved in the other sociological conception, self-presentation. Presumably, just as an actor conveys impressions of a particular character to the audience, so in everyday life an individual conveys particular self-images to others, thereby managing the impressions they receive. For some social psychologists, impression management is the central and incontrovertible aspect of social interaction (Schlenker, 1980). In bare outline, managing impressions requires: "(a) an awareness of the interpretations that others place upon our acts, (b) a desire to maintain face or the appropriate situated identity, (c) a wide range of self-presentational skills, and (d) the willingness to use this repertoire of impression-management strategies" (Snyder, 1981, p. 120).

Another perspective emphasizes the motivational basis of social behavior. One focus is on the rewards that can be obtained in social interaction: the kindliness or physical attractiveness of others; their approval, agreement, or praise; their assistance in obtaining goods or escaping from danger; and the pleasures of social relaxation, the stimulation of conversation, or the excitement of a party (Lott & Lott, 1974). The way these rewards are balanced against costs and the consequences for relationships constitute the thrust of exchange theory (Thibaut & Kelley, 1959).

Another focus within the motivational perspective is on needs or instincts. The instincts may be of the Freudian variety, or the innate tendencies may be the primary drives of learning theorists, but in terms of social behavior the most relevant innate motivational tendencies are those posited by ethologists in their attempt to understand animal behavior. Some ethologists believe that in motivational terms, humans are just like other animals. Thus Lorenz (1966) views aggression as an instinct or drive that must be discharged. In the course of evolution, conspecifics developed appeasement behavior, which temporarily turned off aggressive drive, and when appeasement responses evolved into rituals, they became the basis for the love bond. In a similar vein, Eibl-Eibesfeldt (1971) assumes that evolution has produced strong, friendly, loving, and aggressive tendencies that are built in and must be expressed in behavior. Most psychologists regard these views as applying more to animals than to humans. There is a general agreement, however, on a built in tendency of humans to form attachments, starting in infancy (Bowlby, 1969), and there is strong evidence from research on primates that deprivation of the opportunity to form attachments causes abnormal social behavior (Harlow & Harlow, 1962).

Currently, cognitive theories of social behavior are receiving the most attention by social psychologists. Social behavior is assumed to be mediated and caused by hypotheses, expectations, attributions and in general, by the processing of information. Darley and Fazio (1980) have outlined how cognitions can determine interpersonal behavior, starting with an initial assumption that the perceiver has somehow developed expectancies about the target person:

> (2) The perceiver then acts toward the target person in a way that is in accord with his or her expectancies of the target person. (3) Next, the target interprets the meaning of the perceiver's action. (4) Based on the interpretation, the target responds to the perceiver's action, and (5) the perceiver interprets the target's action. At this point the perceiver again acts toward the target person and so can be regarded as reentering the interaction sequence at Step 2. (p. 868)

This attempt to describe the self-fulfilling nature of dyadic interaction is a good representative of cognitive theories, which emphasize perceptions, expectancies, attributions, and their impact on social behavior.

This summary of theories of social behavior has leaned heavily on quotations both to avoid the possibility of misinterpretation and to offer the flavor of each approach. There is a tendency among theorists and their adherents to extend theories beyond the area from which they originated. This expansionist tendency is understandable, for we seek theories of the greatest generality. The net effect in our field, however, has been to weaken theories by extrapolating them to areas of behavior to which they may not apply.

Interpersonal Dimensions.   For several decades psychologists have been aligning the personality traits that refer to interpersonal behavior along two axes to form an interpersonal circle. Traits adjacent or close on the circle are positively correlated; the wider the separation, the lower the correlation. Traits at opposite sides of the circle are negatively correlated. The best known of these attempts at a taxonomy of interpersonal traits is that of Wiggins (1979), which includes the following bipolar dimensions: ambitious-dominant versus lazy-submissive, arrogant-calculating versus unassuming-ingenuous, cold-quarrelsome versus warm-aggreeable, and aloof-introverted versus gregarious-extraverted.

Similar taxonomies have been suggested by Becker and Krug (1964), Benjamin (1974), Carson (1969), Conte and Plutchik (1981), Kiesler (1983), Leary (1957), and Lorr and McNair (1963, 1965). There is agreement on one of the axes of the interpersonal circle: dominance-submission or one of its variants, such as power versus autonomy. Concerning the other axis, there is agreement only on its valence being positive versus negative. One group of theorists emphasizes the affective aspect of this axis: love versus hate, friendly versus hostile, and warm versus cold. The other group focuses on the instrumental aspects of aggression or its opposite: quarrelsome versus agreeable.

There are of course other ways to classify interpersonal traits, and Kelley (1983) has offered a scheme based on three kinds of interpersonal processes. The first kind changes dependence on the partner and is linked to the traits of affiliation-aloofness, involved-detached, and gregarious-withdrawn. The second kind alters the commonality of interest and is linked to loving-hating, warm-hostile, and cooperative-competitive. The third kind leads to shifts between individual and joint control and is linked to dominant-submissive, assertive-accommodating, and defiant-compliant.

2 Social Rewards

What are the incentives that motivate people to seek one another? One is defense against threat, the group being a more powerful deterrent than an individual. Another is seeking help in performing a task, cooperation succeeding when individual effort is insufficient. People may wish to engage in social comparison to check out the normativeness of their affective reactions or to validate social reality. They may seek guidance and control from others, preferring at least a minimal social structure in which they are directed and therefore do not have to make decisions, a phenomenon called *escape from freedom* (Fromm, 1941). They may also wish to barter goods, services, or information.

Social incentives are relevant to social psychological theories that emphasize the balance of rewards (Thibaut & Kelley, 1959), the equity of rewards (Walster, Walster, & Berscheid, 1978), and the role of rewards in interpersonal attitudes (Lott & Lott, 1974). With rare exceptions, however, no one has compiled a list of the appropriate rewards or suggested which are balanced or which are involved in equity. One exception is a book on social incentives by Veroff and Veroff (1980). What they call "incentives," however, would be labelled *social motives* by most psychologists, as may be seen by two on their list: curiosity and integrity. Although these incentives are relevant to broader issues of social behavior, they are not relevant here.

The other exception is a list of interpersonal resources by Foa and Foa (1974). In their developmental schema, the initial resource received by an infant is an undifferentiated combination of warmth, softness, food, and care. This diffuse pattern differentiates during infancy into service and love. Service, which consists of caring for the infant, differentiates during childhood into goods, and then goods differentiate into money. Meanwhile, love differentiates into status, from which information splits off. The outcome of these developmental processes is six interpersonal resources: services, goods, and money in one subgroup, and love, status, and information in the other. They are also classified along a dimension of *particularism,* which refers to whether the resource depends on the person who offers it. Status, love, and services usually depend on who is dispensing them and so are more particularistic than are information, money, and goods, which may be received from virtually anyone. The other, presumably orthogonal dimension is *concreteness,* which is roughly synonymous with tangibility. Services and goods are tangible, love and money are less so, and information and status are the least concrete.

These interpersonal resources and the dual classification comprise a promising approach to social rewards, one that has spurred research on social perceptions of the rewards (Turner, Foa, & Foa, 1971). On examination, however, the list appears to consist of two kinds of rewards. Four of them—money, goods, services, and information—can be bought and sold every day in the marketplace. Money can buy any of the other three, or they can be bartered for one another. As such they are economic rewards, which may involve social interaction, but they are not specifically interpersonal rewards. Thus, love is ordinarily not exchanged for money, not even in a bordello, sex obviously being different from affection. Love and status are clearly interpersonal rewards and belong on any such list. What these authors call "status" might better be labelled *praise,* as may be seen in a typical status item (Turner et al., 1971), "The person praises you." Praise may be offered for good performance, whether the job involves money, goods, services, or information, but these four are ordinarily not exchanged for praise.

The thrust of this argument is that four rewards on the list by Foa and Foa (1974) are economic rewards that may be obtained nonsocially as well as socially. Money can be extracted from bank machines, goods may be purchased through the mails, services can be performed in the absence of the owner (one's car, for instance), and information is available in books, newspapers, and television. They are not intrinsically social rewards but economic resources, a distinction that harks back to Goffman's (1961) differentiation of social exchange from economic exchange. Affection and praise are truly social rewards, for they can be obtained only in social contexts. Such rewards are ordinarily delivered only in the context of a relationship, such as that among family, friends, or lovers. These relationships have been labelled *communal,* in contrast to *exchange* relationships (Clark & Mills, 1979). These researchers showed that when a communal relationship (friendship) was desired, receiving an economic reward diminished liking for the donor.

Social rewards also occur among strangers in social contexts involving no particular interpersonal relationship, and the list is not limited to affection and praise, powerful though these two may be. Two major classes of social reinforcers are distinguished: stimulation rewards and affective rewards.

STIMULATION REWARDS

Presence of Others

Our species is highly social, and we usually avoid extended periods of isolation. Thus, the mere presence of others is a reward, though it may appear superfluous to label it a *social reward* when such presence defines social behavior. Nevertheless, this reward resembles other benefits in that humans and social animals seek it.

When others are present, there is often a shared activity, even when no interaction occurs. People watch television and movies together, attend concerts, football games, and convention speeches in crowded halls, browse through art museums together, and even study together. Most people prefer to share activities, even eating meals, rather than to perform them alone.

The presence of others, like all the stimulation rewards, may be regarded as a dimension that is aversive at the extremes and pleasurable in the middle. The complete absence of others is unpleasant enough to be used to punish children with temporary isolation or criminals with the isolation cell. At the opposite extreme, the excessive presence of others shrinks personal space and denies privacy. A crowded elevator or bus squeezes strangers into physical contact, and an overpopulated cafeteria affords little room to eat or converse. The issues of crowding and privacy have been extensively researched (Altman, 1975; Freedman, 1975), as has isolation among primates (Harlow & Harlow, 1962). We know less about the middle of the dimension of the presence of others, but its reward value undoubtedly depends on both details of social contexts and the personality of the participants.

Attention from Others

When others are around, there need be no contact or interaction, and this minimal social stimulation may suffice when the others are strangers. When the others are known, however, we usually want not only their company but their attention. We want to be recognized and acknowledged. Such regard is so common that it is noticed mainly when absent. No one likes being ignored, which spawns feelings of rejection, hurt, or anger. Being ignored even by strangers who are waiting for an experiment can be upsetting (Fenigstein, 1979).

The opposite extreme is excessive attention. When children are being socialized, the close scrutiny of an adult is likely to reveal dirty hands or face, an unbuttoned garment, or torn clothing; observation by elders often leads to corrections of speech or manners; observation of peers may lead to teasing. Such practices tend to make us wary and uncomfortable when we are stared at or examined closely. And being conspicious often causes embarrassment or even fear, especially when we speak or perform in front of an audience. These tendencies occur in most people, though a small minority thrive on attention and may seek the spotlight even when such attention is inappropriate.

Responsivity

When others are merely watching or listening, social interaction is minimal. When they respond, social interaction can occur to its fullest extent, as each person talks or gestures in turn or sometimes overlaps the others. Why is responsivity rewarding above and beyond mere presence of others and their attention? One possibility is the indeterminacy of the other's response, which makes it novel and therefore interesting. Even if a tennis player is practicing and not competing, it is more fun to hit the ball with another player than against a backboard; the response of the backboard is well known and always the same, but the response of the other player continually changes. Predictability breeds boredom. Longtime friendships and marriages may pall because the partner's responses are so predictable as to lack any novelty. Responsiveness has been found to be important in the "robot mothers" of infant monkeys; the infants strongly prefer mothers capable of rebound and movement to absolutely still mothers (Mason, 1970).

One extreme of responsivity is its absence. When people respond with monosyllables or with a lack of interest, the conversation dies. If people merely repeat themselves or mouth dull platitude's, listeners become bored. When confronted with such monotony and tedium, people's reactions vary. Some are not especially bothered, but others become irked and restless.

The opposite end of the dimension, excessive responsivity, may also be aversive. One should be wary about asking certain people "How are you?" because the answer might please only a physician conducting a physical examination. Others may be too loud or brash in their responses, and some tend to be hysterical in their emotional reactivity. Between this extreme and opposite extreme of unresponsiveness lies the appropriate degree of responsiveness that is so rewarding.

Initiation

The last stimulation reward involves not merely responding but starting the interaction. There are people who respond if spoken to but who are too reticent to speak first. To initiate an encounter is to risk rebuff. To make the first move, one must think of a good way to begin, which involves some social skill. It is easier to remain passive and respond only to another's lead, especially with strangers or casual acquaintances. Taking the initiative requires confidence, at least some social skill, and perhaps even leadership qualities. Those who get things started socially, usually extraverts, tend to be valued by others (Hendrick & Brown, 1971).

The absence of initiation is rarely a problem, for sooner or later someone will say something and get the conversation going. The exception may be a dyad of shy people. At a party I introduced two shy psychologists and wandered off. Later I discovered that neither said a word, and after a minute or two of rocking on heels, one of them walked away.

Excessive initiation can be aversive in its intrusiveness. The person may come too close, invading the other's personal space; be more friendly than the situation warrants; seek disclosures that are too private; or make disclosures that imply too much intimacy or personal friendship. Clearly, the excesses of initiation are more negative than the insufficiencies.

ACTIVITY AND STIMULATION

The stimulation rewards are summarized in Table 2.1. Again, each reward may be regarded as a dimension that starts with too little and ends with too much; the reinforcing part of the dimension is in the middle. Although we

TABLE 2.1
Stimulation Social Rewards

Reward	Absence	Excess
Presence of others	Isolation	Crowding
Attention from others	Shunning	Conspicuousness
Responsivity	Boredom	Overarousal
Initiation	No interaction	Intrusiveness

do not want to remain alone, we wish to avoid the crowding that limits our movement, privacy, and personal space. Similarly, we want a modicum of attention from others but become uncomfortable when totally ignored or made to feel conspicuous. Though the extremes of these first two rewards are aversive, the extremes of responsivity and initiation are not especially aversive, except for intrusiveness.

The four rewards are aligned in order of increasing activity on the part of the person delivering the reward. Mere presence requires nothing more than filling space or engaging (in parallel) in the same activity. Looking at or listening to another person represents only a small increment in activity, but it is the beginning of social interaction. Responsivity represents a leap upward in activity, for now the person is reacting appropriately to the other's behavior. Finally, initiation marks the peak of activity in that it is self-starting instead of being reactive.

Each increment in activity intensifies social stimulation and consequently elevates the recipient's level of arousal. The lowest level, presence of others, provides some stimulation or arousal, as in a crowd watching a football game. Working side by side with others also has been found to be arousing (Zajonc, 1965). Attention from others is highly stimulating and can cause either a pleasant excitement or an unpleasant feeling of being too conspicuous. And a still higher level of stimulation results from responsivity or initiation.

We can appreciate these differences in stimulation and arousal when we inquire about technological or animal substitutions for people. The radio is sometimes almost as good as the presence of others, perhaps because the auditory stimuli (talk or music) deny that one is completely alone. Media of communication, however, cannot substitute for any of the more socially stimulating process rewards. Television cannot be considered because its strong visual stimulation acts as a distraction, not a substitute for people, and conversations over telephones are little different from conversations in person. Computers may substitute for social responsivity because part of the feedback they offer is indeterminate and therefore novel. Many of them are capable of benefiting from experience, and some can be hooked up to a mechanical voice that offers a simulated conversation with the user. Responsivity is enhanced by competition in recent generations of computer games. Here the user competes with the computer, which replaces a live opponent. Such computers offer the responsivity that is the hallmark of real-life social interaction: I talk and you answer, or I try one tactic, and you respond with your own.

For most people, pets are better social substitutes than are technological devices. Cats and dogs may share an activity, and they attend to their owners and even respond to them, although initiation is usually too much to expect. For each of the stimulation social rewards, dogs would seem to offer more than cats. Cats are considerably more independent of their owners than are dogs. A dog may be said to have a master, but not a cat. Thus, a dog is more likely to be present and to share an activity, such as taking a stroll. A dog is more likely to look at and listen to its master than is a cat, and dogs are more responsive, both emotionally and socially. All this should come as no surprise—although cat lovers may be offended—in light of the fact that dogs are the more sociable animals. The more sociable the species of the pet, the more likely it is to offer social rewards, especially those involving greater activity, stimulation, and hence, greater social interaction.

The stimulation rewards just reviewed are assumed to be virtually universal in their appeal. If so, what is the role of personality traits? Presumably, they affect the incentive value of rewards. Consider the risky sport of skydiving. It is exciting for a sensation seeker (Zuckerman, 1979) but scary and aversive for a fearful person. Similarly, personality traits can enhance or diminish the potency of social rewards or even render them unpleasant.

The four stimulation rewards are so designated because presumably they offer a specifically social kind of arousal. The personality trait involving a strong need for social stimulation is sociability. The term *sociability* is used here not in the sense of being extraverted, although it is a component of extraversion, but in the sense of a need to be with others. So defined, it has been assessed by the following items (Cheek & Buss, 1981):

1. I like to be with people.
2. I welcome the opportunity to mix socially with people.
3. I prefer working with others than alone.
4. I find people more stimulating than anything else.
5. I'd be unhappy if I were prevented from making many social contacts.

The presence of others, which includes sharing activities, is more prized by sociable people than by nonsociable people. No one likes enforced isolation, but highly sociable people are more likely to chafe at being alone and therefore avoid such occupations as writer or forest ranger. Unless there has been enforced seclusion, however, presence of others is only a weak reward for sociable people, who require more intense social stimulation than may be found merely by the company of others.

Aside from sociability, there is no extant personality trait relevant to presence of others. What about the need for privacy? For some people it is powerful enough for them to seek it as others seek social stimulation, whereas for others the need is so weak that they do not mind the absence of others. The need for privacy may originate in the requirements of certain vocations. Composing music, painting, writing, and solving mathematics problems all require solitude. Similarly, certain leisure-time activities such as reading, solving crossword puzzles, meditating, or even just listening to music may best be done when one is alone. These vocational and avocational activities may be so rewarding that people come to value the solitude associated with them—that is, the pleasures of solitude outweigh the benefits of social stimulation. Furthermore, the presence of others obviously can interfere with any of the activities that require concentration, and therefore others' company can become intolerable. Another reason to avoid others is suspicion that they might steal one's ideas or might even cause harm. There are people in the normal range, this side of paranoia, who may still believe that others are spying on them, a distrust nurtured by well-known illegal activities of the police and various governmental agencies.

In brief, a need for privacy may arise from the pleasures of the solitary life or the potential aversive consequences of others' presence. This need clearly opposes sociability and therefore the two would correlate negatively. If the correlation were moderate, the trait of need for privacy might contribute to our understanding of motivation to approach or avoid social contexts. Thus there might be people who are high in both sociability and the need for privacy—a full-time novelist who strongly values social stimulation, for example.

More than any other stimulation reward, attention from others represents a dimension that is reinforcing only in the middle range for most people, but this range can be shifted one way or the other by personality traits. Other things equal, sociable people are expected to be less tolerant of being ignored and more amenable to additional attention. A stronger tilt in the dimension is expected in exhibitionists, who find being ignored so unpleasant that they may behave or dress outrageously merely to be noticed. The other extreme, the conspicuousness that most people find unpleasant is pleasing to the exhibitionist, for whom there cannot be an excess of attention. Individual differences in exhibitionism have been assessed by Paivio, Baldwin, and Berger (1961):

1. I like to recite poems in front of other people.
2. Every time I get a chance to do something in front of class I take it.
3. In school, I always raise my hand if I know the answer.
4. Even if I know the answer, I usually do not raise my hand. (reversed)
5. If I wrote a prize-winning poem, I would rather have someone else read it in front of the class. (reversed)
6. If my paper is hung on the bulletin board, I'd rather *not* have my name on it. (reversed)
7. I like to show things I make to other children.
8. I would like to make something while the whole class watches.
9. I like to show my work to my classmates.
10. I like to sing in front of others.

11. I like to tell a story in front of class.
12. I would like to be on the stage in front of many people.
13. If my paper is hung on the bulletin board, I'd like everyone who sees it to know it's mine.

This scale obviously is for children, and most of the items pertain to school behavior. Although children may admit to exhibitionistic tendencies, adolescents and adults are likely not to do so. Therefore, a better way of assessing this trait may be to evaluate its opposite, audience anxiety. Paivio et al. (1961) found that their audience anxiety scale correlated $-.55$ with exhibitionism, but the correlation probably would have been higher if non-audience items had been omitted from the exhibitionism scale—the bulletin board items, for instance.

Clearly, an adult questionnaire of exhibitionism would be of value, but those available tend to contain items on extraversion. Therefore, the following items are suggested as a measure of adolescent and adult exhibitionism:

1. I would enjoy being interviewed on television.
2. I can't stand being ignored.
3. There is nothing more rewarding than an appreciative audience.
4. I like to be noticed.
5. I sometimes put on a show to get attention.
6. I am a bit of a show off.
7. I would rather act in a play than write one.
8. I would have no trouble in demonstrating products to people in a department store.
9. If I were giving a lecture, I would prefer a large audience to a small one.
10. I admire John Hancock, who wrote his name larger than anyone who signed the constitution.
11. I sometimes dress just to catch the eye of others.
12. Being conspicuous does not bother me at all.

An opposite of exhibitionism is shyness, which involves one's reaction when with others: tension, concern, feelings of awkwardness, self-consciousness, or discomfort, and inhibition of normally expected social behavior. So defined, shyness has been assessed by these items (Cheek & Buss, 1981):

1. I am socially somewhat awkward.
2. I find it hard to talk to strangers.
3. I feel tense with people I don't know well.
4. When conversing, I worry about saying something dumb.
5. I feel nervous when speaking to someone in authority.

6. I am uncomfortable at parties and other social functions.
7. I feel inhibited in social situations.
8. I have trouble looking someone right in the eye.
9. I am more shy with members of the opposite sex.

The reward of responsivity is linked to the personality trait of sociability by definition, for back-and-forth stimulation is precisely what sociable people seek. It needs only to be added that sociable people are also most likely to offer this stimulation reward and therefore to be seen as friendly, affable, or even hearty.

Concerning initiation, people who desperately need this incentive have a strong need for social interaction but feel too awkward and inhibited to take the first step. Such people represent a combination of high sociability and shyness. Unsociable people have only weak motivation to engage in social interaction, and shy people suffer discomfort when interacting. Thus, shy, sociable people should find initiation by others to be especially rewarding.

Shy, unsociable people may best be regarded as introverts. Though this is a departure from previous usage (Eysenck, 1970), it seems better to capture the behavior of introverts than the combination of low sociability and low impulsivity. The mirror image is the extravert, of course, who is sociable and unshy. Extraverts are the only ones with both the motive and the lack of inhibition to initiate interaction consistently and often. The various links between stimulation rewards and personality traits are reviewed in Table 2.2.

AFFECTIVE REWARDS

The stimulation rewards occur naturally in social contexts, and they vary in the degree of social stimulation or arousal they provide, hence their name. The affective rewards involve specific social responses that typically induce in the recipient a positive affective response, hence their name. In order of

TABLE 2.2
Stimulation Rewards and Traits

Presence of others	Sociability, need for privacy
Attention from others	Sociability, exhibitionism, and shyness
Responsivity	Sociability
Initiation	Sociability and shyness

increasing intensity and implied depth of relationship, the affective rewards are respect, praise, sympathy, and affection.

Respect

The term *respect* is used in the sense of deferring to those of higher status. Though praise is frequently associated with respect, for we may respect those who are praiseworthy, we tend to defer to those whose exalted status requires that their position be honored even if they do not deserve praise. High status may be ascribed—that is, assigned by society to particular social roles. Thus, children are expected to respect the higher status of parents; children, their teachers; workers, their bosses; athletes, their coaches; and people in court, the judges. Although those in superordinate positions expect deference or even demand it, they still are pleased when they receive it. Of course, respect is more rewarding when it is offered voluntarily instead of being produced under pressure.

The opposite of respect is obviously disrespect, a refusal to acknowledge the other person's superior status. Some children talk to their parents as if they were peers, and some students treat their teachers as classmates. Some parents and teachers do not mind such egalitarian behavior, but most cannot maintain discipline unless their superior status is acknowledged, and they also are insulted personally when they do not receive respect. The extreme of disrespect occurs when the status of superordinates is ignored and they are insulted and treated as subordinates. This insolence usually induces a violent reaction, which is sometimes the reason for the subordinate's behavior.

The fact that respect has an opposite makes this reward a bipolar dimension. As such, it contrasts with the stimulation rewards, which consist of unipolar dimensions: from zero to excess, with no opposites. Each affective reward has its opposite and so is a bipolar dimension—not surprising when we realize that most emotions are bipolar.

Praise

When we praise others for accomplishments based on demonstrated talent or superior character, such admiration approaches respect. Praise, however, is offered for a wide range of accomplishments, some of them as minor as good grades, winning a game, obtaining a job or a raise, or winning a beauty contest. In contrast, respect is offered only when the accomplishment is significant or important to society, based on a nontrivial talent, and widely heralded. Praise is typically offered for an immediate accomplishment, whereas respect is typically offered for past accomplishments.

What is praised? We applaud intrinsic qualities, a good example being physical attractiveness, which does not enhance status or gain respect. We often say good things when others are friendly, cooperative, or helpful. We may flatter a man's cooking, a woman's driving, or an adolescent's haircut. We also offer admiration for others' car, house, furniture, or even their children and pets. In brief, we may extol others' significant accomplishments (which comes close to respect), praise their personalities or appearance, or admire their possessions or relatives.

Can there be excessive praise? Yes, when compliments are exaggerated, the recipient may suspect an ulterior motive—that is, the praise is offered as part of an attempt at ingratiation (Jones, 1964). When a person's virtues are being extolled to others, the recipient may become acutely embarrassed. Most of us have experienced the discomfort of such overpraise.

No documentation is needed for the statement that praise is reinforcing. We work hard for other's admiration and we like people who offer it. Whatever may be said about praise may be said in reverse about its opposite, criticism. We despise disparagement, work hard to avoid it, and devalue those who offer it. Praise and criticism are of course the endpoints of a bipolar dimension. The zero point lies in the middle: no praise or criticism. It is a reasonable guess that criticism deviates more from the zero point and is more punishing than is praise rewarding. Furthermore, this asymmetry probably holds for all four affective rewards: The negative end is more punishing than the positive end is rewarding.

The potency of praise and criticism depend on whether they are directed toward one's personality or merely a particular behavior or something peripheral to oneself. To admire a woman's intelligence is a stronger reward than admiring her intellectual performance on a particular task, for the first refers to an enduring ability whereas the second refers to a transient behavior. Also, praising a man's driving ability tends to be more rewarding than praising a man's automobile. Criticism is more punishing when it refers to an enduring characteristic: To call someone a liar or a psychopath is a more hostile act than to point out a single incident of lying or cheating. Similarly, calling attention to a man's baldness is more aversive than directing attention to his need for a shave. Of course, praising or criticizing a particular behavior or possession may strongly imply an enduring trait (intelligence, taste, attractiveness), in which case the distinction being drawn here becomes blurred.

Sympathy

Let us immediately distinguish sympathy that is offered directly to another person verbally or nonverbally from sympathy that is felt but not expressed. We may feel sympathetic toward a stranger who has suffered misfortune or loss but we do not ordinarily make a sympathetic response. We experience sympathy when we come across a blind or crippled person or when we learn that a famous person is terminally ill, but we do not usually convey sympathy to any of these people. The overt manifestation of sympathy, the reward, is delivered principally to friends and family. The closer and more intimate the relationship, the more sympathy is offered.

Sympathy is usually expressed verbally in terms of regret and sorrow. It may also be offered nonverbally, as when the distressed person is held, stroked, or even cradled. Such soothing, which represents the extreme of sympathy, is offered mainly to close friends, family, or lovers, and then only when the other person is acutely distressed.

Can there be too much sympathy? Rarely, for distressed people welcome the comfort of another's nurturing responses. There are times, however, when the sympathy is disproportionate to the distress, when the victim is made to feel even worse because of what the excessive sympathy implies. If I reassure you when you need little reassurance, the implication is that you are even worse off than you had believed. Thus, there are occasions when the sympathetic person might better hold back on solace so that the victim might more easily reassert normality.

Unlike the other affective rewards, sympathy consists of reactive behavior. We try to allay the fear of a person in a panic, calm a screaming infant, reassure those who have suffered loss or rejection, and console those who are hurt, or sick, or have suffered misfortune. Not all misfortune and distress call for sympathy, however, and when the cause is stupidity, ineptitude, or sloth, we tend not to feel sorry for the unfortunate person. Instead, we may react with contempt for people whose minor misfortunes or failures are caused by their own laziness or carelessness; or scorn for people so soft and immature as to be unable to sustain minor troubles without whimpering; or we may ridicule those who exaggerate their rejections, failures, or minor hurts.

Affection

Affection is a broad term, which varies from the mild liking of acquaintances to the deep loving of romantic partners (Rubin, 1970). We are not ordinarily affectionate with acquaintances; although we may like them, the relationship is too casual for demonstrations of affection, which are ordinarily reserved for close friends, lovers, and family members. As a rule, we express fondness only to those who reciprocate, for affection usually involves give-and-take interaction. There is an exception: For the first few months of life, the infant offers little reciprocal affection, but this does not prevent the parents from cuddling, hugging, and kissing the child.

Praise and sympathy can intensify a relationship. When people admire us or offer sympathy, we like them better, and friendship may even be increased by respect. More than any of these rewards, however, it is affection that intensifies relationships. Thus affection is not only the most potent reward but also the one most likely to lead to a deeper reciprocal relationship.

Can there be too much affection? Yes, if the recipient feels smothered, as when a mother loves her children so much that she cannot let them love another person or become independent. Yes, if the affection implies a closer relationship than the recipient desires. Gestures of affection are inappropriate or embarrassing when made by a casual acquaintance. And in a pair of lovers, demonstrations of love from the one deeply involved may be annoying to the one less involved.

If affection is a potent social reward, hostility is an even more potent punisher. Just as liking someone can intensify a social relationship, so disliking someone can destroy it. As affection can vary from liking to loving, so hostility can vary from disliking to loathing. Consistent with the other affective rewards, the bipolar dimension here is tipped toward the negative end, and it would appear to be more punishing to be hated than it is rewarding to be loved. The affective rewards are summarized in Table 2.3, but several issues require elaboration. They are discussed under the headings of dimensionality, gender differences, development, personality traits, and social influence.

Dimensionality.   Each of the affective rewards has been regarded as a bipolar dimension, reward being opposed by punishment. Bipolarity is easy to discern for respect, praise, and affection because each has an obvious opposite that is aversive. The opposite of sympathy is not at all obvious. The only choices appear to be contempt, ridicule, and disdain, none of which is entirely satisfactory.

It has been assumed that the negative end of each dimension is more potent in its punishment than the positive end is in its rewarding properties. Thus the pain of hostility or rejection is worse than the pleasure of love or acceptance, the hurt of criticism is worse than the ego-boost of praise, and

TABLE 2.3
Affective Rewards

Rewards	*Opposite*
Respect	Insolence
Praise	Criticism
Sympathy	Disdain
Affection	Hostility

so on. If the assumption that these bipolar dimensions tilted toward the negative side is true, is there an explanation? One possibility lies in the relative frequency of affective rewards and their opposites. Generally, respect is offered more frequently than disrespect, praise more often than criticism, and affection more often than hostility. Perhaps disrespect, criticism, and hostility are more potent than their positive counterparts because they are less frequent, on the assumption that we habituate to frequent events and thereby are less affected by them.

Another possibility is that negative events are innately more potent than positive events. It is known that avoidance conditioning is quicker and more resistant to extinction than approach conditioning, and Kahneman and Tversky (1984) have demonstrated that the risk of loss is more aversive than the chance of equivalent gain. Thus it may be that the greater potency of the negative end than the positive pole of the affective rewards is merely one instance of a generality.

Gender Differences.   Although there are no obvious gender differences in the value of the stimulation rewards, men and women regard the affective rewards differently. Respect seems to be more important to men, perhaps because they usually occupy roles of higher status and in vocational and social contexts they struggle more to attain positions of respect. There is no obvious gender difference in praise or even in the basis of the praise. Despite the prevalent folklore, most men like to be praised for physical attractiveness, and most women like to be praised for competence. Concerning sympathy, women seem to place a higher value on it than men (Buss, 1966) and are more likely to offer it, presumably because their stereotyped roles tend to be more nurturant. Moreover, women are allowed, even encouraged, to express feelings of distress openly, and they are allowed to be (or feign being) helpless, which is forbidden to men. As for affection, there is no obvious gender difference in its reinforcing value, but there is in its expression. Many men do not know how to receive affection when it is openly delivered and may become embarrassed, whereas women welcome open expressions of affection and offer it easily. Thus, although men's and women's need for affection may be roughly equal, women are more likely to offer and receive this social reward.

Development.   The affective rewards show diverse developmental trends. Soothing, the earliest form of sympathy, is in great demand by infants, and this demand is usually met. Thereafter, soothing slowly gives way to verbal sympathy, with less of the holding, stroking, and calming characteristic of soothing. Praise is not an important issue during the first year of life, for the infant cannot clearly distinguish it from affection or the generalized approval that parents bestow on their infants. As young children begin to understand the spoken word, praise becomes important and remains so throughout development. Respect does not come into play until children are of school age; children and adolescents are typically on the giving end of respect, not the receiving end. Respect does not become a significant reinforcer for them until, as adolescents or young adults, they can assume roles that warrant respect. The deference that derives from significant accomplishment is delayed even longer.

Affection undergoes the most pronounced and interesting developmental shifts. During infancy, expressions of love pour forth from both parents, and these are reciprocated within the limits of its mobility by the infant. Thereafter, the expression of affection by hugging, kissing, stroking, and touching tends to wane throughout childhood and into adolescence. The basis of affection undergoes a similar developmental course. Infants at first receive unconditional love; they do not have to do anything but merely exist. Later, however, parental affection waxes and wanes with the child's behavior, and love is no longer unconditional.

Personality Traits.   Who would be keenly aware of status and be especially reinforced by receiving respect? The answer would seem to be formal people, who know their place on the social ladder, emphasize the implicit rules of social behavior, place special emphasis on manners and politeness, and value dressing and speaking appropriately and maintaining appearances. A trait measure of formality has been developed and validated against observed behavior (L. Buss, 1984). Its items are:

1. I believe it is important to behave with good manners.
2. I consider myself a formal person.
3. I feel quite at home at formal functions.
4. I have a strong sense of propriety.
5. I tend to behave in a dignified fashion.
6. I believe that physical expressions of intimacy are not proper in public situations.
7. I enjoy being spontaneous and expressive, even when it is not appropriate. (reversed)
8. It does not bother me to express my true feelings at social gatherings. (reversed)
9. Social standards of behavior are too confining for me. (reversed)
10. My manners are better than most people's.

Those who score high on this questionnaire are expected to value respect inordinately, to demand it, and to offer it frequently. Those who score low (informal people) tend to disregard status, sometimes to the extent of ridiculing what they see as pomposity, and they place little value on deference. Thus, formality may correlate with authoritarianism (Adorno, Frenkel-Brunswik, Levinson, & Sanford, 1950), one aspect of which is a strong concern for status.

The trait of self-esteem appears relevant to both praise and affection. Most psychologists assume that accomplishments and such valued personal attributes as attractiveness and a sunny disposition are major sources of positive self-regard. Acknowledgment of such attributes or accomplishments through praise necessarily elevates self-esteem, and it requires no special psychological knowledge to know that affection makes the recipient feel valued and worthwhile. All of us prize events that initiate such feelings, and so praise and affection are universal reinforcers. For those low in self-esteem, however, these social rewards are not just pleasant but necessary. Those with low self-esteem need repeated bolstering by others. Those high in self-esteem can manage with less praise or affection because of an intrinsic feeling of self-worth.

There are several questionnaires that assess self-esteem, their similarity being revealed in high correlations. One of them words most of the items so as to reverse self-esteem in an attempt to minimize the tendency to deny being conceited (Cheek & Buss, 1981):

1. I have a low opinion of myself. (reversed)
2. I often wish I were someone else. (reversed)
3. Things are all mixed up in my life. (reversed)
4. I'm fairly sure of myself.
5. I am a failure. (reversed)
6. I am basically worthwhile.

This scale correlates with .88 with Rosenberg's (1965) scale, one of the best known self-esteem questionnaires.

The last affective reward, sympathy, is most likely to be offered to those who are often distressed, troubled, and upset. These would appear to be people who are high on emotionality, a personality trait with an inherited component (Buss & Plomin, 1975). The updated version of the emotionality scale contains the following items (Buss & Plomin, 1984, p. 99):

1. I frequently get distressed.
2. I often feel frustrated.
3. Everyday events make me troubled and fretful.
4. I get emotionally upset easily.

The personality traits associated with the affective rewards are listed in Table 2.4. Most of the traits describe those who especially need the rewards and therefore overvalue them, but one trait also suggests who is most likely to offer the reward. Formal people not only seek respect but are more likely to offer it. For the other two personality traits, there appears to be no obvious relation between the trait and the likelihood of offering an affective reward. Thus those who are low in self-esteem are not necessarily more affectionate; some of them may offer more praise in an attempt at ingratiation, which might lead to being liked and therefore boost self-esteem. However, this suggestion is highly speculative and rests on the assumption that people low in self-esteem are capable of social manipulation and at the same time are oblivious to the fact that any praise so extracted would in reality add nothing to their intrinsic worth. Concerning emotionality, those who are high in this trait are expected to receive more sympathy for reasons already mentioned, but they are not especially likely to offer sympathy.

It is possible that personality traits may affect the cost–benefit issue that occurs in bipolar rewards. The formal person who especially values respect surely finds disrespect to be especially aversive; the person low in self-esteem places a more positive value on praise but probably finds criticism more negative than most people would. Do the personality traits make the affective rewards so potent that a person will risk receiving the opposite end of dimension (hate, not love; rejection, not acceptance)? Or would the occurrence of the negative end of the dimension be so devastating that a person low in self-esteem, for instance, would not seek praise because of the risk of receiving criticism. This issue harks back to the research of Kahneman and Tversky (1984) on economic rewards. The difference here is that social rewards are part of an entirely different value system, and the issue is complicated by the presence of personality traits, something that decision theorists rarely consider.

Social Influence.   The four affective rewards increase our attraction to those offering them, intensify relationships, and render us more susceptible to others' influence. We are glad to do what they want for no other reason than it pleases them. This is the nature of friendship or love: We cannot be commanded to do what others want but can be lured or enticed. Others need not be aware of their influence, and awareness does not lead inevi-

TABLE 2.4
Affective Rewards and Traits

Respect	Formality
Praise	(Low) self-esteem
Sympathy	Emotionality
Affection	(Low) self-esteem

tably to social manipulation, but the potency of the affective rewards makes them available as a means of social influence.

Affection is an especially potent reward and therefore a two-edged sword. When affection must be shared with other friends or with siblings, jealousy becomes a problem. Children balk at sharing parental love with brothers and sisters, and they may be sensitive to even the slightest imbalance in others' favors. Even equity in the distribution of parental affection may not stop resentment, for many children demand preferential treatment. Jealousy is less of an issue among friends, but it is common among lovers: The more intense the affection, the less lovers can bear sharing it. A husband who was previously not jealous sometimes becomes so when his wife becomes a mother and lavishes love on the newborn infant.

Another problem, common to both affection and praise, is the consistency with which they are offered. If they are offered on a variable ratio or variable interval schedule, the expectation of receiving them tends not to extinguish. At same time, the recipient inevitably becomes insecure and anxious, never knowing when approval and affection are forthcoming.

An infrequent reaction is suspicion that one is being manipulated by affective rewards. The other person may be using deference or praise for the purpose of ingratiation, or affection to be bartered for nonsocial rewards—hence the labels of gold digger and fortune hunter. The reaction of suspicion is ordinarily accompanied by reactance to loss of control (Brehm, 1966) and even anger at being manipulated. Who is likely to be suspicious? Those who score high on Machiavellianism (Christie & Geis, 1970) or on the paranoia scale of the Minnesota Multiphasic Personality Inventory.

Social influence is most likely to be attempted by those of subordinate status, who cannot exercise control through dominance or economic power. Thus children may withhold affection or even manifest dislike when they cannot get their way with parents or other caretakers. For women in traditional marriages, the social rewards open up an avenue of influence over their husbands, who can be manipulated through praise, affection, and sympathy. In structured social relationships, such as teacher–student and boss–worker, subordinates can manipulate superiors through judicious use of deference and praise.

STIMULATION VERSUS AFFECTIVE REWARDS

To furnish coherence to a complex array of incentives that occur in social contexts, two distinctions are necessary. First, truly social rewards are differentiated from economic rewards, which can be bartered and can be obtained in nonsocial contexts. Social rewards, as defined here, can be obtained only interpersonally, and they are not ordinarily bartered. When a friend does a favor and asks for money, the friendship is weakened or destroyed. When a spouse withholds love until money or goods are forthcoming, the marriage would appear to be in trouble. Thus, economic rewards may be exchanged for one another and social rewards may be exchanged for one another, but when the boundary between the two kinds of reward is breached, any interpersonal relationship is weakened or negated.

The second distinction is between two kinds of social rewards: stimulation and affective. Each stimulation reward is regarded as a unipolar dimension, the middle being reinforcing and the extremes being aversive; this is especially true of attention from others. Each affective reward consists of a bipolar dimension, with one pole being completely positive and the other, aversive.

There are no apparent gender differences for stimulation rewards, but there are for the affective rewards: Men seem to want more deference, and women seem to want more affection and sympathy. There are no apparent developmental trends for the stimulation rewards, but there are for all four affective rewards. Soothing yields to sympathy, gestures of affection wane, praise waxes, and deference awaits adulthood.

The difference between the two kinds of social rewards is especially clear when each set is aligned in order of intensity. The stimulation rewards form a sequence that increases in intensity of induced arousal from mere presence through the initiation of social contact by another. The affective rewards form a sequence based on increasing depth or intimacy of relationship. Thus deference may be offered by an acquaintance, praise by an acquaintance or friend, sympathy only by a friend or member of the family (with rare exception), and affection is exchanged only between good friends, lovers, or family members.

Which kind of social reward is more fundamental in a biological sense? One way of answering this question is to examine what humans share with other highly social species, especially primates. It is a strong need for social stimulation. Though infants require care and affection, and adults may be reinforced by any of the affective rewards, none of these rewards appear to be crucial for juveniles or adults of highly social species. But presence of others, their attention, and their responsivity seem to be crucial, for social animals and humans strive to attain these social rewards.

Humans have more complex interpersonal relationships than other social species and can verbalize the experience of needing social rewards by reporting being lonely. In the present framework, loneliness may consist of the absence of either stimulation rewards or affective rewards. What the person misses is the presence of others and the sharing of activities, receiving attention, or the more arousing stimulation of responsivity; or the person may be dysphoric because of the lack of respect, praise, sympathy, soothing, or (perhaps especially) affection. This distinction in which kind of social rewards are absent is related to an earlier distinction between social and emotional loneliness (Weiss, 1973). The emotional person, lacking sympathy and affection, is likely to be depressed, whereas the socially lonely person, lacking companionship and stimulation, is expected to be socially anxious.

Loneliness has been studied as a personality trait, the only available measure including both kinds of loneliness (Russell, Peplau, & Cutrona, 1980):

1. I feel in tune with the people around me. (reversed)
2. I lack companionship.
3. There is no one I can turn to.
4. I do not feel alone. (reversed)
5. I feel part of a group of friends. (reversed)
6. I have a lot in common with the people around me. (reversed)
7. I am no longer close to anyone.
8. My interests and ideas are not shared by those around me.
9. I am an outgoing person. (reversed)
10. There are people I feel close to. (reversed)
11. I feel left out.
12. My social relationships are superficial.
13. No one really knows me well.
14. I feel isolated from others.
15. I can find companionship when I want it. (reversed)
16. There are people who really understand me. (reversed)
17. I am unhappy being so withdrawn.
18. People are around me but not with me.
19. There are people I can talk to. (reversed)
20. There are people I can turn to. (reversed)

In a subsequent study, subjects were asked to rate how socially lonely and how emotionally lonely they were, and these ratings were correlated with items on the loneliness scale: "Social loneliness was more strongly associated than emotional loneliness with not feeling 'in tune' with other people, not feeling part of a group of friends, and not having a lot in common with other people. In contrast, emotional loneliness was more strongly correlated with feeling that there is no one to turn to, feeling no longer close to anyone, and feeling that nobody really knows one well" (Russell, Cutrona, Rose, & Yurko, 1984, p. 1317). Also assessed were the subjects' close relationships and feelings of intimacy, as well as their network of more casual relationships. Regression analyses revealed that a lack of friendships better predicted social loneliness, whereas the absence of dating relationships or a romantic link better predicted emotional loneliness, leading the authors to conclude, "Social loneliness motivates the person to seek out activities and groups he or she might participate in, whereas emotional loneliness leads the person to seek a one-on-one intimate relationship" (p. 1319).

The two kinds of social rewards also differ in whether they can be used to influence others. Respect, praise, sympathy, and affection are such potent reinforcers that we are glad to do what others want when they offer them, which ordinarily occurs in the context of a relationship. The stimulation rewards, in contrast, are usually not a source of social influence, presumably because they are less personal, less potent, and involve no necessary relationship. These various contrasts are summarized in Table 2.5.

In addition to suggesting possible answers to questions about social interaction, the present formulation proposes further questions. There may be a hierarchy of social rewards that holds for virtually everyone, but perhaps there are several clusters of rewards, some stimulating and some affective, each for a different kind of person (the differences presumably being in pattern of personality traits). If there are hierarchies or clusters, are they the same for men as women? Do particular social rewards link up with personality traits not mentioned previously? Another issue concerns who offers social rewards. Sociable people are likely to be responsive, and nurturant people are likely to be sympathetic, but what about the other social rewards? Who is affectionate, and who offers praise?

Consider also continuing social relationships among friends, lovers, or family members. Are secure relationships based on a match between rewards sought and offered? Do mismatches cause relationships to fracture? It has been assumed here that the affective rewards are crucial to relation-

TABLE 2.5
Stimulation versus Affective Rewards

	Stimulation	Affective
Underlying psychological dimension	Arousal	Intimacy
Kind of loneliness	Social	Emotional
Biologically fundamental	More so	Less so
Used for influence	No	Yes
Dimensionality	Unipolar	Bipolar
Gender differences	No	Yes
Vary during development	No	Yes

ships, but in a minority of instances the stimulation rewards might also be important. Consider a marriage in which each spouse receives sufficient praise, sympathy, and affection from the other. One spouse might be so extraverted as to require unusual responsivity, and if it were not forthcoming from the other spouse, the result would be boredom. More than one relationship has been dissipated by the boredom that is common when couples have lived together for years. Thus the presence of affective rewards may be necessary for a relationship to flower, but the sufficient condition for its enduring may be the additional presence of stimulation rewards.

NOTES

Two types of loneliness have been distinguished by Weiss (1973). Social loneliness occurs because of the absence of friends with whom one can interact and share activities. In my terms, stimulation rewards are missing. Emotional loneliness, derives from the absence of a close relationship, familial or romantic, in which there can be intimacy. In my terms, the affective rewards of sympathy, soothing, and love are missing. The two kinds of loneliness also relate to Rubin's (1970) distinction between liking and loving.

Weiss (1974) went on to outline a set of social provisions that might be offered by various relationships. The provisions supplied by three kinds of relationships appear to overlap three of the social rewards. Thus an attachment relationship offers safety and security, which are analogous to the social rewards of soothing and sympathy. Other relationships allow the sharing of interests, which is analogous to presence of others and their attention. Some relationships offer reassurance of worth through acknowledgment of the person's abilities, which is analogous to praise and possible respect. The other three kinds of relationships do not touch on the social rewards: opportunity to offer nurturance, possibility of receiving assistance through cooperation, and the possibility of receiving advice and guidance.

Friendships, especially those involving same-sex companions, can be approached from the perspective of the social exchange of rewards (Thibaut & Kelley, 1959). A semester-long study compared the development of close and nonclose friendships among college students (Hays, 1985). For both kinds of friendship, companionship was found to be the most frequently reported reward, which is consistent with my suggestion that the stimulation rewards are basic to all kinds of social interaction. Also consistent was the fact that over time, the other's presence became increasingly aversive: As friends continually rub against each other, friction develops. The largest differences between close and nonclose friendships were in the categories of confidence and emotional support. Neither precisely matches any of the social rewards on my list, but emotional support is not far from soothing. The major gender difference was not surprising: more casual affection among women and more shared activities among men.

There is a large literature on attractiveness, much of it summarized by Byrne (1971). His approach emphasizes reinforcement, that is, the stimulus values of people that make them attractive to others. The most prominent features are physical attractiveness, similarity of interests, and positive personal evaluations (equivalent to praise).

Another way of approaching social rewards is through equity theory (Walster, Walster, & Berscheid, 1978), which makes three assumptions about interpersonal relationships (there is a fourth assumption dealing with groups, but that is irrelevant here). First, individuals try to maximize rewards and minimize costs or punishments. Second, inequitable relationships lead to distress. Third, such distress leads to an attempt to restore equity. Thibaut and Kelley (1959) add that each of us has a particular set of expectations for each relationship; we evaluate benefits and costs not only in terms of these expectations but also in terms of opportunities for other relationships. These theories have derived from and led to a large set of empirical data, usually centered on economic rewards. It would be of considerable interest to determine how well equity and balance theories work when applied to the social rewards specified in this chapter. Furthermore, with rare exception, the social psychologists who have theorized about these issues tend not to consider the personality of the subjects. For example, does a person with low self-esteem enter a relationship with the same expectations or other possible options as a person with high self-esteem?

It is rare for an author to write an entire book on a single social reward, but Derber (1979) has offered a sociological perspective on attention: "The quality of any interaction depends on the tendencies of those involved to seek and share attention. Competition develops when people seek to focus attention mainly on themselves; cooperation occurs when the participants are willing and able to give it" (p. 3). He suggests that in informal settings most people seek most of the attention, and this tendency originates in American individualism and self-interest. Consistent with a sociological view, Derber emphasizes class and gender variables as determinants of who gives and who receives attention, thereby presenting an approach complementary to the one adopted here.

3

Attachment and Love

In the course of mammalian evolution from lower mammals to primates to our species, childhood became an increasingly larger part of the life span. Although there are powerful advantages of this extended childhood in socialization and the opportunity to try out new behaviors in the comparative safety of play, there is the serious disadvantage of the child's inability to survive on its own. This helplessness is especially pronounced in human infants, who cannot walk until roughly 1 year of age and who, early in life, must be carried by a parent. Human infants cry when they are uncomfortable, thereby bringing to them the caretaker, almost always the mother. The nurturance of the mother tends to be rewarded by the infant's responsivity or its smiles. The mother, of course, is strongly motivated to nourish and protect her child. It is only natural, then, that a strong social bond develops between infant and mother, a bond called *attachment*.

ATTACHMENT

In common with infants of other social mammals, human infants appear to be strongly motivated to obtain security and social stimulation. These needs may be supplied by several caretakers, but usually the mother provides both, and in the interest of simplicity only the mother–infant dyad is considered.

Security

Even casual observation of infants reveals that they enjoy being held and touched. They prefer to cuddle with soft, furry surfaces, especially when these are warm. This fundamental mammalian tendency may be seen in house pets, and Harlow and Harlow (1962) demonstrated it in rhesus monkeys. They allowed infant monkeys access to a robot mother constructed of wire mesh and offering milk or a robot mother covered with soft terry cloth. The infants spent most of their time clinging to the terry cloth mother, leaving occasionally to suckle from the wire mesh mother.

The very young tend to be startled easily and threatened by the sights and sounds that pose no problems for older children and adults. The reasons for the infants' excessive arousal are perhaps lack of experience with novel stimuli to which they will gradually habituate and lack of instrumental means of coping with stimuli (escaping from aversive stimuli, for instance). Whatever the reasons, infants regularly become fretful and fussy and therefore need to be calmed. The best way to soothe upset infants is to pick them up and cradle them, offering contact comfort, softness, and warmth. If these are not sufficient, infants usually can be pacified by rocking and soft singing or murmuring, or the last resort of suckling, which can calm even babies who are not hungry. Infants also seem to crave at least minimal affection, which usually takes the form of mothers' hugging and fondling them, kissing them, and murmuring endearments, the tone and softness of which convey love to infants.

Human infants, lacking the advanced cognitions and language they later develop, may be regarded as little different from other primate infants in their social behavior. Beyond infancy, specifically human tendencies appear. The need for security remains, but it wanes as children habituate to neutral novel stimuli and as they develop ways of coping with everyday events. The mother remains a sure base of security, a shelter from a potentially threatening world. As young children locomote better, they no longer need to touch the mother, so long as she can be seen or eventually heard. Young children still seek hugging and kissing, but the frequency wanes, and affection need not be expressed by contact; reasonable substitutes are verbal affection ("I love you") or praise for being good-looking, good, or talented. Furthermore, various partial substitutions can be employed for security: a pacifier for mother's breast, a security blanket or doll for being held, magic (kissing away the hurt), and verbal sympathy for contact soothing.

The developmental course of expressions of soothing and affection may be different for boys and girls. Among families that follow traditional gender-role socialization, girls are allowed to be fondled, kissed, and told that they are loved. Girls are also allowed to keep security blankets and dolls beyond infancy, and they are allowed to cry when unhappy, frustrated, or mildly hurt. Boys are told, explicitly or implicitly, that "crying is for sissies" and only girls resort to dolls or security blankets. Hugging and kissing are regarded as unmanly and therefore discouraged. Although traditional gender socialization is not as strict or popular as in previous generations, the majority of boys and girls are still enculturated in the old ways. As a result, girls are allowed to express more insecurity and fear, and they have available social responses from others that can allay insecurity (hugging, kissing, and terms of endearment). Boys, though not totally deprived of these soothing responses from parents, are gradually expected to deny fear and insecurity as unmanly signs of weakness.

Stimulation

Infants require the social rewards that cause arousal, especially attention from others and responsivity. The need for something like responsivity in primate young was demonstrated by Mason (1968), who offered infant rhesus monkey a choice of robot mothers, both covered with soft, clingable material and both suspended from the ceiling. One was anchored to the floor and was therefore stationary. The other was not anchored and could therefore swing or rotate when nudged:

> Since the movements of the robot are essentially unpredictable, it can withdraw from the infant without warning, or sneak up on it from behind and deliver a gentle rap on the head; its comings and goings demand adjustments from the infant that are not required of the animals reared with stationary devices. The robot stimulates and sustains interaction; it is withdrawn from, pursued, pounced on, and wrestled with. (Mason, 1968, p. 89)

The swinging robot mother produced more normal monkeys, who explored more and were quicker to approach and interact with humans. These facts underline a theme expressed earlier: Stimulation is a crucial aspect of social contact.

Mason (1970) went on to assume that the need for stimulation (curiosity) is opposed to the need for security. There is an optimal level of arousal, below which stimulation is sought and above which security is sought. He tested this assumption by having two trainers available to interact with infant chimpanzees. The trainers wore distinctive masks and clothing, and over a period of time each trainer stuck to his own script when interacting with the chimpanzees. One soothed the animals, held them, and let them cling; the other never held them but instead engaged in roughhouse play to the delight of the young animals. At first there was no preference, but the infant chimpanzees eventually sought out the energetic, playful trainer more often. When the chimpanzees were aroused, however, this preference was reversed. Whenever they were placed in an unfamiliar room or administered the activating drug, amphetamine, they reached out to be held and soothed. Clearly, young primates need to feel sufficiently secure (low arousal) before they attempt to satisfy the opposing need for stimulation (high arousal).

Social contact is not the only source of stimulation, for there are many nonsocial kinds of stimulation available to infants once they are sufficiently secure to explore the environment. We know that crying human infants explore their surroundings more after being picked up and held than without such soothing (Korner & Grobstein, 1966). During the first few months of life, infants manifest intense curiosity, and their attention can be easily captured by novel movements or sounds. As they gradually acquire control of their limbs and become mobile, they actively explore the environment and manipulate anything they can hold. Such manipulation foreshadows the enjoyment of making things and having an impact on the environment.

The pioneering work of Bowlby (1969) led to an outpouring of research on attachment. In describing some of the infant's accomplishments, Bowlby (1967) wrote:

> When a baby is born, he cannot tell one person from another and indeed can hardly tell person from thing. Yet by his first birthday he is likely to be a connoisseur of people. Not only does he come quickly to distinguish familiars from strangers but amongst his familiars he chooses one or more favorites. They are greeted with delight, they are followed when they depart; and they are sought when absent. The loss causes anxiety and distress; their recovery, relief and a sense of security. (Foreword)

Mothers do leave their infants alone or with others (who may be unfamiliar) and return later. This oft-recurring situation has been studied intensively in the laboratory, and infants have been classified on the basis of their reactions to the mother's leaving and her return (Ainsworth, Blehar, Waters, & Wall, 1978). They suggested three types of infants and several subclasses, but only the three major classes have received attention from most subsequent researchers.

The *secure* infant allows the mother to leave with little or no protest and greets her warmly on her return. The *avoidant* infant allows the mother to leave without protest, behaves with her no differently than with the stranger, and avoids or ignores the mother when she returns. The *resistant* infant becomes upset when the mother leaves, when she returns the infant's efforts at contact-seeking are not effective, and the infant is hard to soothe, often resisting contact or any social interaction with the mother. These three kinds of reactions tend to be stable over many months (Ainsworth et al. 1978), and avoidant infants have been found to be more dependent on their preschool teachers (Sroufe, Fox, & Pancake, 1983).

In seeking the origins of these attachment types, developmental researchers have focused on the mother's behavior. Thus, mothers of avoidant infants are reported to be tense, irritable, lacking in caretaking skills, and less responsive when the infant cries, and mothers of resistant infants are reported to be unskilled and insensitive caregivers (Egeland & Farber, 1984). It has also been found that the mother's overstimulation causes avoidance, her understimulation causes resistance, and her sensitivity leads to a secure attachment (Belsky, Rovine, & Taylor, 1984).

Clearly, the mother's behavior is an important determiner of which type of attachment her infant develops, which is consistent with the passive model of personality development outlined in chapter 1. The active model suggests that the infant is not merely a passive recipient of environmental inputs—in this instance, from the mother—but has his or her own dispositions, which influence and modify the impact of the environment. The relevant dispositions would seem to be temperaments.

Temperaments are defined as personality traits that not only appear very early in life but also have a strong genetic component (Buss & Plomin, 1984). These inherited tendencies begin before environmental events can have much influence. The personality dispositions are not immutable and can be modified during the course of development, although there are undoubtedly limits set by the genes. A comparable example would be physique, which can be altered by diet and exercise but only within limits. Thus the fact that temperaments start before the environment has much influence does not mean that the importance of environment should be denied, and both determinants would seem to be important in understanding types of attachment.

Only three personality traits meet the aforementioned definition of temperament. Sociability and emotionality were mentioned in chapter 2, and the third temperament is activity. All three have been observed during the first half year of life, and a body of research on twins has documented their heritability (see Buss & Plomin, 1984, for a summary).

Infants have little control of their affects, and from the beginning they can best relieve distress by showing it and obtaining help from the mother. The facts point to emotionality as a crucial temperament in infancy. The emotional infant becomes distressed more frequently and intensely, by definition, and therefore has a stronger need for security; in the face of social novelty, the emotional infant tends to be more upset than curious. He or she clings to the mother, resists separation from her, and reacts to intrusion by wariness or crying. It follows that, other things equal, emotional infants are likely to become insecurely attached, falling into either the avoidant or the resistant category.

The primordial emotionality is assumed to differentiate into fear and anger, most infants tending to be more of one than the other. The angry infant reacts to separation from the mother with temper tantrums or sullenness, and pacifying the infant may be difficult even when the mother returns. Such a resistant infant may also be expected to display intense jealousy and perhaps even aggression when the mother lavishes her attention and affection on someone else. The fearful infant reacts to separation from the mother by withdrawal and ambivalence. Wanting the mother's presence and soothing, this infant is fearful of being abandoned and so displays the behavior of the avoidant infant.

As mentioned earlier, the need for security is opposed by a need for stimulation. Variations in the need for social stimulation define the temperament of sociability. Sociable infants want more of the stimulation rewards: presence, sharing of activities, attention, and responsivity. If they do not receive these social rewards from the mother, they may seek them elsewhere. The balance between security and stimulation needs is tilted toward stimulation, which bears on the issue of attachment types.

Insecure infants are wary and fearful when the mother leaves and they are left with a stranger (stranger anxiety). Other things equal (especially emotionality), a sociable infant tends to tolerate the higher arousal of social novelty because of his or her need for social stimulation. Even if a sociable infant were initially anxious, his or her need for the stimulation rewards would overcome the anxiety. Furthermore, sociable infants tend to meet more strangers and remain in their company without complaining, which means that the novelty tends to habituate and fearfulness wanes. An infant low in sociability needs less social stimulation, by definition, and therefore has less motivation to tolerate the fear associated with the mother's absence or the presence of strangers. His or her avoidance of or escape from strangers prevents habituation from occurring, and fear does not wane. It follows that infants low in sociability may be more susceptible to stranger anxiety and insecure attachment.

The third temperament, activity, is defined in terms of tempo and vigor: the sheer output of physical energy. An active infant may wear out a mother with his or her energy; the infant needs space to move about and reacts badly to immobility. Infants with a slower tempo are easier to manage and are regarded as placid. These differences in energy level of the infant are important mainly when there is a mismatch with the mother's activity level. The problem occurs when the mother is low in activity and the infant, high; the mother may regard her child as *difficult to manage,* and this labelling may interfere with the attachment bond. The impact of the infant's activity temperament is neither as strong nor as direct of the impact of his or her emotionality and sociability.

The research on temperament and attachment is difficult to interpret because investigators have studied personality traits present in infants but not necessarily those with an inherited component. Egeland and Farber (1984), for example, reported that temperament did not affect attachment, but their "temperaments" did not include emotionality or sociability. Though there is no confirmatory evidence on the effect of temperaments, there is evidence consistent with their impact. It comes from comparisons of securely attached infants with those who are insecurely attached. Ambivalently attached infants cry nearly twice as much as securely attached infants as early as the first few months of life (Ainsworth et al., 1978). Securely attached infants are more sociable than ambivalently attached infants with peers (Easterbrooks & Lamb, 1979; Pastor, 1981) and with strange adults (Thompson & Lamb, 1983).

These findings can be interpreted in wholly environmental terms, but this would appear to be an oversimplification. The child's early attachment to the mother and the effect of this attachment on subsequent social behavior is probably determined by a combination of the mother's behavior and the child's temperaments. An example of this multiple causation may be found in a study that compared secure with insecure in infants (Crockenberg, 1981). Early irritability in infants led to insecure attachment only in infants whose mothers tended to be unresponsive.

The mother's responsivity would seem to have two origins. The first is a combination of her motivation to care for her child and her ability to do so. This determinant has been emphasized by developmental psychologists who study the mother's sensitivity to the needs of her infant, which presumably leads to a securely attached infant. The second determinant consists of the mother's personality, especially the two temperaments most relevant to attachment: emotionality and sociability. Of particular interest is the match between the child's and mother's temperaments. If the child and his or her mother are both low in emotionality, there should be few problems in the interaction, for neither one becomes upset easily. If the child is emotional and the mother is not, there will be emotional turmoil because of the child's temperament, but these problems will be minimized by the mother's lack of emotionality. She will regard the child as difficult but will tend to react calmly to the child's fears or tantrums and therefore partially counteract the child's emotionality. If the child is unemotional, he or she will offer fewer problems, but an emotional mother will tend to magnify these problems. By presenting a more stressful social environment, she will elevate the child's low level of distress. She may also offer the child an emotional model to be copied. Still, the mother's contribution would appear to be less than the contribution of inheritance, and the child is likely to remain on the low end of emotionality. If both child and mother are high in emotionality, the child suffers from double jeopardy. The child's natural tendency to become upset is likely to be intensified by the mother's emotional reactions and by observational learning of her behavior.

Concerning a match in sociability, if both mother and infant are high in sociability, the mother will be comfortable with the infant's demands for her and others' presence and attention, for sharing activities, and for the mutual give-and-take that occurs beyond the necessary feeding and mainte-nance routines (see chapter 2). Similarly, if mother and infant are low in sociability, both will be comfortable with the lower frequency of social contact, attention, sharing, and responsivity. Problems may arise, however, when there is a mismatch in sociability temperament. Parenthetically, it may seem paradoxical that a mother's inborn sociability may differ from that of her infant. However, the mother contributes only half of her offspring's genes, inherited personality traits are likely to be polygenic, and the lottery that occurs at conception allows for divergence between parents and children.

If the infant is sociable and the mother unsociable, the mother is likely to regard the infant as excessively demanding. The infant may want more of her presence, attention, sharing of activities, and responsivity than she finds comfortable and regards as adequate. As a result, she is likely to be bothered by her infant and frustrate his or her need for greater social contact. The infant, deprived of the social rewards he or she seeks, may become irritable, give up the attempt, and settle for a lower level of social contact, or turn to others for the requisite social interaction. The attach-ment will be insecure. If the infant is unsociable and the mother sociable, she is likely to be disappointed that the child does not seek her out and wish to maintain social contact as much as she expects. She may feel rejected and will have no choice but to accommodate to her infant's weaker need for social interaction. As a result, she may be less affectionate and initiate fewer contacts. If she has other children who are more recep-tive to such social contacts, she is likely to prefer them to the child whose sociability does not match her own. If this mother–child pair were seen in a laboratory setting after their behavior patterns had become established, an observer might emphasize the mother's apparent indifference to the child. The child's low sociability could be neatly explained by insufficient stimula-tion and social reinforcement by the mother. This explanation might be correct in some instances, but often the mother is merely reacting to her infant's sociability, not causing it.

The temperaments of the mother and infant, and the consequences of matches and mismatches for the infant's temperament have already been discussed, but the events of attachment may serve to initiate new personal-ity traits. Infants vary in their need for the affective social rewards, espe-cially love. If the infant receives the love needed, the infant is likely to reciprocate with affection and start on the road toward being an affectionate child. If the infant does not receive sufficient love, he or she may become clinging and whiny in an attempt to obtain the attention and affection it craves. When displaced by a younger sibling, such a child tends to become jealous; if no subsequent events alter the course of the child's development, the child would become high in the trait of jealousy.

An infant may cling also because he or she has not received enough soothing or because the mother has not been available as a safe haven; the trait of dependency may have been initiated. In contrast, the infant may emerge from the attachment era secure in the knowledge that his or her mother is almost always available to soothe him or her and offer the tranquility that is sometimes needed. This infant is on the way toward autonomy, for he or she has learned that when his or her independent efforts at exploring the environment get it into trouble, there is always a safe haven to run to. Such a secure infant is likely to be pliable when his or her parents begin the process of socialization. An insecure infant may become negativistic, resisting the efforts of those who have failed to be available when needed. Furthermore, the insecure infant may start to distrust its caretakers and generalize this distrust to others around it. The secure infant has every reason to trust others and is likely to continue this trust.

Thus the events of the attachment period can set in motion tendencies that may develop into the personality traits observed in older children. The traits are not sufficiently developed in infancy for them to be assessed adequately, and therefore, the measures of these various traits are discussed in subsequent chapters, which deal with older children and adults.

SELF–ESTEEM

In this formulation, self-esteem consists of two elements. One is a residual, core self-esteem that is continuous throughout life and originates largely during infancy in the context of attachment. The other element is less stable and is determined largely by events after infancy. To understand why a two-tiered model is necessary, consider a hypothetical example.

During a lifetime, most people suffer enough misfortunes to cause considerable misery, but the misfortunes are spread out over time. There are rare instances, however, when calamities pile up in time and one is overwhelmed by rejection and loss, usually self-cause. Thus, a man might be fired from his job, shunned by his former friends, rejected by his family, and excommunicated by his church. Suppose, then, that all external sources of self-esteem were cut off. Would there be a residual feeling of self-regard, a belief by the man that he was still worthwhile? For some people, the answer would be No; for others, Yes, there is something left over when external sources of self-esteem have been removed. This residual core of self-esteem might be sufficient for them to get going again and lift themselves out of a pit of despair.

Core self-esteem is assumed to originate in psychological events known to occur in infancy. Aside from being tiny and helpless, which stimulate nurturance in parents, newborn infants offer little reason for being loved. They are usually not physically attractive, they sleep most of the time, and they demand considerable care. Nevertheless, most infants are loved intensely and unconditionally by their parents. Why? Observe parents when a child is born and discover the child is loved because the infant is theirs. The infant need not be beautiful, accomplished, or well-trained. The child merely has to be there, and parents will lavish enormous attention, care, and love. Under this regime, the infant learns that the most important people in the world (parents) find him or her valuable merely because he or she exists. During the infant's first year of life, parental love requires no conditions.

Infants who are loved unconditionally during the first year of life are expected to develop a robust *core* of self-esteem. Infants who receive less unconditional love are expected to develop a smaller, weaker core. An insufficient core is also the expected outcome when unconditional love is terminated after only a few months. In rare instances, parents continue unconditional love for several years, producing an insufferably egocentric child who thinks that he or she is the center of the universe.

Sooner or later, unconditional love ends. Parents and other caretakers vary their affection in accord with the young child's behavior. Hugs and kisses now occur less spontaneously and more in response to the child's behavior. And the negative side of the coin is introduced: punishment, criticism, dislike, and rejection. Young children quickly learn the contingencies of social reinforcement. Now praise and affection are delivered not just for being there but for doing something right. Thus parental love becomes conditional, and external sources esteem depend on how the child behaves. In traditional families, mothers tend to emphasize affection and fathers, discipline. As a result, more of the mother's love is unconditional, and more of the father's love is conditional. As gender roles change and families drift away from traditional modes, this distinction may fade away.

Conditional affection can be withdrawn at any time and therefore cannot contribute to an individual's residual or core self-esteem. Instead, such affection accrues *peripheral* self-esteem, which can also develop from positive relationships with siblings and peers. In addition to affective rewards, the child gradually accrues peripheral self-esteem from the other external sources: body (including attractiveness), abilities, vicarious esteem, control of others, and morality. These various sources accumulate a stable, enduring periphery of self-esteem, which is no less important than core self-esteem. An adult of 25 years, for instance, may be able to look back on a history that includes some measure of attractiveness and body dependability, esteem derived from being a member of a family and other groups, some measure of dominance or other means of controlling others, at least minimal adherence to a moral code, and a fair amount of praise, affection, and even respect from others. This accumulation over decades of life is the stable part of peripheral self-esteem, which changes only gradually.

Peripheral self-esteem also includes an unstable part that varies considerably from day to day and week to week. We are all familiar with the ups and downs of daily life, the victories and defeats, acceptances and rejections, successes and failures. These daily or weekly events are assumed to affect only the outermost part of peripheral self-esteem — the unstable part, which bounces like a cork in the sea.

This model of self-esteem, though speculative, can account for conceited and excessively humble people. It relates core self-esteem to attachment in infancy. Children with secure attachment are expected to have an adequate core of self-esteem. Those who are insecurely attached are expected to have an insufficient core and therefore to rely excessively on their own accomplishments or praise and affection from others to bolster their self-esteem. If securely attached infants developed any problem with self-esteem, it would be on the conceited end: unconditional love maintained for too many years, which would lead to an exalted sense of self-worth.

ROMANTIC LOVE

The mother–infant bond is merely the first of a series of love relationships that occur throughout life. Older children may develop childish infatuations and starting at puberty, young adolescents daydream about popular singers or even peers. Romantic love comes to full bloom in adolescence, when its parallels with mother–infant attachment become evident. Before discussing these parallels, we must first distinguish romantic love from other close relationships.

The distinction has been made concrete by a questionnaire on liking and loving (Rubin, 1970). The loving items are:

1. If ____ were feeling badly, my first duty would be to cheer him (her) up.
2. I feel that I can confide in ____ about virtually everything.
3. I find it easy to ignore ____'s faults.
4. I would do almost anything for ____.
5. I feel very possessive toward ____.
6. If I could never be with ____, I would feel miserable.
7. If I were lonely, my first thought would be to seek ____ out.

8. One of my primary concerns is ____'s welfare.
9. I would forgive ____ for practically anything.
10. I feel responsible for ____'s well-being.
11. When I am with ____, I spend a good deal of time just looking at him (her).
12. I would greatly enjoy being confided in by ____.
13. It would be hard for me to get along without ____.

The complete list of items is presented because love is so rarely assessed. There are several friendship measures, however, and therefore it is necessary to present only a sample of Rubins 13 liking items:

1. When I am with ____, we are almost always in the same mood.
2. I think that ____ is unusually well adjusted.
3. I would highly recommend ____ for a responsible job.

These liking items reflect admiration and a sense of companionship with the other in the absence of intense feelings. The loving items, according to Rubin (1970) have three major components: affiliation and dependence, predisposition to help, and exclusiveness and absorption. These three components might also be part of a close friendship, which means that the liking items may reflect not only qualitative differences between liking and loving but also quantitative differences in the intensity of any relationship. Notice that the loving scale there is no mention of sexual attraction, a deliberate omission by Rubin so that he could compare liking and loving. There is of course no sexual attraction between mother and infant, an important difference between that bond and romantic love. If sexual attraction is excluded, however, the similarities between the two kinds of love are striking.

The most observable parallel is intimacy. There is mutual touching, caressing, and fondling, and the partners are usually close in space or actually in bodily contact. There is mutual smiling, and the smiles are loving. This intimacy is accompanied by an exclusivity that advertises to others that this relationship is not to be shared. The affective rewards are offered mainly by the mother in attachment because the infant may not be capable of sympathy, soothing, or praise, but it is capable of affection; in romantic love, of course, these rewards are exchanged. When the dyad is separated, the isolation breeds desolation; when the pair is reunited, joy abounds.

In both relationships the love is unconditional. Just as mother and infant are aware of no deficiencies in each other, so lovers can see only the virtues of each other. It is a reasonable hypothesis that the euphoria of romantic love derives from the boost in self-esteem that comes from this unconditional affection. What can be better than to be valued by the most important person in the world?

Does this unconditional love lead to increments in core self-esteem? The theory of self-esteem outlined earlier would be simpler if the answer were No, for then the origin of core self-esteem would be limited to the events of infancy. The answer, however, must be a tentative Maybe. If the love from the romantic partner is intense and remains unconditional for months, it might elevate core self-esteem. This possibility would be strengthened if the romantic phase of the love relationship ended with either companionate love or at least friendliness. If it were to end in bitterness and acrimony, these negative aspects might undo any increments in core self-esteem. Admittedly, these ideas are speculative, but romantic love, until recently, has been the province of poets and philosophers, not of scientists. The hypotheses offered here are thus less anchored in facts that would otherwise be the case.

Just as the mother–infant bond eventually ends, so romantic love has a limited life span. After a period of infatuation, each lover's eyes open and see for the first time the other's defects. In both kinds of relationship, the love is so impossibly unconditional and the intimacy so close and exclusive that they cannot be maintained. The close physical contact becomes less frequent, the attention and responsivity of one or both partners diminish, and the affection that was once exclusive may perhaps be shared with another. The outcome is inevitably a loss of psychological closeness and in many instances, jealousy and rage at the other. Thus there are parallels between mother–infant attachment and adult romantic love in both the psychological features that characterize them and in the course of the relationship. It must be added, though, that most close relationships may proceed through a similar course of initial excitement (accompanied an unrealistic view of the other), followed by a return to reality and a painful loss of innocence.

Is mother–infant attachment a precursor of romantic love? In the sense that one inevitably follows the other, No. In the sense that the attachment bond of infancy appears to be needed for the development of normal social relationships thereafter, the answer is a very tentative Yes, based on the sparse evidence we have of the consequences of poor attachment. Not everyone experiences romantic love, and it may be asked who is most likely to fall in love this way, perhaps repeatedly. Here there is no answer, only ignorance.

Finally, what is the role of personality traits in romantic love? Their role is limited to their impact on the course of the relationship. Self-esteem would seem to be crucial. A person who is low in self-esteem tends to be insecure about the other's love (Do I deserve it?), may need excessive affection, praise, and reassurance, and becomes jealous easily (Another person is surely more attractive than I). Lovers become upset when they are separated, and a person high in emotionality would become especially distressed, by definition. Some people have a strong need for privacy, perhaps because they are low in sociability, an issue discussed in chapter 2. Feeling constricted, they may need time away from the loved one. If the partner were offended by this need for privacy, it might cause a rift in the relationship and the infatuation phase would end prematurely. Again, these guesses are designed to fill in gaps in knowledge, which are large in the area of romantic love. Some would argue that our ignorance is beneficial in sustaining the mystery surrounding this most intimate of human relationships.

NOTES

Ainsworth (1979), like many attachment theorists, believes that individual differences in attachment derive from environmental events: "To what extent is the pattern of attachment of a baby attributable to the mother's behavior throughout the first year, and to what extent is it attributable to built-in differences in potential and temperament? I . . . have concluded that in our sample of normal babies there is a strong case to make for differences in attachment quality being attributable to maternal behavior" (p. 933).

Sroufe (1985) states the case against temperament in stronger and more explicit terms. He notes that no single behavior can serve as an index of attachment, and infants assigned to any attachment category differ considerably in their behavior. Previous attempts to relate temperament to individual differences in attachment have failed. Temperament theorists can account for attachment behavior after the fact, Sroufe claims, but have offered no predictions; and it does not suffice merely to assert that temperament affects attachment behavior.

Sroufe's critique is telling and requires answers if the temperament position is to give any credence. Concerning the empirical issue, previous research on temperament and attachment has used a measure that has no known inherited component (Carey, 1970; Carey & McDevitt, 1978). A better test would be to use the EAS temperament measure (Buss & Plomin, 1984), which is known to have a genetic component. Concerning predictions, they have been made in the temperament book just mentioned and also in this chapter. Emotionality, activity, and sociability have been demonstrated as traits during the first year of life. Sroufe (1985) insists that any personality traits believed to influence attachment would have to be demonstrated during the first few *weeks* of life, but this demand rests on assumptions about the early origin of individual differences in attachment that have no empirical basis; it is just as reasonable to assume that temperaments first observed after several months of life would have an important impact on attachment. The EAS temperaments can be observed during the first few months of life, though there may be measurement problems because of the limited behavioral repertoire of infants of this age. These temperaments may explain why some children are relatively unaffected by deprivation in infancy (Rutter, 1979).

The broader theoretical issue involves the consequences later in childhood of individual differences in attachment in infancy. The consequences for important personality traits have been demonstrated, and explanation for these later dispositions becomes an issue. Sroufe and Ainsworth maintain that the mother's behavior and the mother–infant relationship are the sole determinants of these later tendencies. This is an extreme position, one that neglects temperaments, which have been shown to be the source of a variety of other individual differences that appear during childhood. It is possible that enduring tendencies are established solely by the mother's behavior, but the more likely explanation includes the inherited dispositions called temperaments.

Do the mother's personality traits contribute anything to the attachment bond? Cairns (1979) concludes that the answer is No and suggests that perhaps the infant normalizes the mother: The needs of the infant and the desire of the mother to help cancel out any personality differences. This idea seems appropriate for infants and mothers who occupy the middle range of dimensions of personality traits. For the extremes, however, such normalization would appear dubious, especially when the personality traits match. Thus a highly emotional infant is unlikely to cancel out the distress of a highly emotional mother. Concerning a mismatch, consider a highly sociable mother and a relatively unsociable infant. The infant presumably would be less motivated to interact and less responsive than the mother would prefer. After months of attempting to induce a higher level of social interaction, the mother would give up. If the pair were seen in the laboratory at the end of this time, the mother's relative lack of initiative would be seen as the cause of the infant's low responsiveness. Though investigators of infant behavior often emphasize relationships rather than the behavior of the infant in isolation from the mother, researchers rarely consider the issue of matches and mismatches in personality traits or complementarity versus conflict between infant and maternal environment.

In this chapter, as in most discussions of attachment, the focus is on mother–infant attachment. Regarding the mother as the crucial parent during the early months of life makes sense for tradition-bound families and for animals. Fathers do play an important (though secondary) role even in traditional families, but in this country at least, more families are nontraditional: "Not long ago, men in our culture neither sought nor assumed active responsibility for the rearing of their children. This was especially true during the children's early years: Infant care was clearly perceived as the province of women. Today, however, increasing numbers of men appear eager to play an active and important role in child rearing . . . " (Lamb, 1979, p. 938). It has been documented that young children have a favorite adult whom they prefer over all others. In the past this adult was almost always the mother, but with each passing year it becomes more likely that this figure might just as easily be the father (for a review, see Lamb, 1976). When father–infant attachment is studied as closely as mother–infant attachment has been, perhaps novel patterns of individual differences will emerge.

The psychological literature on romantic love has been sparse, probably because most investigators study love in a more general sense, including love of siblings, parents, children, and friends. A recent example of such research is a large scale study by Sternberg and Grajek (1984). Analysis of many measures yielded a general factor of love, which could be decomposed into several clusters of different affective bonds. Concerning the general factor, "Its aspects include especially (a) deep understanding of the other, (b) sharing of ideas and information, (c) sharing of deeply personal ideas and feelings, (d) receipt and provision of emotional support to the other, (e) personal growth through the relationship and helping of the other in his or her personal growth, (f) giving help to the other, (g) making the other feel needed and needing the other, and the giving and receiving of affection in the relationship" (p. 327). These aspects of love can be seen to be sufficiently general to encompass not only romantic love but also filial and parental love and close friendship.

If so, what distinguishes romantic love from other bonds of affection? One answer, already discussed, has been offered by the items that distinguish liking from loving (Rubin, 1970), but some of the loving items might apply to an especially close bond of friendship or that between parent and child. A list that is more exclusive to romantic love has been offered by Tennov (1979), who renamed the phenomenon *limerence:* obsessive thoughts about the other, acute longing to be loved by the other (a feeling that is limited to one other person), imagining doing things with the other, fear of rejection, euphoria when the other reciprocates love, great intensity of feeling, accentuating the other's virtues and ignoring faults, and intensification of the feeling through adversity.

That lovers are drawn closer by opposition, especially by parents, has been celebrated in literature and also documented by Driscoll, Davis, and Lipetz (1972), who called it the "Romeo and Juliet effect." They collected the self-reports of a sample of married and unmarried couples; the assumption is that romantic love flourishes among the unmarried couples. Parental interference was defined as being more critical of the partner and a higher frequency of negative behaviors toward the partner. There was no relationship among married couples between the intensity of romantic love and parental interference, but for unmarried couples the correlation was .50. Concerning romantic lovers, the authors wrote: "These persons are intensely in love and may be disappointed and critical when their partners are not 'knights in shining armor' or 'fairy tale princesses...' Also suggested is oscillation between needs for reassurance and testing due to their intense involvement..." (p. 9). In brief, the results suggested a clear demarcation between romantic and conjugal love.

Any relationship may contain social rewards that are intrinsic and extrinsic to the bond. What is the effect of making one or another kind of reward salient? To find out, Seligman, Fazio, and Zanna (1980) asked a dating couple to check a list of reasons why each went out with the other. One list was intrinsic, for example, enjoyment of each other; the other list was extrinsic, for example, because friends would think more highly of the person. One group was exposed to only the extrinsic reasons and the other group, to only the intrinsic reasons. Making the extrinsic reasons salient diminished liking but not loving. This study, taken in conjunction with other research, suggests that romantic love is a special bond, which differs not only from less intense relationships but also from the strong bonds that occur in an enduring marriage, a parent–child relationship, and a close friendship. The only relationship that may approximate romantic love is the mother–infant bond of attachment.

4 Dominance

Social behavior includes not only nurturance and affection but also power relationships in which one individual is ascendant over others. Such ascendance tends to involve dominance, which occurs in highly social animals as a major source of social organization. In primates, as in other highly social animals, the strongest and most ferocious animals tend to enforce their will on weaker, smaller animals, thereby gaining greater access to females, food, or merely a place to sit or sleep. Dominant animals tend to move where they please with no concern about irritating lesser animals. Subordinate animals pay close attention to dominant animals, get out of their way, and readily surrender rewards when challenged. The simplest kind of dominance involves a linear relationship: A dominates B, who dominates C, and so on. Coalitions can form, however, and there are status relationships in primates. Nevertheless, in most primates dominance is achieved by means of coercion or threat of physical harm. The picture is more complex in human social relationships, for the aggression is not the only means by which dominance can be achieved. Aggression is still a primary means, however, and it is the major means of achieving dominance among children.

AGGRESSION

There is a crucial distinction between angry and instrumental aggression, made some time ago (Buss, 1961) and now widely accepted. In angry aggression the person is irritated or even enraged, and the reward (in cognitive terms, the intent) is the victim's being hurt or harmed. No one has explained why an angry person is pleased at the discomfort or pain of the victim, but it appears to be a universal phenomenon. In instrumental aggression, the aggressor is rarely angry, and the reward is not hurt or harm to the victim but any of the usual rewards by anyone: food, money, perquisites, goods, or services. Such economic rewards are achieved by seizing them or coercing the victim to abandon the attempt to achieve them. This is of course dominance through aggression.

The clear conceptual distinction between the two types of aggression may become cloudy in everyday life. Angry aggressors are rewarded primarily by the pain and suffering of their victims, but there may be additional incentives in the form of the usual economic rewards that are available after successful aggression. Instrumental aggressors are rewarded primarily by the economic rewards that follow coercion, but they may also be reinforced by a feeling of power over those they have vanquished. Adding to the complexity is a third kind of motivation: intrinsic pleasure in fighting. A love of fighting, sometimes playfighting and sometimes serious contests, is usually seen in children, but it may also be observed in some adults, usually men, who tend to deliberately pick fights in places like bars. The reward is intrinsic to the activity and requires no incentive beyond the sheer enjoyment of the act. Of course, successful aggression may yield economic rewards and dominance over the other, but presumably these are secondary to the primary reward of just enjoying the fight.

Successful fighting can lead to three other rewards. The first is obedience from the loser, who does what the dominant person wants or suffers the consequences. The extreme case is the Mafia threat, "Make him an offer he can't refuse," which implies giving in or being killed. Closely linked is the second reward, which might be called social effectance: being able to influence the behavior of others. Obedience is merely one example of social effectance, for it might be possible to influence another's behavior or decisions even when obedience is not the central issue. The third reward involves self-esteem, for the victor can acknowledge superior strength, ferocity, or skill. Dominant animals exude confidence as they move among conspecifics; dominant humans are not only confident but high in self-esteem. In brief, there are several kinds of incentives available to the successful aggressor: These include hurt or harm to the victim, a variety of economic rewards, obedience, impact on others, and elevated self-esteem.

Reaction of the Other

In the face of aggression, there are two possible reactions: submit or resist. The submission may be as total and complete as when the other person is holding a gun or is clearly physically too powerful. Some people willingly submit totally to the control of the person attempting to dominate. Such people tend to be insecure, lacking in self-esteem, and incapable of counteraggression. Beyond avoidance of punishment, their sole reward comes from identifying with the dominant person and sharing vicariously in the aggressor's status.

The submission may be only temporary, however, especially in people of high self-esteem and assertiveness. The boy who submits to his older brother may be biding time until he is strong enough to rebel. The girl who obeys her mother may be copying the latter's methods, waiting for the day when she can assert her own dominance. Such temporary submission is easier to bear and is adaptive in that it can lead to subsequent dominant behavior through observational learning.

The aggression of parents against their children has been receiving considerable attention in the media under the heading of child abuse. On the basis of retrospective reports, it has been suggested that parents who beat their children, often incurring serious injury, were themselves beaten as children. Though we must be careful in asserting explanations for a relationship based on retrospective reports, one obvious explanation is observational learning: parents may find themselves acting toward their children as parents had acted toward them.

Returning to transitory reactions to aggression, I suggest that one determinant is the manner or style with which aggressive responses are delivered. Some peers and some parents are sadistic in their beating of others, and some are ferocious in their anger; both accompaniments of aggression are frightening to the victim and are likely to result in enduring anxiety. Some aggressors, especially mothers, may react to the hurt of their victim with guilt or the anticipation of rejection and therefore attempt to undo the harm by being soothing and protective. Such behavior may have the desired effect of minimizing dislike toward the aggressor, but it sends a mixed message to the victim: I am willing to hurt you, but I really love you.

A common response to aggression is passive resistance, a frequent reaction of young children, especially 2- and 3-year-olds whose negativism is well-known. Passive resistance does not openly challenge the dominant person and therefore is more likely to be tolerated without a counter-reaction of punishment.

The probability of punishment is precisely the problem with active resistance. Open rebellion is such a direct challenge that the dominant person must immediately reassert authority by threat or aggression. Why, then, does anyone rebel? One reason is the possibility, however faint, that the rebellion will succeed, but the major reason for active resistance may lie within rebels themselves. They may be so young and egocentric, as 2- and 3-year-olds tend to be, that they have difficulty accepting orders. Or they may be so independent or so uncontrolled in their anger, as are some adolescents, that they resist any authority. These problems are associated with immaturity, which in most instances will be corrected over time. A small minority of youngsters, however, never adjust to the need to submit occasionally to those who are stronger. Their reward is an occasional small victory over authority and a pride in their unwillingness to accommodate to the demands of authority, whatever the cost.

When the aggressor is a playmate, friend, sibling, or casual acquaintance, the most likely reaction is resistance. It is in such dyadic conflict that stable relationships develop, but stability is the end-point of much struggling between members of the pair. The conflict may be shortlived, however, when one member submits quickly and offers no further resistance. A third option is avoidance of the other person.

When the aggressor is a parent or other authority figure, avoidance is not an optimal option, and the most frequent response is submission. If the dominant person is a beloved parent or admired authority figure, the submission is likely to be voluntary and accompanied by idolatry and attempted imitation of nondominant responses. If the dominant person is not admired, submission is grudging and may shade into negativism. The least frequent response to authority is open, active rebellion, but parents and authority generally have all the cards, so active resistance cannot endure. Those who try it either lapse into passive resistance or attempt to escape—for example, the running away from home or school by children and adolescents, or desertion by soldiers.

Relevant Traits

The most obvious personality trait relevant to dominance achieved through aggression is aggressiveness. Those who are rewarded by winning fights are likely to develop an enduring tendency to fight. The two major modes of aggression are physical and verbal. Though the traits of verbal and physical aggression are correlated (Buss, 1961), each must be regarded as a separate disposition: Verbally aggressive people may not be physically aggressive, and violent people may not be verbally aggressive. There are many questionnaires of aggression, but the one that makes the distinctions needed here is one of the oldest (Buss & Durkee, 1957). When the inventory was constructed, an attempt was made to minimize defensiveness in responding, for aggression is socially proscribed and most people do not readily admit to it. Therefore, most items either contain justification for aggression or assume that anger is already present. The items pertaining to physical aggression are:

1. Once in a while I cannot control my urge to harm others.
2. I can think of no good reason for ever hitting someone. (reversed)

3. If somebody hits me first, I let him have it.
4. Whoever insults me or my family is asking for a fight.
5. People who continually pester you are asking for a punch in the nose.
6. I seldom strike back, even if someone hits me first. (reversed)
7. When I really lose my temper, I am capable of slapping someone.
8. I get into fights about as often as the next person.
9. If I have to resort to violence to defend my rights, I will.
10. I have known people who pushed me so far that we came to blows.

The items that assess verbal aggression are:

1. When I disapprove of my friends' behavior, I let them know it.
2. I often find myself disagreeing with people.
3. I can't help getting into arguments when people disagree with me.
4. I demand that people respect my rights.
5. Even when my anger is aroused, I don't use strong language. (reversed)
6. If somebody annoys me, I am apt to tell him what I think of him.
7. When people yell at me, I yell back.
8. When I get mad, I say nasty things.
9. I could not put someone in his place even if he needed it. (reversed)
10. I often make threats I don't really mean to carry out.
11. When arguing, I raise my voice.
12. I generally cover up my poor opinion of others. (reversed)
13. I would rather concede a point than get into an argument about it. (reversed)

The inclusion of items referring to anger (to minimize defensiveness) has the effect of mixing angry aggression with instrumental aggression in both the verbal and physical aggression scales. There is also a scale that assesses anger or irritability (Buss & Durkee, 1957). These items are:

1. I lose my temper easily but get over it quickly.
2. I am always patient with others. (reversed)
3. I am irritated a great deal more than people are aware of.
4. It makes my blood boil to have people make fun of me.
5. If someone doesn't treat me right, I don't let it annoy me. (reversed)
6. Sometimes people bother me just by being around.
7. I often feel like a powder keg ready to explode.
8. I often carry a chip on my shoulder.
9. I can't help being a little rude to people I don't like.

10. I don't let a lot of unimportant things irritate me. (reversed)
11. Lately I have been kind of grouchy.

Notice that almost all the items refer to the emotional state of anger rather than to the behavioral consequences of anger. The scale does not assess whether people actually aggress when they are angry, nor was it constructed to do so, but it is the only scale that attempts to measure the anger component. The problem here is that both dominant and submissive people may score high on this scale. Thus a dominant person who is both instrumental-aggressive and angry-aggressive would score high, but a submissive person who is enraged about being the victim of aggression might also answer most of the questions in the direction of irritability. Submissive people need only to inhibit counteraggression, but they are free to become enraged.

The victims of aggression, who have struggled but consistently lost fights, are likely to carry an enduring burden of resentment. Resentment can also originate in jealousy over others' good fortune or over losing the affection of a loved one. Both kinds of items are found in the following resentment scale (Buss & Durkee, 1957), but the items relevant to the present discussion are those that do not involve jealousy:

1. I don't seem to get what's coming to me.
2. Other people always seem to get the breaks.
3. When I look back at what's happened to me, I can't help feeling mildly resentful.
4. Almost every week I see someone I dislike.
5. Although I don't show it, I am sometimes eaten up with jealousy.
6. I don't know any people that I downright hate. (reversed)
7. If I let people see the way I feel, I'd be considered a hard person to get along with.
8. At times I feel I get a raw deal out of life.

Victims of persistent and enduring aggression are likely to become chronically fearful. Though there are several copyrighted anxiety scales available, one of the briefest and most recent is available for general use (Buss & Plomin, 1984):

1. I am easily frightened.
2. I often feel insecure.
3. When I get scared, I panic.
4. I have fewer fears than most people my age. (reversed)

SUPERIORITY

Dominance can also be achieved by demonstrating superiority over others, which ordinarily occurs in competitive situations. The competition may be explicit and formal, accompanied by a set of rules. Thus in contests for political office, there are legal ordinances, although there are also unwritten codes involving morality. Debates, whether political or not, are governed by statutes that are spelled out in detail, and most organizations abide by Robert's Rules of Order. Virtually all athletic contests have detailed regulations such as not hitting below the belt in boxing, and beauty contests specify details of dress. Humans being what they are, some bending of the rules is inevitable and tolerated, but serious breaches are regarded as bad sportsmanship or worse.

Much competition is not explicit but implicit. In the workplace, there are often several workers vying for a single promotion; in universities several assistant professors struggling to achieve tenure, knowing that it will not be granted to all of them. In industry, in schools, and in the arts, men and women strive for the honors and prizes that are dangled before them. Salespersons can win a dazzling trip to Acapulco, students can become valedictorians or members of honorary societies, musicians can be judged the best among peers, and scientists can achieve professional recognition that ranges from local acclaim to the Nobel prize. When these public rewards are sought, the inevitable head-to-head competition is rarely acknowledged and remains just below the surface.

Whatever the nature of the competition and its setting, it tends to be fierce and the outcome for the winner is a demonstrated superiority over others. To achieve such status requires skill or talent, work habits, discipline, and the requisite motivation that may carry the day in the face of all obstacles. In most technologically advanced societies, enormous variations in talent are acknowledged in the form of graded competition. Beauty contests, for example, range from local to statewide to national. The loser of the national contest can console herself with the knowledge that she is a statewide winner, and the loser of the state competition knows that she previously won the local contest. Another way of spreading superiority around is to arrange for several prize winners. Thus in the Olympics there are gold, silver, and bronze medals, so that even the third place finisher is recognized as superior to all but two; and it is an honor to be selected to compete in the Olympics even if the athlete winds up in last place during the competition.

The usual rewards for success in competition are admiration for the winner's attributes (beauty, talent, discipline, and so on) and recognition for demonstrated superiority. The winner receives a medal, banner, badge, or document proclaiming superiority over rivals in the struggle for supremacy.

If you have beaten me in a fair contest, whether the competition is explicit or implicit, your dominance has been socially validated. It matters not whether I complain about the contest or refuse to accept the outcome, for social reality states that you have superior status over me.

Also well known are the economic rewards that often go to the winner: money, goods, and a variety of perquisites. Accompanying these is a heightened self-esteem, an acknowledgment by oneself of one's beauty, skill, or determination. Movie actors may believe in themselves, but their self-evaluation must be enhanced when the belief is confirmed by winning an Academy Award for best actor.

Reaction of the Loser

The reaction of those who fail in a contest depends on the degree of loss and the character of the losers. In a debate, beauty contest, athletic game, or election, the outcome may be so onesided that the loser is humiliated. When the loser's inferiority is made plain to everyone, it makes sense to surrender any hope of winning a subsequent competition. Many people overvalue their own attributes or undervalue those of competitors, but head-to-head competition shines a bright light of reality on such evaluations. It may then be time for a reevaluation and a decision to avoid competition subsequently. This decision is facilitated by the presence of low self-esteem in the loser.

Even when the loss is decisive, however, some people persist in further competition. They may do so because the rewards are so powerful or because their high self-esteem demands that they attempt further demonstration of their own talents. Of course, if the contest had been close and the outcome in doubt until the very end, the loser would have good reason to persist in further attempts to establish superiority. One reason for losing is youth and its associated inexperience; another is insufficient preparation or practice. These can be remedied and the previous outcome reversed. Thus the loser may emerge with an even greater determination to establish dominance or with a sense of sorrow, distress, lowered self-esteem, and a decision to avoid further competition.

Relevant Traits

The crucial trait involved in demonstrating superiority in relation to others is clearly competitiveness. This disposition, one component in achievement motivation, is closely linked with independence to form a second order factor of competitive striving for money (Jackson, Ahmed, & Heapy, 1976). Independence or autonomy needs to be kept distinct from competitiveness, although both are involved in dominance: in any event, striving to obtain only money is too narrow a perspective on competitiveness.

Competitiveness also emerged as a factor in a questionnaire on Type A behavior (Matthews, Krantz, Dembroski, & MacDougall, 1982), but the factor loadings for the only two items—competitive in sports and preference for winning rather than having fun in games—were too low to be meaningful. Clearly, achievement motivation and Type A behavior contain an element of competitiveness, and it is certainly no criticism of those who developed measures to assess these complex traits that clearcut measures of competitiveness have not emerged from their research. There is a set of competitiveness items, however, that emerged from an attempt to relate personality traits to performance at work. The competitiveness factor of the Spence and Helmreich (1978) WOFO consists of these items:

1. I really enjoy working in situations involving skill and competition.
2. When a group I belong to plans an activity, I would rather organize it myself than have someone else organize it and just help out.
3. It is important for me to perform better than others on a task.
4. I feel that winning is very important in both work and games.

The second item appears to assess initiative more than competitiveness, but the other three are apt. One problem with these items is that they were designed for situations that occur at work, and it would be preferable to have a questionnaire that was more general in orientation.

In the present context such a measure would take into account several theoretical issues. Competitiveness is a motivational trait, which means that items should reflect a strong desire to participate in contests involving skill and determination. The emphasis should be on the struggle to beat the other person, not on the rewards that might be obtained, for these might vary from one person to the next. The focus should be on winning, for this is the essence of striving for superiority. The competitive person likes to play games because of the opportunity to win, not just for the joy of playing. There are those who love to play games and who enjoy the suspense that accompanies the competition but who might be merely excitement seekers rather than competitors. Furthermore, competitiveness cannot be gauged merely by success in competition, for there are many reasons, other than motivation to win, that determine such success—physical or intellectual prowess, skill, luck, and the ability of one's opponents. It is the striving to win that is crucial here, not the percentage of wins. Of course, if a person regularly chooses weak opponents to guarantee winning, this is an unequivocal indicator of competitiveness.

Competitiveness is also distinct from mastery or competence: the motive to develop one's talents and to excel at work or play. It is true that one measure of competence is establishing that one is superior to another person—mastery can be combined with competitiveness—but it is also possible to exclude competition and establish mastery merely by meeting one's own goals or meeting social standards.

In brief, a questionnaire measure of competitiveness needs to exclude the related but distinct trait of mastery and any relevant abilities (a person may be capable but competitive or competitive but not capable). The focus should be on motivation to win, not on any particular reward that may accrue from winning. Such motivation can be assessed by inquiring who seeks out competitive situations, enjoys them, feels deprived without them, struggles to win even against formidable odds, endures the discomfort or pain of training in order to win, believes that nothing comes close to winning, might try anything to win (including bending the rules), is furious or otherwise upset after a loss, and cannot understand people who lack competitiveness.

The following 10 items appear to meet these criteria:

1. I get a kick out of matching my ability against other people's.
2. I need to be the best in my group.
3. I hate to lose.
4. I am willing to make sacrifices in order to win.
5. It bothers me to meet someone more attractive or talented than I.
6. In sports, the most important thing is winning.
7. I like it when there is a clear winner and loser.
8. Only people who lack motivation are good losers.
9. The only response to losing is to try harder next time.
10. I enjoy being challenged by another person.

ASSERTIVENESS

This means of attaining dominance might also be called "bossiness," but *assertiveness* is preferred as a broader and more neutral term. The developmental precursor is assumed to be the negative behavior of children roughly 2 years of age, the "terrible twos." Having separated self from others, they strive for self-determination by demonstrating that they have a choice. Many activities are initiated by adults, who tend to dominate young children, and therefore self-determination can best be demonstrated by a refusal to go along (I won't).

Most children gradually give up this negativism for more mature and positive ways of asserting self. It starts with a determination to "do it my way," and proceeds to bossiness over other children, as the child attempts to direct the course of joint behavior. Such bossiness usually starts with children who are younger, especially younger siblings, and gradually extends to peers. Children who cannot subjugate peers in this way may develop a preference for being with younger children who can be dominated.

This developmental trend appears to be paralleled by a similar trend in verbal interaction. Some children insist on taking over a larger share of the conversation and on having the last word. They tend to interrupt others, resist interruption by others, and seize the lion's share of the verbal interaction.

These trends continue through adulthood, their outcome being the variations evident in adult assertiveness. As might be expected, a major reinforcer is a sense of self-importance that accrues from dominating others. The other reward is the sense of having social impact, of being able to control the behavior of others, which is one kind of power.

The reaction of the other person varies from submission to resistance. Those who will not be dominated counter assertion with their own assertion, the inevitable outcome being an argument. Much bickering involves a struggle to seize the verbal initiative, resist being interrupted, and insist on doing it one's own way. The parallel to aggression should be evident, but assertion involves no necessary punishment or threats of punishment. One way of avoiding a quarrel is to yield the floor or to do it the other person's way. Such surrender may occur because of submissiveness or a lack of motivation to resist on this particular occasion or to dispute with this particular person. In the latter case, submission tends to be accompanied by annoyance or anger, as well as subsequent motivation to resist restriction of one's freedom—a phenomenon called *reactance* (Brehm, 1966).

Relevant Traits

No one has developed a distinct self-report measure of assertiveness, perhaps because the relevant items are mixed with other kinds of dominance items. Such a mixture reflects stereotyped notions of dominance, as may be found in the acts that are nominated by college students as involving dominance (D. Buss, 1981). A subset of these dominance items, however, refer to precisely the kind of assertion described here:

1. I demanded that he run an errand.
2. I told her to get off the phone so that I could use it.
3. I interrupted a conversation.
4. I chose to sit at the head of the table.
5. I yelled in order to get my way.
6. I decided which programs we would watch on TV.
7. I told him which item he should purchase.
8. I challenged someone to discuss her position.

9. I forbade her to leave the room.
10. I monopolized the conversation.
11. I walked ahead of everyone else.

Such specific acts may be used to assess traits such as assertiveness, and this is precisely the aim of the act frequency approach (D. Buss & Craik, 1983). The traditional approach is to use more general items, which refer to larger classes of behavior. Again, such items may be found only in combination with other items designed to assess a more broadly defined dominance. The items most relevant to the present account may be found in a dominance questionnaire by Ray (1981). A group of items such as the following might comprise a questionnaire of assertiveness as it has been defined here:

1. Are you the sort of person who always like to get their own way?
2. Do you tend to boss people around?
3. Do you dislike telling others what to do? (reversed)
4. Do you tend to dominate the conversation?
5. Do you give in to people rather easily? (reversed)
6. Do you like having the last word in an argument or discussion?
7. Are you pretty good at getting your own way in most things?

Those who chronically resist this kind of domination are expected to be dominant themselves. After a prolonged period of being bossed, some people react by being consistently rebellious. The appropriate trait measure is the negativism scale of the Buss–Durkee Inventory (1957):

1. Unless somebody asks me in a nice way, I won't do what they want.
2. When someone makes a rule I don't like, I am tempted to break it.
3. When someone is bossy, I do the opposite of what he asks.
4. When people are bossy, I take my time just to show them.
5. Occasionally when I am mad at someone, I will give him the silent treatment.

Those who repeatedly resist being dominated by an assertive person tend to be assertive themselves, though they may be less so than the one who is originally bossy. Furthermore, their self-esteem is likely to be high or at least moderate. Those who submit to another's assertiveness tend to be low in this kind of dominance, and other things being equal, their self-esteem is likely to be depressed.

LEADERSHIP

When dominance is sought or attained through aggression, competition, or assertion, the conflict is open and explicit. In the last avenue to domination—leadership—conflict may or may not be present, and the issue of dominance may be implicit rather than explicit. As defined here, *leadership* involves taking the initiative, being decisive, and assuming responsibility for what the group does. The group may consist of just two people or many, but the emphasis in the present context is on two or three people and an unorganized group.

Leaders tend to be the ones who have an idea of what to do next and are willing to put forth the idea. They are the ones who offer suggestions and who say in effect, "Follow me." In addition to displaying initiative, they are likely to make a decision when one is needed. Thus when others cannot make up their minds or when there are several possibilities, leaders tend to select one course of action for the group. By implication, leaders cannot be obsessive. Leaders also tend to take responsibility for the actions of the group because they are willing to take personal risks. Those less willing to take risks are glad to have someone else assume this burden, and the question may arise as to why anyone should take the chance of being blamed for a group action. There appears to be a specific social norm for a leader's being responsible. In addition, leaders are willing to tolerate the possibility of blame in order to assert leadership.

The three components of leadership are separable. Thus a leader might show initiative but not decisiveness or responsibility, decisiveness but not initiative or responsibility, and responsibility but not initiative or decisiveness. Any single component rarely occurs in isolation, however. If one appeared without the other two, the leadership would probably be brief. Thus, the three are surely correlated and are most likely to appear together.

If leadership carries with it the risk of blame, it also has its rewards. Others tend to admire the one who makes decisions and takes responsibility. When the group has some identity or is organized, prestige is associated with leadership. As with the other forms of attaining dominance, leadership offers a feeling of power over others—in this instance, the power extending to deciding the actions of the group. And leadership ordinarily carries with it various perquisites, which range from merely going first or being at the head of the table, to access to cars or servants (the more organized and formal the group, the greater the perquisites). In the interpersonal contexts that are the focus of this book, perquisites tend to be minimal and of little consequence as rewards. The last reward, common to all behavior that results in dominance, is a boost in self-esteem that is the inevitable consequence of comparing oneself with others: Anyone who can get others to follow must possess qualities that demand respect and there-fore self-respect.

The response of others depends on their personalities. If they include leaders, there is likely to be conflict over who makes the decision and which course of action should be taken. Such conflict is bound to continue until one person emerges as leader. When someone steps forward to make a decision and takes responsibility for it, there is a double security for the followers: the feeling that the person in charge has the knowledge and capability to decide correctly and carry out the decision and the knowl-edge that this person will be held responsible for the consequences. In most groups, the majority lack the initiative or energy to step forward and take charge, and they are satisfied to have someone else make the decisions.

Relevant Traits

The components of leadership are assumed to be initiative, decisiveness, and responsibility, and one would think that there are appropriate trait measures of each. Responsibility tends not to be represented in trait measures, though it may be regarded as one aspect of social maturity. Initiative and decisiveness are included in the dominance acts assembled by D. Buss (1981):

1. I set goals for the group.
2. I volunteered an idea in order to start the group conversation.
3. I took the lead in livening up a dull party.
4. I organized a protest meeting.
5. I took the lead in organizing a project.
6. I took the initiative in planning the party.
7. I settled a dispute among other members of the group.
8. I issued orders that got the group organized.
9. I assigned roles and got the game going.
10. I made decisions without consulting the others involved in them.
11. I took command of the situation after the accident.
12. I made the final decision.

Notice that the first six items refer to initiative: getting the group organized or starting people on a particular path, as the leader steps forward and suggests that others follow. This kind of behavior would be difficult for a shy person or someone low in sociability. I assume that the combination of shyness and low sociability equals introversion and that the combination of unshyness and high sociability equals extraversion. Thus other things being equal, we would expect that leaders lean toward the extraverted side of the bipolar dimension. This expectation does not imply that all leaders are extraverts or that extraversion is a necessary condition for leadership. Given that an introvert would have more difficulty in stepping to the front and initiating an activity, however, an association between extraversion and leadership appears likely.

The last six items on the list deal with decisiveness, as the leader assumes control and imposes coherence on the group. At issue here is taking charge and telling others what to do or deciding what the entire group will do. Extraversion is not necessarily involved, but decisiveness does seem to require determination and resoluteness. Just as initiative may be assessed by the first six items on the list, so the trait of decisiveness might be assessed by the last six. However, there is a more traditional self-report measure of decisiveness, which appears as a Directiveness factor on a questionnaire of assertiveness devised by Lorr and More (1980):

1. I have no particular desire to be the leader of the group. (reversed)
2. I shy away from situations where I might be asked to take charge. (reversed)
3. I let others lead when I'm on a committee. (reversed)
4. I would avoid a job which required me to supervise other people. (reversed)
5. I work best when I'm the person in charge.
6. I seek positions where I can influence others.
7. I am usually the one who initiates activities in my group.
8. In an emergency I get people organized and take charge.

Notice that half the items refer to the avoidance of leadership and are therefore reversed for scoring. Also, the seventh item deals with initiating activities, which obviously is correlated with decisiveness but which I regard as differentiable from it. Not everyone who initiates activities or makes suggestions for others to follow will necessarily possess the determination to take command of others, and not everyone who takes command will necessarily be the one who originates activities.

In brief, the traits relevant to leadership are initiative, decisiveness, and responsibility, though trait measures seem to be available for only the first two. There are also traits relevant to the remainder of the group: those to whom leadership is directed. Those who merely follow are expected to be low in initiative and decisiveness; and they rarely seek to lead or find themselves in a position of leadership, so responsibility is not even an issue.

Those who resist presumably have a strong need for independence. Striving for autonomy resembles assertiveness but does not involve domination. There are trait measures of autonomy, but they tend to involve a reluctance to comply in the face of group pressure. Thus the independence factor of Lorr and More (1980) contains these items: My opinions are not easily changed by those around me; and I follow my own ideas even when pressured by a group to change them. Other measures of autonomy deal with independence of functioning, such as being able to fend for oneself and not needing the help or supervision of others. What is needed in the present context is a measure specifically designed to assess the autonomous reaction of people who resist being led.

FOUR PATHS TO DOMINANCE

The different kinds of dominance behavior are summarized in Table 4.1. Aggression, superiority, and assertion share a common feature: there is a winner and a loser. Leadership differs in that the leader is not necessarily a winner and a follower is not necessarily a loser, for there is often no contest about who makes the decisions. Aggression and superiority are linked by the common feature of competition, the outcome being possible hurt or harm for aggression but not for superiority demonstrated in competition. Aggression and assertion apply pressure to the target; if animals could talk, they would display dominance not only by aggression and threats but also by being bossy. Assertion resembles leadership only in the initiative demanded, either by the bossy person's making demands or the leader's imposing a course of action on others. Furthermore, when a leader becomes dictatorial, leadership shades into assertion.

There are developmental differences among the four behaviors. Aggression first appears in infancy as soon as the child has sufficient mobility and control to hurt another. Assertion, in the form of insisting on having one's way, appears in the second year of life and flowers in the third year of life. Competition must await the child's understanding of a contest and therefore does not usually begin until the fourth or fifth year of life. Leadership would seem to start at about the same time as competition, the child being able to initiate activities, get others to follow, and being old enough to imitate the taking command displayed by older children and adults.

A boost in self-esteem is the common reward of all four forms of domination, for there is an explicit or implicit demonstration of superiority over another person. Three of the four kinds of domination result in social impact—an implied or direct control over another person—but success in competition does not. However, success in competition and leadership both garner admiration and prestige, either for the skill and persistence needed to win or for the initiative and decisiveness that define leadership. All four modes can result in economic rewards, but they are most likely to occur only for successful aggression and competition.

The reaction to dominance varies with the kind of domination that occurs. The loser of an aggressive encounter must submit to the winner or

TABLE 4.1
Dominance

	Aggression	Superiority	Assertion	Leadership
Method	Hurt, harm, threaten (physical, verbal)	Win in competition (skill, persistence)	Boss, monopolize conversation	Initiative, decisiveness, responsibility
First seen	Early childhood	Childhood	Early childhood	Childhood
Reward (all: transient reaction of other)	Obedience, social impact, economic rewards	Admiration, prestige, economic rewards	Feeling of control, social impact	Admiration, prestige, perquisites (identity)
Instrumental	Counter-aggression, submission, avoidance	Continue competing, avoid competing	Refuse to submit, submit	Resist (active or passive) follow, avoid
Affect	Anger, hostility, fear	Distress, dejection	Annoyance, anger, reactance	Anger, security
Relevant traits				
Dominant one (all: self-esteem)	Aggressiveness	Competitiveness	Assertiveness	Initiative, decisiveness
Dominated one resister	Aggressiveness, resentment	Competitiveness	Assertiveness, negativism	—
Nonresister	Submissiveness, fearfulness	Low self-esteem	Low self-esteem	—

face subsequent hurt. The loser of a competition can cry "foul" or otherwise attempt to undo the outcome, but such behavior would brand that person as a poor loser. In both assertion and leadership, however, there is an option available to the person being dominated. It is to leave the interaction and not accept being bossed or led, an option available to peers of roughly equal status but not open to those of lower status or strength.

The affect common to the dominated person in all four paths to domination is anger, though the loser of a competition is more likely to be frustrated and upset than angry. Aggression elicits the most powerful emotions and is the only behavior to induce fear. A loss in competition is special in that it may cause an emotion not present in other forms of domination: dejection. A felt loss of freedom (reactance) is most likely to occur as a result of being bossed; reactance rarely occurs in a follower because the person would refuse to follow the course of action suggested by the leader.

Each variety of domination is closely linked to a personality trait that follows from the way the behavior is defined: aggressiveness for aggression, competitiveness for superiority, assertiveness for assertion, and a combination of initiative and decisiveness for leadership. The relevant trait for all four forms of dominance is self-esteem. Dominant behavior inevitably boosts confidence, not only in humans but in other animals. Ethologists have observed that dominant animals move about the group, facing down any challengers and manifesting all the facial and bodily expressions of a supremely confident animal. The cognitive analogue of confidence would seem to be self-esteem, which we cannot infer in animals but know exists in humans. Dominant humans have established their control or superiority over others by any of the four social behaviors already discussed. With continued episodes of such demonstrated superiority, one consequence must be an elevated sense of self-worth.

If dominance can elevate self-esteem, so can high self-esteem lead to dominance. Those who value themselves tend to enter competition confident of winning, perhaps because one basis for the high self-esteem may be prior success in competition. In a game such as tennis, for example, players who think they are better than the opponents are likely to play up to their ability, whereas players of lower self-esteem tend to choke in crucial situations because of doubt about winning. It requires good feelings about oneself to interrupt another, monopolize a conversation, or boss others. And leadership requires a faith in one's ability to suggest the correct solution, make the right decision, and especially to take responsibility for the outcome. Notice that aggression has been omitted from this sequence of self-esteem to domination. High self-esteem does not inevitably lead to successful aggression or to the motive to aggress, though it may be a powerful determinant of the other three forms of dominance.

The self-esteem of the dominated person does not necessarily suffer. There is no humiliation in being beaten up by a stronger aggressor or by being led by a decisive leader. Self-esteem may drop, however, when one is bossed by a peer or when one loses in competition, though even in these situations there may be mitigating circumstances that can save the self-esteem of the dominated person. In brief, self-esteem is more closely linked to domination than to being dominated.

There may be important variations within each of the four ways of establishing dominance, especially in the consequences for subsequent behavior. If the aggression is purely instrumental and is restricted solely to obtaining an extrinsic reward, the victim may be upset or angry. These emotional reactions escalate rapidly when the aggression is angry aggression and the victim is hurt or harmed, and the reaction of others is more likely to involve retribution. Similarly, a winner with good manners usually elicits mature behavior from the loser, but a bragging winner who rubs the losers' nose in their loss is likely to elicit anger and perhaps aggression. Similarly, assertiveness can be exercised in a polite way, with profuse use of "I beg your pardon" and "excuse me." Such good manners may conceal the domination or at least render it implicit, thereby minimizing negative affective reactions from the person being bossed. And a leader can take charge in an unassuming way, minimizing the decisive and responsibility aspects. A truly subtle leader appears merely to surrender to the mandate of those being led, covertly taking charge of the group. In brief, the style of each mode of domination plays a major role in the reaction of those who are dominated.

The four paths to dominance vary in whether there are gender differences. There is a well-documented and consistent gender difference in aggression: Boys are more aggressive than girls, and men are more aggressive than women. Laboratory research has shown that men are more physically aggressive (Buss, 1966), and they score higher on the verbal aggressiveness scale of the Buss–Durkee (1957). Also, males are more likely to curse than are females.

Gender differences for the other three paths to dominance are problematical. Women are just as likely to be bossy as are men, although they are trained to inhibit assertiveness with casual acquaintances and strangers and also when the target is a man who might construe the behavior as putting him down. There are two related issues here: One is whether the group consists of only women, and the other is how public the social behavior is. Women may be just as competitive and as likely to seek leadership as men but only in relation to other women or when they are not being observed. They compete less against men and are less likely to assume leadership when men are present. These tendencies are presumably products of gender role socialization. Another product is the limitation on the kind of competition open to women; traditional socialization trains women to compete in baking contests and beauty contests but not in "rough sports" and politics. Gender roles are changing, however, and a minority of women are expected to be no different from men in assertiveness, competitiveness, and leadership. Indeed, there are women's workshops that train them to be more assertive and to seek leadership in the presence of men. In brief, males are more aggressive than females, but gender differences in the other three paths to dominance are weaker and tend not to appear when the interaction is same-sexed.

NOTES

Virtually all the research in this area has dealt with a variety of behaviors under the headings of dominance or power. The concept of power usually applies to adults, whereas dominance applies to both children and adults, and the concept therefore can be studied developmentally.

Gellert (1961) observed dyads of 4- to 6-year-old preschool children in a playroom. Each dyad was observed three times, and a stable pattern of dominance and submission was found for most of the children. Thus dominance may be established as early as the first few years of life.

One place to investigate dominance behavior in older children and adolescents is a summer camp, which lasts long enough for stable relationships to occur. Savin-Williams (1976) observed the behavior of 13-year-old boys in such a camp and obtained sociometric rankings of dominance. Both observations and rankings yielded a stable hierarchy: "Although the dominance ordering is not invariant—for example, Beta dominated Alpha in 32% of their dominance interactions together—there was a clear tendency for some boys to dominate other boys consistently and for those boys to dominate other boys, etc. This stability increased during the course of the camp period" (p. 975). Almost all the indices used in observing dominance involved aggression (physical or verbal) or assertiveness. Athletic ability correlated .71 with dominance position; such ability presumably led to success in athletic competition. Thus, in terms of the analysis of dominance discussed earlier in the chapter, three of the four means of attaining dominance were represented: aggression, assertion, and competition.

In a subsequent summer camp, the subjects were of both genders and ranged in age from 12 to 14 (Savin-Williams, 1979). The data for boys yielded essentially the same findings as before: dominance based on physical aggression, threats, and taking away objects. Again the dominance hierarchy was stable for boys, but it was less stable and there was less agreement on the sociometric rankings for girls. There was also much less aggression among the girls, who established dominance by bossiness and shunning. In describing the upper extreme of the dominance hierarchy, Savin-Williams (1979) wrote: "The most dominant child has been characterized as being older, taller, heavier, tougher, and healthier and more popular, athletic, daring, and attractive to other group members" (p. 933). It is not much of a presumption to suggest that being daring and attractive are attributes that should result in leadership, the fourth means of attaining dominance.

The gender difference in dominance is especially likely to become manifest when a dyad includes both sexes. Megargee (1969) had dyads work on a task that required one of them to be the boss and the other the worker. The subjects varied in self-reported dominance. When a dominant woman was paired with a submissive man, she tended to reveal her dominance by choosing him as leader. Thus, her dominance was manifested subtly, not by becoming the boss but by deciding who would be the boss.

In a subsequent experiment, Snodgrass and Rosenthal (1984) assigned one member of each dyad to be the leader and the other, the follower. Female leaders were observed to be just as dominant with male followers as with female followers. Female leaders, however, rated themselves as less dominant with male followers than with female followers. Thus in the 1980s women may dominate men when they have been assigned the role, but they still cannot perceive themselves as doing so or perhaps just refuse to admit it publicly.

The concept of power extends beyond psychology into sociology, economics, and political science, disciplines too far afield to discuss here. Two exceptions might be worth mentioning, however. Wrong (1979) has reviewed the many concepts of power in the social sciences. He draws an important distinction between *power to* and *power over:* "Clearly, everyone seeks to acquire the power to satisfy their wants and achieve their goals, but this is implied by the very concepts of 'want' and 'goal' themselves. It does not, however, follow from this truism that everyone seeks power *over* other people, that is, strives to produce intended effects on the actions and attitudes of others" (p. 220).

The other exception is a classification offered by Lasswell and Kaplan (1950), who suggest eight different means of attaining power. In the following list, the means are first, then the resultant kind of power: power, political power; respect, councilorship; rectitude, mentorship; affection, personal influence; well-being, violence; wealth, economic power; skill, expertness; and enlightenment, advisory influence.

A classification with more of the flavor of psychology and sociology was compiled by French and Raven (1959). They include reward, coercion, expert power (an expert, such as a physician or lawyer), legitimate power (societal, institutional), and referent power (being an admired person whom others wish to emulate).

Much of the psychological research on power has been conducted by students of David McClelland, who has his own book on power (1975). He postulates four developmental stages, only the third of which is relevant here: assertion and control of others through physical aggression, bargaining, persuasion, and physical assertiveness. McClelland's principal contribution in this area, however, may be using imagery in the Thematic Apperception Test to assess individual differences in the motivation to seek power.

The first TAT measure of power was developed by Veroff (1957), who later (1982) called his trait fear of weakness to contrast it with a subsequent TAT measure called hope of power; the two correlate .42. Uleman (1972) distinguished between trying to gain a base of power and using it to influence others. Although this differentiation may be hard to maintain when scoring imagery on the TAT, it would appear to be meaningful when applied to behavior.

The most comprehensive work by any of McClelland's students is a book on power by Winter (1973), who introduced the concept of hope of power. He suggested three dimensions of power-related concepts: inequality of strength or status, legitimacy or morality of the act, and resistance of the target. Although they were arranged in a three-dimensional schema (p. 9), the schema was not used in Winter's scoring of TAT power imagery, which appears to be the most popular (see Fodor & Farrow, 1979; Fodor, 1984, for example). The themes scored for power are getting or keeping power or influence, assaults, threats, controlling others, helping when asked, influencing or bribing others, arguing, trying to impress others, arousing strong positive or negative emotions, and a concern with reputation or prestige. This list reveals the mixture of behaviors that can lead to power, which is defined as roughly synonymous with dominance. If these various instrumental behaviors are not kept separate, however, we cannot distinguish between the dominant person who achieves power through aggression from one who achieves power through competition, assertiveness, or leadership.

These four means of attaining dominance have been implicated as possible precursors of coronary artery disease, for they comprise the essential elements of the personality syndrome called Type A. There is a Type A questionnaire for children that assesses aggression, competition, and leadership (Matthews, 1980). The two factors on this instrument, which correlate .41, are as follows:

Competitiveness
1. When this child plays games, he/she is competitive.
2. This child works quickly and energetically rather than slowly and deliberately.
3. This child is a leader in various activities.
4. He/she seems to perform better when competing against others.
5. When working or playing, he/she tries to do better than other children.
6. It is important to this child to win, rather than have fun in games or schoolwork.
7. The other children look to this child for leadership.
8. This child is competitive.

Impatience-Aggression
1. When this child has to wait for others, he/she becomes impatient.
2. This child does things in a hurry.

3. It takes a lot to get this child angry at his/her peers. (reversed)
4. This child interrupts others.
5. This child gets irritated easily.
6. This child likes to argue or debate.
7. This child is patient when working with children slower than he/she is. (reversed)
8. This child can sit still long. (reversed)
9. This child tends to get into fights.

The second scale is a mixture of impatience, aggression, and irritability, whereas the first scale combines leadership and competition. We should not be surprised that dominant children will not tolerate waiting for others or that they might become irritated with their peers; one of the rewards of being dominant is not having to tolerate aversiveness from others. Investigators of Type A behavior have collected evidence that it is a contributor to coronary artery disease (see Matthews, 1982 for a review). If this evidence holds up, it would suggest that dominance or power has physiological costs.

Aggression has been interpreted in terms of coercion, a topic issue closely linked to dominance (Tedeschi, Smith, & Brown, 1974). Coercion derives from the use of punishments or the threat of punishments, and these are classified as noxious stimulation, deprivation of expected gain, and social punishments (presumably shunning or rejection). Aggression is of course a possible last resort, which has been summarized in terms of making an offer that cannot be refused. Tedeschi et al. (1974) phrased it this way: "If a person cannot persuade, bribe, manipulate, or otherwise induce a target to comply with the source's wishes ... the latter's power may ultimately rest upon his ability to restrain, transport, immobilize, injure, or destroy the target" (p. 550).

Two aspects of dominance, aggressiveness and competitiveness, appear regularly in questionnaires of masculinity–femininity. On a currently popular questionnaire, that of Spence and Helmreich (1978), the 8-item M–F scale contains an aggressiveness and a submissiveness item, and the 8-item M scale contains a competitiveness item. Self-reports may be misleading, however, with the respondents merely reflecting stereotypes that are expected rather than behavior that actually occurs. The larger literature was reviewed by Maccoby and Jacklin (1974), who reported compelling evidence for greater aggression among males but only equivocal findings on competition. They wrote "Most research on competition has been conducted in contrived situations ... that do not correspond well with the naturalistic conditions under which competitiveness is often most intense; hence the failure to find consistent sex differences in existing studies of competition has not closed the issue" (p. 274). They also conclude that although boys tend to dominate other boys, there is little evidence that boys dominate girls.

Thus, except for aggressiveness, there is reason for cognitive dissonance here. Boys tend to be socialized to be competitive, assertive, and to attempt to lead, whereas girls are either not socialized in these directions or are even urged to avoid them. Yet, the research on the nonaggressive aspects of domination has yielded sparse evidence of a gender difference. Two possibilities remain: Either the research is basically flawed, as Maccoby and Jacklin (1974) suggest, or the stereotypes of masculine and feminine behavior and their socialization have been exaggerated and do not encompass reality.

5 Prosocial Behavior

There is an enormous literature on prosocial behavior, much of it summarized in the encyclopedic volumes of Ervin Staub (1978, 1979). In the last decade or so, researchers have concentrated on altruism, in part because of the thrust of the sociobiological perspective. Though various kinds of prosocial behavior are examined here, the focus is narrowed by two considerations. One is that personality variables must be prominent, either as inputs into prosocial behavior or as consequences. The second is a developmental perspective that centers on the child's progress from egocentricity and selfishness to a social orientation and unselfishness; the endpoint of such development is social maturity.

SOCIAL MATURITY

Social maturity includes emotions, instrumental behavior, and cognition. There is no implication that they necessarily operate in isolation, but they can be separated conceptually and the exposition will be helped by doing so.

Emotional Maturity

The earliest response to another's distress is crying, as has been observed in newborns who cry when they hear the wailing of another infant (Simner,

1971). Beyond the neonatal period, infants may laugh when they hear laughter or may smile in response to another's smiling. Though some psychologists regard these emotional reactions to another's emotional behavior (especially distress) as primitive empathy (Hoffman, 1977), perhaps the behavior should be considered as social contagion. It is well known that people laugh more in response to humor when in an audience than when alone, and older children and adults may go off on laughing spells as first one and then the other almost reflexively laughs at the other's laughter. Thus infants' early positive or negative reactions to another's emotional state may be an early form of empathy, but social contagion might account for this behavior, thereby obviating the need to invoke empathy so early in life.

Young children may also become distressed when another person has been hurt or suffered misfortune because as observers they feel helpless. Older children and adults also become upset when they cannot alleviate another's suffering, and there is no sadder sight than watching parents sit helplessly while their infant is ill or even dying. When a family member dies, the living relatives mourn for the death of the loved one and are saddened by their own loss. The point being made is that the distress reaction to another's hurt, harm, or misfortune may be caused by helplessness or one's own loss. We should expect individual differences in this tendency to become upset, and they have been assessed as part of an empathy questionnaire (Davis, 1983). The relevant items, part of a factor called personal distress (Davis, 1983), deal with such topics as: going to pieces when someone needs help, feeling helpless in an emotional crisis, being apprehensive in an emergency, and losing control in emergencies. This personal distress scale correlated .59 and .53 (men and women, respectively) with the fearfulness scale of the EASI (Buss & Plomin, 1975). Given the general emotional nature of the items on the personal distress scale, they should correlate even higher with the emotionality scale of the EASI. In brief, the tendency to become upset in the face of another's distress may derive mainly from the trait of emotionality, which has been shown to have a genetic component (Buss & Plomin, 1975).

When there is an emotional reaction to another's good or ill fortune and both social contagion and helplessness can be ruled out, a case can be made for emotional empathy (by usage, *sympathy* refers to an emotional reaction only to another's suffering). Thus, if a friend or relative wins a lottery, an election, or an important athletic contest, one might be happy for this person even without observing his or her emotional reaction. Similarly, when a friend suffers a loss and is not present, one may be saddened. Perhaps a friend is acting foolishly or committing a social blunder without knowing it and therefore without displaying any embarrassment; one may feel ill at ease or experience pity, even though the friend has no emotional response that might cause social contagion.

Emotional empathy is especially prevalent when two people are close friends or members of the same family. There is an extension of self to the other, so that whatever affects one person also affects the other. This kind of identity tends to occur for parents with their young children, for siblings who have grown close, and for lovers. In each instance, there appears to be a partial merging of the self with the other so that self-interest includes the other. Such empathy can occur even in the absence of a close relationship if the observing person has been through the experience that the other is currently undergoing. Thus a mother may vicariously experience what another mother is feeling when the latter is in childbirth, an Olympic gold medal winner knows emotionally what another winner is feeling, and a recently divorced person knows what another is going through when the latter is being divorced. The gut feelings involved in these various acts are difficult to experience unless one has been through the same situation but easy to share vicariously if one has.

As might be expected, there are individual differences in emotional empathy, and a questionnaire bearing this name was developed by Mehrabian and Epstein (1972). The items were divided into seven subscales, which included, among other things, emotional contagion, appreciating others' feelings, being emotionally responsive, being upset easily, and being sympathetic. A more coherent scale emerged from a factor analysis of empathy items, the factor also being called *emotional empathy* (Davis, 1983):

1. I am often quite touched by the things I see happen.
2. I would describe myself as a pretty soft-hearted person.
3. Sometimes I don't feel very sorry for other people when they are having problems. (reversed)
4. When I see someone being treated unfairly, I don't feel very much pity for them. (reversed)
5. When I see someone being taken advantage of, I feel kind of protective toward them.
6. I often have tender, concerned feelings for people less fortunate than me.
7. Other people's misfortunes do not usually disturb me a great deal. (reversed)

Several items, especially item 6, appear related to the trait of tender-mindedness (Cattell, 1973), a trait observed more in women than in men. Women also score higher than men in all extant questionnaires of emotional empathy (Davis, 1983). Women's greater empathy may develop because they are traditionally socialized to nurture the young, but it may also derive from their greater tendency to sustain close friendships and their stronger sense of family.

Progressing from being upset at another's distress to experiencing emotional empathy represents one aspect of emotional maturity. Another is the developmental sequence that starts with jealousy in early childhood and ends with eventual sharing of affection and attention. Jealousy is not limited to humans and may be seen in household pets. Some dogs are disturbed by the arrival of an infant in the home, which deprives them of some of the attention and love they had been given previously. Such jealousy in the next older human sibling is so common that most books on parenting describe ways of dealing with it. Although not as important, the movement from insisting on being the center of attention to sharing attention with others is a common developmental theme. Some adults have never learned to share the spotlight and remain rooted in exhibitionism.

Concerning individual differences in jealousy, there appears to be no measure that specifically assesses them. It seems likely, though, that any adult who persists in childish feelings of jealousy as a personality disposition will probably suffer from generalized resentment. To the extent that this assumption is correct, the relevant measure would be the resentment scale of the Hostility Inventory (Buss & Durkee, 1957).

Instrumental Maturity

Egocentricity in the behavioral domain emerges as selfishness. Infants are unlikely to share their toys or any of their prized possessions. They may hand over a toy momentarily but demand it back quickly. It is not clear whether children would start sharing goods, services, and privileges if they were not trained to do so, but socialization training to share appears to be universal, and there is strong pressure for children to split economic rewards with those around them. Similarly, as children develop, they are taught to share the work. When others ask for help, children are expected to cooperate; when there is a group task, children are expected to do their part even when there is no immediate selfish reward. Some children are socialized more thoroughly, and some children accept it more than others. The result is individual differences among adults in the extent to which they share economic rewards and cooperate in work. There are apparently no self-report measures of these dispositions, perhaps because cultural pressure is so great that people will not admit to being selfish or uncooperative.

There is also a developmental progression from helplessness to self-help. Infants are unable to care for themselves and require the ministrations of adults. As they mature, most children prefer to do things for themselves and wave off the assistance of adults. They want to feed themselves, dress themselves, and walk to school unaccompanied by a parent. Parents and others encourage this instrumental independence, and children are expected gradually to seek less help from others, which produces individual differences. Some older children and adults continue to rely heavily on others for support, and others are so independent that they refuse to ask for aid even when it is strongly needed.

Women are traditionally brought up to depend on others for help and sympathy, and they tend to disclose their personal problems to female friends and prefer shopping with others. Men are traditionally reared to be rugged individualists who can make it on their own and who regard disclosure of personal problems or the seeking of sympathy as being childish or feminine. In terms of traditional socialization, women's sociability is likely to be channelled into close personal friendships, and they depend on these friends. Men's sociability is more likely to be channelled into play or work groups, and they have few or no intimate friends and reject sympathy or help in solving personal problems.

Seeking help may also be related to the trait of emotionality (Buss & Plomin, 1984), the tendency to become distressed easily and more intensely. Emotional people are more likely to need help and therefore, other things equal, are more likely to seek it. One thing that is not equal is sociability, which means that the person most likely to seek help from others tends to be high in both emotionality and sociability. By this reasoning, those low in emotionality tend not to seek help from others. Thus the help-avoiders tend to be low emotional, low sociable people.

Infants and others who require care must depend on older children and adults to furnish the assistance needed. Who offers such nurturance? Those who occupy vocational roles that involve helping others do so as part of the job: nurses, nursery school teachers, social workers, and therapists. It is no accident that women are disproportionately represented in these occupations, for they are traditionally socialized to be nurturant, partly as preparation for their role as mothers. Within each gender, however, there are individual differences in nurturance, and one questionnaire that assesses this trait is the Inventory of Interpersonal Styles (Lorr & Youniss, 1973). Sample items are: I like jobs where I can help people; I find myself helping friends when I know they are sick; and I am not the kind of person who rushes in to help when he/she hears a hard luck story (reversed).

Cognitive Maturity

Infants start out life without the requisite social cognitions that would alert them to the needs of others. As children mature, they gradually discern that others may need help, and children are socialized to feel obligated to furnish such help. Thus the usual developmental path is from irresponsible to responsible. A small minority of children appear to be incapable of such learning, and when they reach adolescence or adulthood, they are recognized as psychopaths. Within the normal range there are also individual differences, some children having adopted the social norm more than others. Harris (1957) devised a scale of social responsibility for youngsters 9 to 18 years of age, but only the following five items appear to be precisely what is meant here by responsibility:

1. I am the kind of person that people can count on.
2. I am frequently chosen as room helper or to run errands.
3. I would never let a friend down when he expects something of me.
4. Every person should give some of his time for the good of his town or city.
5. People have a real duty to take care of their parents when they are old, even if it costs a lot.

Parents know how egocentric their children are, but it remained for Jean Piaget (1932) to describe the developmental progression from egocentrism to the ability to take the perspective of another. Breaking out of one's own individual cognitive set is important not only for an understanding of cognitive development but also for the development of social maturity. Some people move further along this developmental path than others, and when designing his empathy questionnaire, Davis (1983) came up with items that clustered on a factor of perspective-taking:

1. I believe that there are two sides to every question and try to look at them both.
2. When I'm upset with someone, I usually try to "put myself in his shoes" for a while.
3. I try to look at everybody's side of a disagreement before I make a decision.
4. I sometimes find it difficult to see things from the "other guy's" point of view. (reversed)
5. Before criticizing somebody, I try to imagine how I would feel if I were in their place.
6. If I'm sure I'm right about something, I don't waste much time listening to other people's arguments. (reversed)
7. I try to understand my friends better by imagining how things look from their perspective.

Though these items all refer to cognitions, they also relate to the emotional aspects of social maturity, the scale correlating in the 30s with Davis' scale of emotional empathy.

ALTRUISM

Of all the prosocial behaviors, altruism has received the most attention, perhaps because it paradoxically opposes the general tendency of individuals to act in self-interest. Altruistic behavior involves the helping of others at some cost to oneself. Of the two major kinds of altruism, one consists of relieving the suffering of another person: giving mouth-to-mouth resuscitation to an accident victim and delivering him or her to a hospital; defending a person being attacked; rescuing a person in danger of being trapped in a fire or drowning; offering an organ for an organ transplant; donating blood; offering to replace a person who is being punished; or allowing others to occupy the only lifeboat. In the other major kind of altruism the person who needs help is not suffering pain and is not in danger but has been or will be deprived: offering charity in the form of food or money to poor people, sometimes at considerable loss to the donors; parents going deep into debt to send their children to college; or denying oneself credit so that a loved one can derive greater prestige, as some wives do for their husbands.

These various examples represent the altruistic extreme of a dimension, the opposite end of which is selfishness. Thus, in the face of another's suffering or danger, the observing person may choose not to help or risk danger. Or, to move toward the altruistic part of the dimension, the observing person may decide to risk minimal danger, thereby alleviating only some of the other's suffering. And at the extreme altruistic end of the dimension, the observer may choose to risk considerable danger (entering a burning building, offer one kidney for a transplant) to the greater benefit of the other. Similarly, when the other person has been or will be deprived, the observer may be completely selfish and surrender no economic reward. At the middle of the dimension, the observer may offer some food, money, prestige, or affection, all involving minimal self-denial, and alleviate only part of the other's need. Or the observer may be completely altruistic and go hungry while the other person eats, or wear old clothes and travel in an ancient car while the son or daughter attends an expensive college. The point is that altruism consists of any self-denial that benefits another, although the extreme instances of self-denial, especially those involving great risk, capture our imagination.

When one is made aware of the other's need and something can be done about it, a cost–benefit analysis may occur. The cost involves self-denial of economic rewards or the risk of bodily harm; the benefit concerns how much relief there will be of the other person's suffering or deprivation. Other things being equal, the smaller the costs and the greater the benefits, the more likely that altruistic behavior will occur—a truism that nevertheless needs to be stated. But not everything is equal, and there may be strong reasons for altruistic behavior even when the cost is high and the benefit is low.

Reasons for Altruism

Many of the reasons for altruism have already been discussed as part of the development of social maturity. People may be so upset, depressed, or even disgusted when another person is in desperate need, that they offer help or sacrifice to reduce their own distress. Those most likely to experience such distress are high in the temperament of emotionality (Buss & Plomin, 1984). Observers may experience the other person's distress vicariously and therefore feel so much sympathy and pity that they are driven to help. Such people tend to be high on the trait of emotional empathy (Davis, 1983). Another reason for altruistic behavior is identifying with the person who is in pain or in danger. Such identification could lead to either personal distress, emotional empathy, or both. A more cognitive reason for altruism is the ability to take the perspective of the victim and therefore realize more keenly what the other might be experiencing and the desperate need for help. This ability is of course the trait of perspective taking (Davis, 1983). Another reason might be the ability to fantasy being in the shoes of someone else, which can be differentiated from taking another's perspective. The only attempt to measure this ability is that of Davis (1983), but his items are oriented toward the media: after seeing a play or a movie, I have felt as though I were one of the characters; I really get involved with the feelings of the characters in a novel. Thus there appears to be no trait measure that specifically assesses fantasy empathy as it relates to other people. Another reason for altruism is a strong need to help others, which is reflected in the trait of nurturance (Lorr & Youniss, 1973). All these antecedents of altruism are part of what is considered here to be social maturity, but there is another set of reasons, also linked to social maturity, that fall under the heading of morality.

Following Piaget, Kohlberg (1969) classified cognitive morality in a developmental scheme that has six sequential stages. The first stage consists of selfish and self-centered explanations of choices, and the sixth stage appears to be beyond the reach of most people. The second through the fifth stages bear directly on reasons for altruism. Kohlberg's second stage involves reciprocity or what might be called an enlightened selfishness. Thus, I might help you because I expect that in the future you will help me, or I help you now because you have helped me before. Kohlberg's third stage concerns seeking approval from others and avoiding blame or shame. These motives can lead to altruistic behavior when onlookers can observe whether the person fulfills his or her moral obligation to help (approval) or displays cowardice or selfishness (shame). In the absence of negative social consequences, people at this cognitive stage are unlikely to be altruistic. The fourth stage involves an orientation toward doing one's duty, so that if a person is in a position to help and has the competence to do so, society demands that help be offered. To avoid doing one's duty would be an affront to constituted authority and might disrupt social organization. Thus a physician would have to help an accident victim, even at the risk of being sued later for malpractice. The fifth stage concerns morality, especially the notion that those in need are deserving of help. There is an awareness that others have rights and privileges, and the issue of fairness assumes greater importance: We cannot eat while those around us starve.

In addition to Kohlberg's stages, each of which can be considered to be a moral trait, the trait of responsibility (Harris, 1957) can lead to altruism. These various reasons and the associated personality traits are summarized in Table 5.1, which includes both personal and moral reasons.

The personal reasons all derive from emotional or instrumental or motives for helping another person; these are, respectively, relieving one's own distress or vicarious feelings and being a helpful person (and therefore wanting to help). The moral reasons appear to match four of Kohlberg's stages of morality but also include the personality trait responsibility. It is not just speculation to relate Kohlberg's various moral stages to altruism. In one experiment, a confederate started moaning and groaning, thereby expressing considerable distress (Erkut, Jaquette, & Staub, 1981). The subjects wanted to help but they were also motivated to continue the

TABLE 5.1
Reasons for Altruism and Associated Traits

Reasons	Traits
Personal	
Relieving own distress	Emotionality
Empathy	Emotional empathy
Taking another's perspective	Perspective taking
Wanting to help	Nurturance
Moral	
Reciprocity	Kohlberg Stage 2 (reciprocity)
Seek approval, avoid shame	Kohlberg Stage 3 (good boy orientation)
Sense of responsibility	Kohlberg Stage 4 (duty) and responsibility
Higher morality	Kohlberg Stage 5 (rights of others)

experiment. The greatest incidence of helping at the cost of interrupting the experiment occurred among subjects known to be in Stage 5 of morality; subjects in Stages 3 and 4 tended to help less.

Adaptation and Individual Differences

A basic assumption of the theory of evolution is that each individual attempts to survive and to procreate. Those that are better adapted for survival and procreation leave behind more offspring, and eventually their line tends to predominate in the population. It would seem to follow that each individual would compete with others for resources and for mates, and underlying all motivation would be selfishness. In this theoretical context there is no room for altruism, which must be regarded as paradoxical and maladaptive.

The paradox can be resolved if it is assumed that the proper unit is not the individual but the genes that may be shared by several or many individuals. This is the notion of inclusive fitness (Hamilton, 1964): Individuals will act to sustain not only themselves but also those with whom they share genes. An immediate implication is that the closer the blood relationship, the greater the altruism. Thus parents would be expected to be more generous to their children, and siblings more generous to each other than to cousins or even more distant relatives. Parents may even sacrifice themselves for their children when, by doing so, they would maximize the probability that their genes would continue.

Inclusive fitness can account for the fact that most people tend to be more altruistic to kin and especially closer kin than they do to unrelated people. This fact can also be explained, however, by socialization that teaches us about kinship and the obligations expected of kin. The advantage of inclusive fitness theory is that it can also encompass the altruism displayed by animals. Its disadvantage is that it cannot explain the altruism of foster parents for their adopted children or the cruelty and abandonment by parents of their biological children.

No one questions that altruism can be adaptive. To the extent that this is true and it exists for countless generations, altruism could become part of the biological heritage of human beings, bred into all of us the way speech and two-legged locomotion is part of our biological heritage. This was the idea of Trivers (1971), who suggested conditions favoring the evolution of reciprocal altruism. The territory should be localized to favor continued interaction among the participants. The group should be small and relatively stable, and the individuals should live together for a long time. These conditions would guarantee many social interactions, which in turn might promote interdependence. It would then be adaptive to help someone else, not only because such cooperation could accomplish tasks not easily done by individuals but also because offering help today would guarantee receiving help tomorrow. It would also be necessary for a dominance hierarchy to be weak or absent, else various members of the group would not receive reciprocal treatment and the tendency to be altruistic could not be maintained. In this formulation, it is adaptive to be altruistic toward all members of a small group, and there is no special payoff in being more generous toward kin than toward others.

People do not necessarily engage in adaptive behaviors, as the prevalence of cigarette smoking attests. Individual differences in altruistic behavior are therefore to be expected. Measures of emotional empathy and perspective taking, mentioned earlier, might predict altruism, but there is a self-report measure specifically designed to assess altruism (Rushton, Chrisjohn, & Fekkin, 1981). Unlike most questionnaires, this one lists specific acts and asks the respondent to indicate how often the acts have occurred:

1. I have helped push a stranger's car out of the snow.
2. I have given directions to a stranger.
3. I have made change for a stranger.
4. I have given money to a charity.
5. I have given money to a stranger who needed it and asked me for it.
6. I have donated goods or clothes to a charity.
7. I have done volunteer work for a charity.
8. I have donated blood.
9. I have helped carry a stranger's belongings (books, parcels, etc.)
10. I have delayed an elevator and held the door open for a stranger.
11. I have allowed someone to go ahead of me in a lineup (xerox machine, supermarket).
12. I have given a stranger a lift in my car.
13. I have pointed out a clerk's error in a bank (at the supermarket) in undercharging me for an item.
14. I have let a neighbor whom I didn't know too well borrow an item of some value to me (dish, tools, etc.).
15. I have bought charity Christmas cards deliberately because I knew it was a good cause.
16. I have helped a classmate who I did not know well with a homework assignment when my knowledge was greater than his or hers.
17. I have before being asked voluntarily looked after a neighbor's pets or children without being paid for it.
18. I have offered to help a handicapped or elderly stranger across a street.

19. I have offered my seat on a bus or train to a stranger who was standing.
20. I have helped an acquaintance to move households.

Notice that the recipients of generosity are strangers or casual acquaintances. This is not an accident, for any trait measure would assess altruism as a general tendency, not altruism directed specifically toward kin or close friends. Also, everyone is expected to display at least some altruism toward kin and therefore individual differences would best show up in the relation to strangers. To the extent that altruism is a personality trait, it cuts across the distinction between kin and strangers: Those high in this trait are willing to self-deny and be helpful to others as a general tendency, not as a specific response to blood relatives. This fact bears on formulations of altruism as being biologically adaptive. The inclusive fitness approach assumes an adaptive advantage only when we self-deny and help those who are genetically related. The amount of altruism displayed depends on the overlap in genes, and there should be no individual differences in altruism. Triver's (1971) hypothesis about reciprocal altruism also suggests that we are altruistic only toward some people: those who have helped in the past or who are likely to help in the future. In this enlightened selfishness view, there is no room for a trait in which people are altruistic across the board. The fact that there are individual differences in altruism implies that any explanation based on bio- logical adaptation cannot be the complete explanation. Other causes must be operating, and these are most likely to reside in how people are socialized.

Women are socialized to be more nurturant and helpful than men, and it is no accident that the professions of social worker and nurse are domi- nated by women. In contrast, research has yielded no gender differences in altruism either in experiments on offering help (Maccoby & Jacklin, 1974) or in the trait of altruism (Rushton et al., 1974). As mentioned earlier, however, women are more emotionally empathic than are men. How are we to explain the paradox? One way is to decide that the paradox is more apparent than real. Empathy may not be necessary for altruism to occur, and there are reasons for altruism other than empathy (see Table 5.1); thus it is possible to find a gender difference in emotional empathy but not in altruism. The second way is to question the research that has failed to yield a gender difference in altruism. In this research subjects are asked to help, typically without any particular sacrifice. Perhaps more important, they are asked to help strangers. In everyday life, altruism often involves sacrifice and is limited largely to friends, lovers, and kin, and it is this kind of altruism that should be studied. If this second explanation were correct, it would account for the lack of evidence on gender differences in research with strangers, and it follows that a gender difference would be found if altruism were studied in close relationships.

PARENTAL ROLES

The most common examples of altruism, including extreme instances of self-denial and even sacrifice may be found in the behavior of parents toward their children. Parents engage in a variety of prosocial behaviors toward their children, behaviors that were discussed earlier. In addition, parents distribute economic rewards, shelter their children, exchange social rewards, and dominate their children. In parent–child interaction, we find examples of the kinds of behavior discussed in the last several chapters, which may be organized under the heading of parental roles.

Caretaker

The earliest role, caretaker, starts on the first day of life. Mothers, especially breastfeeding mothers, usually take charge here, but fathers are increasingly feeding, cleaning, clothing, and watching over their children. Parents not only feed, clothe, and shelter their children but also soothe them when they are upset. Such calming of children is the only instance of a social reward being involved in neonatal caretaking, the rest consisting of offering biological necessities.

The caretaker role necessarily wanes in importance as children mature and thus need less nurturance and protection. Parents gradually worry less about biological deficits and about danger, and they become more concerned with providing opportunities and economic rewards. In middle-class America, the caretaking role increasingly becomes one of being a chauffeur, ensuring that the children are well dressed, buying lessons in music, art, ballet, or athletics, and providing the opportunity to attend a good school. Parents soothe their children less as the children mature, and are less involved in dressing, feeding, and cleaning their children, and gradually the caretaking role becomes mainly one of distributing economic rewards and privileges.

Parents vary enormously in caretaking. Some fathers abdicate the role completely, leaving it to mothers. Some parents avoid the more personal aspects and hire others to care for their children. Some parents spoil their children with excessive gifts and privileges, the outcome being adolescents who regard credit cards as their birthright. Other parents deny their children nurturance, one outcome being insecurity; or children are denied economic rewards and privileges, one outcome being a lifelong thirst for these rewards. Some parents are inconsistent in the caretaking role, so that their children may feel insecure or jealous and resentful that they do not receive their fair share. Some parents use economic rewards to purchase affection, thereby poisoning affectionate relationships. And some parents beat their children—the opposite of the caretaking role.

The child's personality can influence how parents play their caretaking role. Children who mature quickly and wish to be independent cause parents to abandon the caretaking role faster than children who retain infantile ways and virtually beg for parental care. Some children are temperamentally emotional and therefore need more soothing, and caretaking is likely to persist longer for these children than for children who get upset less frequently and less intensely.

Partner

The partnership role, which starts soon after birth, consists of an exchange of social rewards, though at first the parent does most of the initiating. Soon, infants discover ways to bring their parents to them, and their smiles, laughter, and responsivity are powerful reinforcers. Although the stimulation rewards are important, the crucial social rewards are affective. At first, affection is offered unconditionally by the parents and later, conditionally. Infants reciprocate, and attachment bonds develop. This is the typical pattern, but some parents neglect their infants or love them only conditionally. Rejected children are likely to feel unloved and inferior. For some children, rejection may be so painful that they are subsequently wary of any close relationship; for others, the denial of love may cause them continually to seek it. We cannot predict which extreme will occur because of our ignorance of these events of early childhood.

Some parents tend to love one child more than another, which inevitably leads to jealousy and resentment. Some parents are so excessive in their affection that children may feel smothered or may be prevented from developing affectionate relationships outside the immediate family; or the children may feel guilty about not reciprocating enough affection.

Children's personality is especially important as a determinant of how the partnership role is played. Children who are temperamentally sociable require considerable social stimulation, perhaps forcing parents to become more interactive than they prefer to be. Children who are jealous, and this may occur even when the parents are blameless, may demand excessive love, perhaps more than the parents can offer; at the same time, such children may throw tantrums if affection is offered to other siblings. Thus parents may find themselves in a no-win situation: not being able to furnish enough affection to the jealous child versus keeping the child infantile by surrendering to its excessive need for affection. The child who is low in self-esteem may also need more love and reassurance than parents can be expected to deliver.

In the second year of the child's life, he or she starts being disciplined by parents. Such discipline is part of the parental role of dominance, which is different from the kind of dominance that occurs among peers. Among peers, the struggle for power may end with one person becoming dominant and achieving a variety of rewards. Between parent and child, the parent uses the dominant role to prevent the child from hurting him or herself or others and from harming or destroying its environment. The only reward for the parent is the knowledge that the child is kept within bounds until he or she matures sufficiently so as not to require parental supervision.

Recall that there are four aspects of dominance: aggression, competition, assertion, and leadership. Competition poses problems, for when parents compete with their children, they are violating the parental role and acting as though they were merely their children's peers. Such competition is entirely inappropriate to the parent–child relationship, and when it originates in the parent's behavior, it can weaken the relationship. Adolescents may compete with their parents, the adolescents desiring to demonstrate their newfound maturity and talents. Such motivation is usually acknowledged by parents, who tolerate it and do not respond as though they had been challenged by a peer. When a father and son or mother and daughter become embroiled in serious competition, the separation between generations disappears and the parent–child relationship degenerates to a struggle for dominance between equals.

A common means of disciplining children is of course physical punishment, and even more common is scolding. These physical and verbal kinds of aggression are important modes of dominating children and of maintaining control over them. In addition to the negative consequences of inducing fear or anger, the parent might serve as a model for the child's observational learning. There is hardly a better way for a child to learn aggression than by observing how his or her parent aggresses. Such imitation learning can be minimized by punishing the child physically in a way that cannot easily be copied: spanking. It is difficult to believe that a child will aggress against other children by attempting to turn them over and paddle their rear. As any parent knows, however, any kind of punishment may eventually be imitated by the child, if not in its original form, then with some minor variation.

One step down from aggression is assertion by the parent. The child is told what to do and what not to do, and when the infant starts becoming sufficiently mobile, the most commonly spoken word by the parent is likely to be "No." (Given the child's self-assertion and a tendency toward negativism, especially during the "terrible twos," the child's most frequent word may also be "No.") As children mature, they need less direction. Throughout childhood there is a continual struggle between dominating parents and gradually less submissive children, which comes to a head during adolescence. Children want less bossiness by parents and more freedom of choice for themselves without any increase in their responsibilities. Parents want the children to assume increasing responsibilities while remaining submissive to parental dominance. When parental bossiness does not work, parents can hardly try physical aggression against their adolescent children. Verbal aggression and scolding are common, but the ultimate weapon usually is control of economic resources. Thus the adolescent can be deprived of allowance, use of the telephone or the car, a vacation trip, or even the freedom to leave the house.

Leadership, the last aspect of domination, tends to be a less contentious aspect of parent–child relationships. Parents necessarily take the initiative and responsibility when their children are young. As the children mature, parents must be ready to relinquish this leadership and to furnish an opportunity for their children to make decisions and to face the consequences of these decisions. Excessively dominant parents tend not to allow their children to display initiative, and excessively nurturant parents tend not to allow their children to pay the price when the children's decisions turn out bad. A major task of childhood is to learn acceptance of the consequences of one's own behavior. There may be no better distinction psychologically between childhood and adulthood than this: Children are not responsible for their own actions, but adults must face the consequences of their actions.

The child's personality is one determinant of the way parents play the dominant role. A child low in activity may require more initiative from the parent, and a temperamentally active child may require more restraint and control as he or she explores possibly dangerous environments and engages in extremely vigorous behavior. Similarly, an aggressive child must be prevented from harming others, and an impulsive child needs to be made to wait or needs to be distracted from proscribed behavior. Thus the child's personality dispositions may move his or her parents toward one or another end of the parental dimension of strict to permissive. The parents' place on this dimension may be determined by their own personalities, the way they were reared, and current child-rearing fads, but these determinants are well known, whereas the child's input is rarely acknowledged.

Socializing Agent

The remaining parental role is especially relevant to this chapter: socializing agent. Although by no means the only socializing agents, parents are the principal ones, especially when their children are young. The content of socialization has already been spelled out; the means involve the three parental roles just described plus rule learning and observational learning. Parents imbue children with rules and injunctions, implemented by principles that may have the authority of law or religion. The major socialization training, however, occurs within the parent–child relationship, and the crucial parental role would seem to be that of dominance. Through leadership, parents can show children how to comport themselves as they progress toward maturity, and they can back up such leadership by being verbally or physically aggressive when necessary. When parents are assertive, telling children what to do and what not to do, they need to proclaim the rationale for their behavior. When such cognitions are added to parental bossiness, children can learn the basis for parental actions. When such actions make sense, children are free to adopt them later in life. When parents are being merely bossy ("Do it because I say so"), there is nothing to help socialize the child.

Thus, the role of socializing agent is enhanced by the roles of caretaker and disciplinarian. The caretaker can manipulate economic rewards to teach the child responsibility and sharing. The dominant parent can set standards as a leader and back up demands by punishing the child (fairness in punishment may be crucial in socializing a child). The only parental role that has little influence on the child's becoming a member of the larger community (being socialized) is that of partner. Social stimulation and exchange of affective rewards are important for the child's personality but not necessarily for learning the lessons of society.

The Roles Compared

The partnership role stands in contrast to the other three parental roles as the only one that is egalitarian. In the other three roles, parents take charge as caretakers, disciplinarians, or socializing agents. They control economic rewards, dominate, or serve as teachers of society's lessons. Only when they exchange social rewards are parents the equals of their children.

The presence of four parental roles can cause trouble in the parent–child relationship, for the roles inevitably conflict. When parents act as disciplinarians, children may feel rejected and unloved. When parents act as socializing agents and attempt to instill values and responsibilities, children may feel that they are not accepted as they are, perhaps because they are inferior or unlovable. When parents are caretakers, they must not only provide food and nurturance but protect children from physical danger and from the consequences of such things as overeating or loss of sleep. When children are forbidden the wrong kind of food, prevented from staying up late, or not allowed to engage in dangerous activities, their anger is likely to spill over into the partnership relationship. Thus the parental role of caretaker can interfere with the exchange of affection and praise between parents and children. The most common conflict occurs between the dominance and partnership. Children who are loved do not expect to be punished; punished children may temporarily hate their parents, and some parents find such hatred so aversive that they cannot punish their children. One traditional solution to these inter-role conflicts is to assign different roles to father and mother. The mother is more of a partner (especially exchanging affective rewards) and a caretaker, and the father is more of a disciplinarian and a socializing agent. This division of labor allows the mother to be more affectionate with her children and to play the typical role of housewife in the family. The father plays a more authoritarian role and can serve as a model for subsequent nonfamiliar authority; he is the one who sets standards and who punishes when they are not met.

This arrangement, though common, is obviously not the only one possible, and as men's and women's roles change, other ways of dividing up parental roles are being seen. What happens when there is only one parent, an increasing possibility in today's society? If the foregoing analysis is correct, the single parent may expect more role conflict. Though children are not fragile, it may be too much to expect them to be tranquil in the face of a single parent playing four related but different roles. If the partnership role were emphasized, the child might become too close to the parent through exchange of the stimulation and affective rewards; discipline and socialization training would be likely to suffer. If the disciplinary and socializing agent roles were emphasized, the outcome might be a good child who would be well prepared for the adult world but lacking in the warmth and affection needed in close personal relationships. If the parent tried to play all the roles equally, the more dominant disciplinary and socializing agent roles would interfere with the partnership role. This gloomy assessment may be an inevitable consequence of the diversity of parental roles.

The particular role a parent emphasizes or prefers is likely to be at least partly determined by the parents' personality traits. A nurturant parent tends to prefer the caretaker role, which allows all the caring behavior that is so strongly motivated: It is no accident that women tend to be higher in nurturance and are more often the caretakers of children. The role of partner would seem to be linked to the trait of sociability, the parent deriving satisfaction from sharing activities and interacting with the children. The disciplinarian role should be associated with several aspects of dominance; specifically, parents who are verbally aggressive are more likely to scold their children, and those who are more decisive tend to be more controlling. Parents who are low in dominance might have trouble in controlling and punishing their children, especially if the parents were also high in nurturance and were strongly reinforced by playing the partnership role. The role of socializing agent might be enhanced by the trait of responsibility, although parental values would probably be a larger determinant.

NOTES

As the chapter began, so this section must begin with the two volumes of Staub (1978, 1979), each a compendium of research and theory about prosocial behavior. The first book (containing material on altruism, empathy, and why people help others) is wide in scope, for it includes social influence, attraction, group membership, social exchange, cooperation, friendship, reactions to transgression, and the impact of mood. The second book emphasizes socialization, identification and internalization, and generally, the development of prosocial behavior.

One approach to altruism emphasizes personal and social norms (Schwartz, 1975). A sequence is hypothesized, the first three segments of which are awareness of the other person's need, awareness of actions that would alleviate the need, and recognition that one's own acts would suffice. Next in the sequence is the arousal of responsibility because of being available, being the cause of the other's trouble, or being in a role that involves help. The arousal of responsibility activates social norms (expectations, obligations) or personal norms (pride, guilt, or aspects of the self-concept). The final steps are a cost–benefit analysis, followed by action or inaction. Three kinds of individual differences would seem to be crucial in this framework: social norms that derive from socialization, self-concept (which is a broad and diffuse disposition), and sense of responsibility.

One of the problems with studying altruistic behavior is that some of the behavior that appears altruistic may derive from selfish motivation. Batson (1984) compares the three major motives for such behavior. The first is obviously selfish: the anticipation of reward or the avoidance of punishment (being labelled as *cowardly* or *self-centered*). The second is not so obviously selfish, for it involves the vicarious arousal of distress when observing the other's suffering, but the implicitly selfish motive here is the reduction of one's own aversive arousal. The third motive is truly altruistic: After the other's perspective is adopted, vicarious arousal leads to motivation to relieve the other person's distress with no special concern with one's own distress. Batson sought to distinguish between the second and third motives, distress and empathy, by exposing subjects to situations in which it would be easy or difficult to leave. According to Batson, O'Quin, Fultz, Vanderplas, and Isen (1983):

> subjects who reported experiencing a predominance of personal distress helped less when it was easy to escape without helping, suggesting that their underlying motivation was an egoistic desire to relieve their own distress. In contrast, subjects who reported a predominance of empathy were as likely to help when escape was easy as when it was difficult, suggesting that their

underlying motivation was an altruistic desire to reduce the distress of the person in need. (p. 717)

When the cost was increased (pain to be experienced by the potential altruist), altruistic helping all but disappeared.

The challenge of sociobiology has inspired psychologists to offer formulations that take into account the distinctiveness of human psychological reactions. Thus, Hoffman (1981) suggests that the concept of inclusive fitness applies to humans, who must recognize the degree of kinship and also engage in a cost-benefit analysis of altruistic behavior. These psychological processes must be included in any theory: "What therefore must have been acquired through natural selection is a predisposition or motive to help that, although biologically based, is nevertheless amenable to control by perceptual or cognitive processes" (p. 128). The predisposition is identified as empathy, which is assumed to originate in individuals either innately (motor and emotional mimicry) or through classical conditioning.

Campbell (1975) sees biological and social forces in continuing conflict and contradiction. In keeping with a Darwinian approach, competition for resources is viewed as inevitably resulting in the selection of biological selfishness. Human societies require cooperation and altruism, however, so every social system preaches altruism (as part of morality) in an effort to overcome, or at least balance the biological tendency of individuals to be selfish.

Genetic similarity theory (Rushton, Russell, & Wells, 1984) makes only a slight change in the sociobiological approach to altruism: Individuals will be altruistic toward any person who is phenotypically similar. The underlying assumption is that the basis of similarity is inevitably genetic, even though the individuals may actually share no genes. Thus redheads are expected to be more helpful to other redheads than to blondes or brunettes. It is not clear what this theory would predict about people who are similar in political attitudes or religion. It does suggest that friends are more likely to be altruistic toward one another, but whether we need a biological theory to account for altruism among friends is moot. Also, there may be an inconsistency between genetic similarity theory and the presence of the personality trait of altruism (Rushton, Chrisjohn, & Fekkin, 1981), which involves individual difference in altruism to strangers with whom there is no necessary similarity. Rushton (1980) has reviewed these and other issues in his book.

Concerning traits, Davis' (1983) empathy questionnaire is the only one derived by means of factor analysis and therefore psychometrically sounder than most, but earlier questionnaires have been the more popular measures of the multiple trait. These questionnaires are reviewed by Chlopan, McCain, Carbonell, and Hagen (1985), who concentrate on two measures. The first is that of Hogan (1969), which has been found to have four factors (Johnson, Cheek, & Smither, 1983). The first three were easy to label: social self-confidence (I have a natural talent for influencing people), even temperedness (I am usually calm and not easily upset), and sensitivity, which appears to be a mixture (I have seen some things so sad that I almost felt like crying, and I like poetry). The fourth factor contained a disparate group of items, the label for which, *nonconformity*, does not adequately describe the cluster. The content of this questionnaire does not inspire confidence that it assesses empathy, and it remains to be seen if such a conglomerate of items relates to empathy in the way most psychologists define it. Johnson et al. (1983) are aware of this problem, which extends into the more general issue of testing and so is beyond the scope of the present discussion.

The questionnaire by Mehrabian and Epstein (1972) is also a mixture of items that fall on different scales that were labelled a priori, but the review of Chlopan et al. (1985) reveals that it predicts empathic behavior in several contexts. A recent study not mentioned in their review is especially pertinent (Wiesenfeld, Whitman, & Malatesta, 1984). College women without children were divided into groups high and low in empathy. They watched brief, silent videotapes of infants who were crying, smiling, or quiescent. Compared to those low in empathy, the highs had a larger increase in heart rate, a greater rise in skin conductance, and a stronger desire to pick up the infants. These findings are consistent with the content of the questionnaire, which emphasizes emotional reactions and which correlates about .60 with the empathic concern factor of Davis' (1983) questionnaire.

Finally, one study has demonstrated that there may be a trait of selfishness–generosity in children (Hetherington & Brackbill, 1963). The tasks involved contributing pennies to the needy, rocks borrowed and later returned, and sharing crayons. The six measures derived from these tasks correlated .58 to .86 with each other, suggesting a trait the authors called parsimony.

6 Public and Private

Infants start life unself-conscious and uninhibited. As they mature, advanced cognitive processes render them susceptible to awareness and self-awareness. As they are socialized and acquire the explicit and implicit rules that govern social interactions, they become conforming and willing to inhibit impulses and emotions. One way of thinking about these issues is to invoke two kinds of distinctions between public and private: behavior that others can see versus behavior that is observable in principle but occurs in private, and overt behavior versus covert impulses, feelings, and cognitions.

OVERT AND COVERT

Virtually all of a newborn's behavior is overt and easily observable. As time passes, some of the infant's behavior becomes covert, and sometimes all that can be observed in adults is the tip of the iceberg—the behavior of a chess player, for example. This development of covertness may be divided into three related trends: (a) inhibition of behavior; (b) development of implicit, cognitive responses; and (c) occurrence of secretiveness and deviousness.

Inhibition

When awake, infants may appear to be little more than bundles of impulses. When hungry or wet, they cry; when the bladder is full, they urinate. For most infants, the pressure to restrain impulses starts during the second year of life, when toilet training begins. Control over bowel and bladder is merely the first step in a sequence that demands increasing suppression of impulsive behavior. Young children must learn not to snatch food when they are hungry, not to grab another child's toy, not to say certain words, and in general, to curb or at least delay a variety of actions.

The inhibition of instrumental acts is accompanied by a damping of affective reactions, or at least the overt expressions of these affects. Temper tantrums, allowed the first year of life, are no longer tolerated by the end of the second year. Crying is expected to diminish during childhood, and it does. Both fear (especially for boys) and anger (especially for girls) are supposed to drop in frequency and intensity. Boys are expected to display and receive fewer signs of affection; in traditional terms, hugging and kissing are unmasculine.

By the time children are well settled in school, at about 10 years of age, they vary considerably in inhibitory control. One reason for such individual differences is the socialization practices of parents and other agents of socialization. Some parental practices are stern and rigid; others are permissive and flexible. Some parents are consistent in their discipline; others are inconsistent. Such variations in the way parents treat their children tend to produce children who vary considerably in inhibition: timid, inhibited children; confident children who are capable of controlling their own instrumental and affective behavior; and children who appear as uncontrolled as infants.

We cannot assume, however, that children start out the same. There are known to be inborn differences in emotionality, the tendency to become distressed. An emotional child, by definition, has more frequent and more intense affective reactions, the presence of which may mistakenly be interpreted as a lack of inhibitory control.

Presumably, impulses do not immediately dissipate when they are controlled. A hungry child still wants to eat, a covetous child still wants the other's toy, and a child who suppresses the outward signs of rage is still covertly angry. The greater the inhibitory control, the more impulses that are delayed or denied expression.

Cognition

The trial-and-error behavior of infants and young children can easily be observed, as they try one response and then another until one succeeds or they give up and move on to other activity. As cognitive development proceeds, overt trial-and-error gives way to implicit trial-and-error. Now possible responses are worked out "inside the head" before trying any one of them. This progression can be seen, for example, as a chess player becomes more skillful. The novice moves a piece to a new square and then discovers how bad the move is. Later, he or she keeps his or her hand on the piece after moving it. The better player imagines the consequences of the move, sees them to be bad, and considers an alternative, all this before the piece is touched. What was originally an entirely overt response is now mainly covert.

There is a similar developmental trend that begins with rote learning and ends with tactics and strategy. In early childhood, learning is mainly associative, consisting of linking stimuli with responses by rote. The outcome is an immediate, impulsive response to a stimulus, the response being reinforced by praise or some other incentive. At approximately 5 years old, children add a new mode of learning, employing considerable imagery and language. Instead of responding reflexively, children now inhibit the rote response in favor of a response based on strategy. Children reflect about outcomes, and their overt responses tend to be reinforced by correctness as well as by incentives. In this reflective kind of learning, there is a time gap between the stimulus and the response, during which children are using their recently acquired cognitive abilities.

At approximately the same age, when children first start school, there is a parallel development in speech. The speech of preschool children tends to be entirely overt. They not only talk to people, pets and toys, but also to themselves. Gradually, however, some of their speech is not actually uttered. They still talk to themselves, but their lips do not move, and they still carry on imaginary conversations with toys or pets but without sounds. Some of their speech has now become entirely covert, and for the remainder of their lives they occasionally will talk silently to themselves.

Another developmental trend starts with play, which at first is entirely overt. Infants and young children merely engage in motor manipulation of toys. Gradually, their play becomes infused with imagery. This broomstick becomes a horse, and that row of boxes becomes a train. Although overt play continues, a portion of it gradually becomes entirely fantasy. In their imagination, children assume various roles and act out entire sequences in their heads. Such imaginative sequences reach a peak among adolescents, whose covert fantasies are often more vivid and rewarding than their overt behavior.

These various cognitive processes, especially covert speech and fantasy, may be directed toward the self. Older children and adults can focus attention on their own sensations, emotions, and moods. They can reflect on their motives, ambitions, and past actions, and they can concoct rich fantasies with themselves as heroes. No one else can become aware of these covert processes unless they are conveyed by speech or some other mode of expression, hence these aspects of the self are called *private*. Some people focus on these private aspects of the self frequently, others rarely. These individual differences have been assessed by the private self-consciousness scale of the Self-Consciousness Inventory (Fenigstein, Scheier, & Buss, 1975):

1. I reflect about myself alot.
2. I'm generally attentive to my inner feelings.
3. I'm always trying to figure myself out.
4. I'm constantly examining my motives.
5. I'm alert to changes in my mood.
6. I tend to scrutinize myself.
7. Generally, I'm aware of myself.
8. I'm aware of the way my mind works when I work through a problem.
9. I'm often the subject of my own fantasies.
10. I sometimes have the feeling that I'm off somewhere watching myself.

Secretiveness and Deviousness

We start out in this world being open and honest, not necessarily because human beings are inherently so, but because we do not know any better. Early in life, infants are not punished for their behavior and therefore make no attempt to conceal anything they do. Once punishment starts, there is a good reason to conceal proscribed behavior. When 3-year-olds are spanked for taking cookies from the cookie jar, they quickly learn to lift the cookies surreptitiously.

With advancing age, there is another reason for secrecy: the desire for privacy. Most children want to do or imagine things that they alone know about. Somehow it is rewarding to be the only one with such knowledge, and therefore most children develop their own idiosyncratic secrets.

After children have mastered speech, the threat of punishment inevitably causes lying. Denial of culpability often evades a spanking or withdrawal of privileges. Who does the parent punish when two children have been fighting and each says the other started it? Often, neither child. Children learn quickly through imitation of older children and adults that lying is a common and useful way of avoiding disastrous consequences. Some school children cut classes and make up fake excuses. As children mature, they learn better excuses and better ways of lying. It is widely believed, for instance, that a liar cannot look you in the eye while lying, so when lying, people tend to gaze directly at you.

Lying is merely one variant of deviousness, an especially human characteristic, but the other forms require more subtlety. Precocious older children and most adolescents learn to feign interest in what the other person is saying if there is a payoff in reward or avoidance of punishment. They may pretend helplessness to get others to do onerous or taxing jobs, a childish tactic that is not unknown in women socialized in the traditional female gender role.

Lying and simulated behavior, when discovered, lead to people being called *two-faced*, an apt phrase that highlights the distinction between covert feelings and overt behavior. We are never more aware of the discrepancy between our psychological inside and outside than when we lie or pretend. Awareness of one's own deceptions may result in feelings of guilt or shame, no special negative reaction, or even a feeling of pride in being able to deceive and manipulate others. Whatever the reaction, such deception is an important aspect of the development of covertness.

The tendency to use others is associated with a historical figure, Niccolo Machiavelli, so it is not surprising that the measure designed to assess the relevant personality trait is called *Machiavellianism* (Christie & Geis, 1970). The scale was found to have several factors, but only the items on the duplicity scale reflect the behavior under discussion:

1.   There is no excuse for lying to someone. (reversed)
2.   Honesty is the best policy in all cases. (reversed)
3.   All in all, it is better to be honest and humble than to be important and dishonest. (reversed)
4.   When you ask someone to do something for you, it is best to give the real reasons for wanting it rather than giving reasons which carry more weight. (reversed)
5.   It is wise to flatter important people.
6.   The best way to handle people is to tell them what they want to hear.
7.   Next to health, wealth is the most important thing in life.
8.   One should take action only when sure it is morally right. (reversed)
9.   Even today, the way that you make money is more important than how much you make. (reversed)
10. Never tell anyone the real reason you did something unless it is useful to do so.

A different approach to assessing the instrumental use of social interaction is to assemble a list of specific acts and have judges rate them for prototypicality. This procedure was followed by D. Buss and Craik (1985), who had calculating acts scaled for how prototypical they are. The seven acts that were judged the most prototypical of calculating behavior were:

1. I made a friend in order to obtain a favor.
2. I asked "innocent" questions, intending to use the information against someone.
3. I pretended I was hurt to get someone to do me a favor.
4. I tricked a friend into giving me personal information.
5. I flattered a person in order to get ahead.
6. I pretended to be sick at work, knowing that I would not be there the next day.
7. I made others feel guilty to get what I wanted.

These items, representing the most typical calculating acts, were part of a larger list that was correlated with the Machiavellian scale (Christie & Geis, 1970), but the correlation was a modest .17. One would guess that the two scales should correlate higher, but the entire Machiavellian scale was used, and it contains factors that, on the surface at least, appear to be unrelated to the tendency to be calculating. If the seven prototypical acts just listed were compared with the duplicity factor of the Machiavellianism scale, the correlation surely would be much higher.

SELF AS A SOCIAL OBJECT

Parents and other socializing agents train children by several methods, the most prominent being instrumental conditioning. Children may be rewarded for being neat and clean, for sharing their possessions, for wearing appropriate clothes, and in general for displaying mature behavior. More often they are punished for being dirty and messy, selfishly clinging to possessions, wearing inappropriate clothes, and in general for displaying immature behavior. Such learning leads to a primitive public–private dichotomy, which requires no sense of oneself as a social object, only the easily learned distinction between the presence or absence of a potential punisher. Social animals easily learn this discrimination and are submissive in the presence of superordinate animals, dominant in the presence of subordinate animals.

There are punishments that are distinctively human, however, especially teasing and ridicule. When children who are presumably toilet trained lose control, they may have to endure raucous laughter. When children or adolescents appear in clothes that are torn, ragged, or even out of style, they may be teased without mercy. Such is the bigotry of some children and adults that any deviation from the norm is greeted with derision or scorn. Thus, children may suffer verbal abuse for being too tall or too short; too fat or too thin; from developing breasts too soon or too late; for developing a deeper voice or a beard too late; or merely for having red hair. Some children and adolescents are stigmatized for defects or disabilities: wearing glasses or a hearing aid, walking with a limp, or stuttering. One outcome of such teaching and ridicule is an acute sense of oneself as a social object. Having been the focus of others' scrutiny, children become keenly aware of their body, appearance, and social behavior. Such a self-focus does not occur in species other than humans, and it involves more than instrumental conditioning.

Sensory versus Cognitive Self

When the sole of one's foot is tickled by another person, there is single stimulation. When the owner tickles the foot, there is the double stimulation: of the foot being tickled and the fingers doing the tickling. Such active and passive stimulation occur only in self-directed behavior, and one outcome is that the passively felt stimulation is weaker (tickling causes more laughter when it is done by another person). The fact that self-induced stimulation is different from stimulation induced externally is one basis for inferring a self. Another is body boundary, the distinction between me and not-me. A third basis for inferring self is the recognition of oneself in a mirror. When a chimpanzee has a red dot placed on its face and looks in a mirror, it tries to touch or remove the dot, thereby revealing that it knows the face in the mirror is its own (Gallup, 1970). Only the great apes and humans are capable of such mirror-image recognition, a fact that has led some scientists to conclude that the great apes have the same sense of self as do humans. However, such recognition, together with body boundary and double stimulation, would appear to be evidence for a sensory self, which may be observed in animals, human infants, and human adults.

There is also an advanced self not found in animals or human infants because it requires cognitions present only in older human children and adults. One basis for inferring such a self is self-esteem. It is analogous to double stimulation in that the agent and recipient are the same person, but it is different in that the self-evaluation requires the ability to make evaluations and direct them toward the self.

Another fact that allows inferring an advanced, cognitive self is the presence of covert thoughts, feelings, images, and ambitions that no one else need know about. The awareness of these private events and their difference from observable behavior, which involve the second kind of public–private dichotomy, is roughly equivalent to private self-awareness.

The last evidence for an advanced self comes from the knowledge that one's own perspective is not the only one and that others have different ways of looking at the world. We also become aware that the way we regard ourselves differs from the way others regard us.

All three aspects of the cognitive self accentuate an awareness of self that is only dimly perceived through the aspects of the sensory self. The sensory self in humans develops during infancy; by 2 years of age, for example, mirror-image recognition occurs in virtually all children (Amsterdam, 1972; Schulman & Kaplowitz, 1977). Each of the three aspects of the sensory self may be regarded as having an analogous aspect of the cognitive self. Thus double stimulation is analogous to self-esteem, body boundary is analogous to the overt–covert distinction, and recognizing one's image as different from that of others is analogous to the distinction between one's and others' perspectives.

Distinguishing between a primitive and an advanced self may help to settle the dust kicked up when scientists compare human and animal behavior. We evidently share a sensory self with other animals, but only older human children and adults possess the cognitive abilities required for an advanced, cognitive self. As these cognitive abilities emerge during childhood, we can trace the development of self from the sensory self of infancy to the cognitive self of childhood and adulthood. Infants cannot be ridiculed because they lack the advanced sense of self that would make them sensitive to ridicule, but older children do possess this awareness and therefore can be embarrassed.

Public Self-Awareness

The public self consists of those aspects that are open to observation by others, the two major headings being appearance and social behavior. Appearance involves clean hands, combed hair, clothes in place and fastened, and the other particulars mentioned earlier. Social behavior involves posture ("don't slouch"), gracefulness or clumsiness of movements, gestures, speech fluency, mumbling ("speak up"), accent, and also politeness and manners.

Any of these particulars may be observed when one is in a conversational group, speaking to an audience, just walking down the street or in a bus or elevator. Others may just casually look, or they may scrutinize closely and stare. With the advent of modern technology, recording devices are now available to substitute for being observed directly. Voice can be tape recorded, face and body can be photographed, and gesture and movement can be video recorded. Any of these devices, which produce records that can be examined later, can induce awareness of oneself as a social object. Such public self-awareness is ordinarily not focused on any particular part of the self. If there has been an abrupt change in appearance (styling of hair, growth of a beard, unusual styling in clothes), the person might feel that others are staring at that specific aspect. Otherwise, public self-awareness consists of a diffuse sense of being the focus of others' attention.

Social contexts vary in how public they are, and people are more likely to be observed in a restaurant when their table is in the center than in a corner. Anyone who speaks to a group tends to be scrutinized more closely than a person who is merely part of a conversational group. Thus conspicuousness is an important determinant of public self-awareness. Another relevant aspect of social contexts is novelty. When we enter a strange classroom, meet a new group of people, or initiate a relationship, we tend to feel that others are observing us and become keenly aware of ourselves as social objects.

The affect accompanying public self-awareness varies considerably. It may be positive, a good feeling that one's appearance or social behavior are sufficiently admirable to be noted by others. Such pleasure in being observed is likely to occur in physically attractive people, public figures (actors, politicians, sports heroes) who are accustomed to being observed because of their reknown, and people who have never been in the spotlight and hunger for it. For most of us, the affect is mildly negative, probably because of the prevalent way that children are socialized. When parents and teachers scrutinize children, the usual consequence is a reminder that something is wrong. Buttons or zippers are undone, hands are unclean, clothes are inappropriate, hair is too long, politeness is lacking, and so on through a litany of mistakes in appearance or social behavior. It is true that sometimes children are praised when they are the focus of attention, but it is assumed here that the majority of comments that follow children's being observed by parents or teachers are reminders of deficiencies. It follows that in adolescents and adults, public self-awareness is usually accompanied by an uneasy feeling that something may be wrong. For completeness, it should be added that a minority of people experience no particular affect when they are observed, presumably because the net effect of prior socialization was neither positive nor negative. In societies that do not single out children for criticism or appearance of social style, it would be expected that there is less awareness of oneself as a social object and when observed; modern China may well be an example of such a society.

American society emphasizes appearance and social style, and socializes children to be keenly aware of themselves as social objects. As the children become increasingly able to regard themselves the way others might, their social self-consciousness intensifies. Parents tend to remind children that others are observing them and admonish, "What will they think of you?" Children are also scrutinized by peers, who jeer and taunt at the slightest deviation from acceptable public appearance or behavior. As others focus on them, so they focus on themselves, and the infant who starts life oblivious to such social scrutiny develops into an adult with at least a minimal self-consciousness.

People are socialized very differently and so it comes as no surprise that there are marked individual differences in the sense of oneself as a social object. The trait is called public *self-consciousness* to distinguish it from the transient state of public *self-awareness*. Public self-consciousness is assessed by the following items, which comprise a factor of the Self-Consciousness Inventory (Fenigstein, Scheier, & Buss, 1975):

1. I'm concerned about what other people think of me.
2. I usually worry about making a good impression.
3. I'm concerned about the way I present myself.
4. I'm self conscious about the way I look.
5. I'm usually aware of my appearance.
6. One of the last things I do before leaving the house is look in the mirror.
7. I'm concerned about my style of doing things.

Several of the items refer to a self-focus on appearance and style of behavior, and it would be surprising if there were not such items. What is the consequence of this focus about the observables of oneself? A reasonable answer is a concern about the opinion of others, for if there is an acute awareness of oneself as a social object, the opinions of others about oneself must be important. Thus there may be a good conceptual reason for the empirical linkage (factor loadings) between the two kinds of items on the public self-consciousness scale.

FORMALITY

There is a fable about a group of porcupines who were huddling together to conserve heat in the face of a bitterly cold wind. When they huddled too close, each was pricked by another's spines, but when they drew apart, they lost too much heat. They finally settled on a distance that would balance the need to conserve heat against the avoidance of being pricked, and this distance was called good manners.

Children are taught good manners as part of the socialization process. They must learn the implicit and explicit rules of social behavior so that social interaction can run smoothly and so that they can take their place as fully functioning members of society. These social rules are most explicit and adherence is most expected when the behavior occurs in public settings. Formal behavior, then, is social behavior that occurs mainly in public contexts and conforms to the rules laid down by society over generations.

Such behavior is easiest to describe in its extreme, when manners assume the mantle of protocol. When a foreign dignitary visits our capital, a series of ceremonies require strict conformity to a set of standards governing even the smallest details of behavior and social arrangements: who precedes whom through a door, who speaks first, the precise title to be used, and at the state dinner, the exact seating pattern, which plates and silverware are used, when the toast is made and its contents, and how the dinner is terminated. We are made especially aware of rules of social behavior when confronted with a member of a culture that is more formal than ours and may be amused, for example, at the bowing of Japanese as a greeting behavior or the curtsying or bowing of British toward their monarch.

Our children are required to learn a less complex and detailed set of rules, which we call politeness. They learn to say sir or ma'am to adults, to append please and thank you to requests, to beg the other's pardon when a minor accident occurs even when not at fault. One set of manners pertains to behavior between the sexes, such that men help women with their wraps, open doors, give up their seats, and do not remain seated while a women is standing; these courtesies appear to be waning as women increasingly reject their role as the weaker sex and as men are less rewarded for chivalry.

Although the rules of governing politeness and manners are explicit and may be detailed in books of etiquette, the standards for demeanor are implicit and are learned largely through imitation. Thus children follow the behavior of their elders and do not whisper in church, laugh during a funeral service, or speak unless spoken to in a court of law. During these and other formal occasions, one's mien should be sober and one's approach to others should be serious. There should be no shouting or raucous laughter, and though smiling may be permitted, decorum is the order of the day.

In formal situations, men are expected to wear a tie and jacket, and as the situation becomes more formal, a suit or even a tuxedo. Women are expected to wear a dress, avoiding the wearing of pants, and the dress should be neither cut too low nor expose too much leg; also jewelry should be sparse and not flashy. Children and adolescents tend to be excused from the extremes of these rules, but they may attend schools that have dress codes that proscribe blue jeans, excessively tight clothes and in general anything that might be construed as "provocative." Such codes are not limited to schools and are also observed in the business world, especially in the more formal contexts of banks and law offices, where length of hair and the presence of a beard may be regulated.

One of the most important set of social rules concerns status. Deference is expected from subordinates even in private social contexts, but expressions that acknowledge status are mandatory in public. Thus a subordinate must use the last name of a boss, but the latter can use the worker's first name. Although we have no royalty in this country, many people have titles, and others are expected to use these forms of address. A physician or a Ph.D. expects to be called doctor, those of higher ranks at a college to be called professor, and governors and senators are addressed that way long after they have vacated office. In traditional families, in which the rules are strictly adhered to, children may be required to greet their fathers with sir.

Social Contexts

Formal behavior is what is generally seen in public, when it can be observed by others, and the rules are relaxed considerably in private contexts. As a result, one of the rules that governs social behavior is a sharp demarcation between public and private behavior. In a restaurant or waiting room, men are forbidden to trim their nails or women to comb their hair or to apply cosmetics. Behavior that is a matter of course when one is alone—yawning, scratching oneself, or personal hygiene—is simply not acceptable in public, and the more formal the social context, the more strict are the rules and the expectation that there will be adherence. Of course, not all public situations require formal behavior. Eating out is no guarantee of a formal atmosphere, for public manners tend to weaken in fast food restaurants and may disappear completely at a hot dog stand. Although formal behavior tends to start in public contexts, such contexts vary considerably in their rules and strictures.

Situations that are more serious in their nature also tend to elicit more formal behavior. Thus we are more rule governed at the office than at home, during working than after working hours, or at a meeting than at a bar. A varsity football game is cosseted with regulations in contrast to the catch-as-catch-can rules of a pickup game of touch football, and a high school basketball game has a detailed set of rules that are never seen in a game of "shirts against skins."

The most public and serious events are inevitably an intrinsic part of the fabric of society and are therefore ceremonial in nature: weddings, funerals, graduations, and inaugurations. When the event is both national and legal, as is a presidential inauguration, for example, the pomp and ritual represent the peak of formality. There is less ceremony in the courtroom (it is restricted to the coming and going of the judge), but the prominence of legal issues and the possibility of incarceration or fines lends a serious air to the proceedings. Informality may be punished as contempt of court, and the judge is not to be approached unless permission is given after a formally worded request.

Another dimension concerns intimacy. Few people are formal with family members, good friends, or co-workers who are peers, for such behavior would be regarded as excessively stiff, unbending, and perhaps even unfriendly. It is in our contacts with strangers or casual acquaintances that we are most aware of status, decorum, propriety, and manners, for it is here that we put on a social mask comprised of behaviors most completely governed by social rules.

Vocational Roles

Vocational roles provide good examples of the range of formal behavior. At the low end is the informal behavior expected of a clown or a forest ranger, but the high end offers the best illustrations of rule-governed behavior. The extreme end would appear to be represented by the military, say an army officer. The uniform contains information that regulates the behavior of other army personnel. Rank is prominently displayed, so that everyone knows who salutes whom and who gives orders that must be obeyed in the chain of command. Badges inform anyone which unit the officer belongs to, and parts of the uniform can also serve this purpose: special boots for paratroopers and hats for units such as the Green Berets. These badges and apparel are especially important when they signify membership in an elite group that commands deference from others. Prominently displayed on the uniform are the officer's medals, which represent a coded presentation of accomplishments, from such trivial ones as good conduct, to being wounded, or even to outstanding bravery. Thus the uniform explicitly informs others how to act (as subordinates or superordinates) and implicity informs them of how much deference should be accorded because of past military accomplishments (the medals or the units). There is of course more than one uniform to be worn, and which one is appropriate is spelled out in detail, often in writing. Punishment is likely to greet any military personnel who are out of uniform because the uniform is incomplete or inappropriate to the occasion. And spit and polish are still expected of shoes and brass. Grooming is also specified, which for men determines the length of hair, whether beards are allowed, and being clean shaven. Nor are bearing and demeanor forgotten, for a soldier is expected to be ramrod straight when standing at attention, eyes to the front, and to have a serious mien. Even the position of the body is prescribed when the soldier is standing at ease, and hands must never be in pockets. In brief, the military role would seem to represent the height of formality in the extent and detail of the rules, the rigid adherence expected, and the strong punishment for deviation from rules of dress and behavior.

The role of judge in a court of law is less formal. The only uniform is a black robe, but it is worn over everyday clothes and has no badges, medals, or other coded ornaments that tell observers anything about the person wearing the robe. Demeanor is expected to be serious ("sober as a judge") even to the point of being magisterial. Above all, the judge is expected to maintain a mask of neutrality, for he or she is there to decide points of law, not guilt or innocence. Thus, although the role is clear and played out in one of the most public of contexts, there is no detailed set of rules. Instead, each judge must attempt to match his or her behavior to a standard of neutrality and command of the proceedings.

The role of diplomat is similar in being extremely public but not having detailed rules. Like a judge, a diplomat must exercise discretion and make choices within a restricted range of behavior, but neither can depend on the rigid set of rules that characterizes the military. The diplomat, however, is required to be formal in attire, sometimes to the point of wearing clothes that are specified in compulsive detail. The demeanor of a diplomat is neither the frozen face of a military man nor the bland neutrality of the judge, but a series of masks to fit each occasion. Such a person must be sober today, mournful at tomorrow's funeral for a head of state, a polite guest at another's reception, and an affable host at the diplomat's own reception. A diplomat may be "onstage" more of the time than a soldier or judge, and in that sense the role is extremely formal.

A drop down in formality is the role of a professor in front of class. He or she ranks much higher in status than the students and is expected to behave like a sage and someone in command. Beyond these requirements, there are no particular rules. Once there were dress requirements, and men did not enter a classroom unless attired in jacket and tie, but now informality reigns and the professor's taste in clothes determines what is worn to class.

This last example makes an important point. In less formal roles, there are fewer rules and little concern when they are violated. As a result, the personality of the individual may be displayed. Thus there are wide differences in the way professors act in class. Some behave little differently than in their homes, and some may be more relaxed and even occasionally outrageous in the interest of keeping the students attentive. Others may put on the mask of professor, sticking to the topic, avoiding humor, and doing only what is necessary to teach; individuality is suppressed and not allowed to intrude into the role.

Roles, then, can be played as though one were wearing a mask the way Greeks did when they staged a play, with little or no intrusion of the personality of the actor. Or they can be played with virtually no mask, the individual's personality largely determining the behavior that occurs. Individuality in role playing tends to occur mainly when the role is informal. When the role is highly formal, the rules are too detailed and adherence to them is too strictly enforced for individuality to break through. Thus, there will be more uniformity in how the roles of military person or judge are played than in how the role of teacher is played.

Formality as a Trait

There is a questionnaire measure of formality, mentioned earlier (L. Buss, 1984). The items include the need for manners, propriety, restraining expressiveness, and being at home in formal situations. No single questionnaire is likely to capture all the individual differences in formality, which may be best regarded as a trait that consists of several components. One is being status-conscious, which means being alert to differences in social rank and therefore offer appropriate respect to superordinates and to insist on deference from subordinates. Formal parents, other things equal, are likely to demand obedience from their children "because I say so."

Formal people, by definition, strictly adhere to social rules, strongly urge or even demand that others do, and disdain of those who ignore, disobey, or flaunt the rules that govern social behavior. Formal people would rather avoid a pleasurable social event than to attend improperly dressed; when invited to a home, they need to know precisely how formal the occasion is and such men are likely to be wearing a suit or jacket and tie when others are dressed more casually. They prefer regularity, discipline, orderliness, and above all, predictability. The extreme of these tendencies would appear to be compulsiveness, which evidently does not cohere as a reliable trait but is seen in certain neurotics. A related tendency is to be serious rather than playful, which is not the same as having or not having a sense of humor. Playfulness is the tendency to laugh easily (including at oneself) and to prefer the spontaneity of situations unencumbered by rules and that allow one the freedom to be expressive. As it is defined here, there is no trait measure of serious–playful, though perhaps there should be.

Formal people believe in the rules that govern social behavior and disapprove of violations of these rules. What would others think of those who are impolite, or who fail to acknowledge status? Surely there would be social censure, and such people would be regarded as unfit to move in appropriate social circles. It follows that formal people are keenly aware of themselves as social objects and of the possible impressions they might make on others. As such, they should be high in the trait of public self-consciousness. Informal people are less concerned about the rules of social behavior, by definition, and therefore, should be low in public self-consciousness.

We know that shy people tend to feel awkward or distressed in the presence of strangers or casual acquaintances. One way to relieve the discomfort would be to learn the rules of social conduct and to play out social roles to the letter. If they can figuratively memorize a social script detailing the rules of social behavior and then read it as would an actor, shy people might be able to get by in social interaction and perhaps even perform well. To the extent that formal behavior provides a facade behind which shy people can hide, formality is linked with shyness, although the correlation is likely to be modest.

An appropriate dichotomy has been suggested by Turner (1976), who distinguishes between institutionals and impulsives. Institutionals are conformists who accept the rules, adhere to them, and scorn those who ignore them. They strongly value self-control and can see the need to deny one's own impulses. Impulsives do not deny their own desires and wish to be expressive even if rules are broken; they believe that it is hypocritical to deny oneself merely for the sake of conformity. They want not predictability but the indeterminacy that occurs when people are allowed to be spontaneous; social rules are anathema. Turner (1976) does not equate his impulsives with those who score high on personality scales of impulsivity. Actually, there is no trait measure of the institutional–impulsive dichotomy, perhaps because such a trait could not be reliably and coherently assessed, but the possibility is intriguing, for the dichotomy would seem to be related to formality.

Formal people prefer rule-governed, predictable situations. When introduced to novel social contexts, they desperately seek to discover how to act, and when visiting other countries, they are anxious not to be regarded as "Ugly Americans." They are likely to gravitate toward the more formal vocations (military, legal, banking), and the converse is true: Vocational training that includes formality is likely to spill over into non-work situations. Thus some naval officers never stop being in the navy even when at home, and they run a tight ship, demanding of their children strong discipline, order, and respect for status.

At the other end of the dimension of formality, informal people find social rules constricting and sometime oppressive. They do not mind dressing up occasionally but prefer the option of wearing whatever is comfortable. Although they acknowledge the existence of status differences, they believe that deference to rank smacks of traditions that may be traced back to royalty and serfs, masters and slaves. They usually know the rules of social behavior, although perhaps not the details of high-level protocol such as which eating utensils or precisely which set of clothes are appropriate, but they believe that the rules are too detailed and excessively and rigidly enforced. They find formal contexts too confining and prefer the informality of situations that allow diversity of dress and spontaneity of behavior.

Informal people like to be allowed to express their individuality and therefore their behavior to represent the impulses of the moment and their enduring personality traits. They wish to interact without the mask that they feel is worn by formal people to conceal their individuality. Informal people avoid occupations and situations that are fully scripted and highly public. Thus they would prefer improvisational acting to reading a script precisely the way the playright wrote it, playing jazz to playing classical music, being a disk jockey to being a radio announcer, and giving an extemporaneous speech to reading the speech.

In brief, when given a choice, formal and informal people select contexts and roles apposite to their personality traits, but often there is no choice. At a funeral or inauguration, for example, there are few options about how to behave. We might detect those who are informal by their becoming tense and impatient over time in such contexts, whereas formal people would be in their element. At an informal party or picnic, however, informal people would be relaxed and spontaneous, whereas formal people might not be at ease and would tend to leave early unless they could find an activity with clear rules, usually some kind of game. While playing games, formal people would be expected to stick to the letter or the law and might be more serious about the way the game is played; they would not like the kind of softball games in which a hitter obtains a beer when reaching first base successfully.

Those at either end of the dimension may be expected to influence how others behave. When people gather at the home of an informal person, they know that they can take off their shoes, sit on the floor, or perhaps even put their feet on the coffee table. At the home of a formal person, people tend to arrive dressed appropriately and stay that way, sit in chairs or couches, and ask the host or hostess for a drink rather than going into the kitchen and fetching one for themselves. Formal people tend to make others aware of themselves as social objects, knowing that formal people emphasize propriety in dress and grooming and decorum in speech and demeanor. Informal people are unconcerned about these issues, which makes others relax and causes no public self-awareness; but informal people may become intrusive in asking others to disclose private feelings or occasionally in being blunt to the point of impoliteness. The point here is that formal people can make others comfortable in the predictability of their behavior but can render a situation stiff and uncomfortable in their zeal for propriety, whereas informal people can make others comfortable by allowing spontaneity and expressiveness but may put others off by excessive candor.

It follows that those at each end of the dimension prefer those who are like them. Consider what might happen if a formal man married an informal woman. The husband would prefer having a formal living room (parlor), eating always in the dining room, and being fully dressed when eating. He would enjoy attending formal parties or dinners, dressing up to go to the theater, and social interactions in which there were at least some people who would defer his status. He might find his wife to be undisciplined and disorderly, blunt and inconsiderate of other people's feelings, offensive in ignoring status, and ignorant of how one sets a table for dinner. She would regard him as being stiff and unbending, intolerant of expressiveness and individuality, excessively mannered and obsequious when confronted with higher status, and unable to throw off the facade of politeness. She might regard him as cold, distant, and excessively preoccupied with the superficials of social behavior, and as unwilling to reveal his true self. One might ask why such people would marry, and the only answer is that people in love tend to act foolishly. Fortunately, such a pairing is rare and unlikely to last, for the dimension of formality requires similarity of partners, not complementarity.

Motivation

Why are people at either end of the formal–informal dimension of social behavior? One motive for following social rules is part of the broader motive to follow all rules and be a good citizen. Such conformity promotes law and order in general, and it facilitates social interaction in particular. Being polite, obeying the implicit rules of dress and demeanor, and attending to others' status tend to make others feel comfortable and avoids embarrassment. Thus, after having eaten a poorly prepared meal, the guests can spare the hostess' feelings by reporting that they enjoyed the meal. There is no moral issue in such minor dishonesty, only a desire to smooth over possible bumps in social interaction.

Some people enter social relationships fearing that they might offend others if they freely express opinions or engage in uninhibited behavior. By following the rules of social behavior, however, Becker (1975) states:

> the individual can navigate without fear in a threatening world. He can even ignore the true attitudes of others, as long as he can get by with the proper ritual formulas of salutation, sustaining conversation, farewells, and so on. The actor has only to be sure of the face-saving rules for interaction. Everyone is permitted the stolid self-assurance that comes with minute observations of unchallenging rules—we can all become social beaurocrats. (p. 61).

Other people enter social relationships determined to be themselves even if they must flout social conventions to do so. Adolescents may wish to challenge the social order to establish their own identity. Some adults have managed to grow up without acquiring the rules that govern public social behavior and are simply oblivious to them. Whatever their previous background, what all these people have in common is motivation to express themselves freely in social contexts, which means that their behavior will be extremely informal.

These various motives may also be regarded in terms of personality traits. Those who are fearful in social contacts with strangers or casual acquaintances are high in the trait of shyness, which has been discussed earlier. Formal behavior may be an excellent option for shy people, for it allows them to conceal their insecurity behind a mask of socially correct behavior, without having to reveal their own individuality. Finally, those who are determined to be informal are likely to be high on the trait of expressiveness (individuality) or on the trait of rebelliousness. Notice that not all these traits can be assessed by appropriate measures; until they are, the possibility remains that the motives or behaviors involved may not cohere as personality traits.

IMPRESSION MANAGEMENT

It is common knowledge that any of us might put on a facade when dealing with other people, but this notion was given impetus by Goffman (1959). Goffman assumed that each person presents a self to others in a manner analogous to an actor playing a role on the stage. Despite the sociological perspective offered by Goffman, self-presentation has been adopted by social psychologists, especially by those who are interested in how we manage impressions. The clearest definition of impression management may have been given by Jones (1964) under the heading of *ingratiation,* which refers to "a class of strategic behaviors illicitly designed to influence a particular other person concerning the attractiveness of one's personal qualities" (p. 11). I prefer to regard ingratiation as a subclass of impression management in which self-presentation occurs only by implication, but more of this later.

When people attempt to influence others in this way, which attributes do they feign or exaggerate? As a rough approximation, there appear to be six kinds: (a) social traits—being warm, pleasant, affable, and sincere; (b) social ability—being knowledgeable, polite, and even sophisticated; (c) ability—intelligence and any particular talent that might be especially appreciated, for example, in music, art, literature, or science; (d) motivation—conscientious, eager to work, and able to meet deadlines; (e) morality—honest, honorable, loyal, and perhaps even altruistic; (f) status—earned or ascribed rank as a member of a family or a vocation, or the winner of a prize; and (g) modesty about one's attributes or accomplishments, which requires some social skill while ensuring that the listener becomes aware of one's positive features.

The Dimension

Impression management may be regarded as dimension that peaks with behavior bordering on the unethical, includes more moderate self-presentation in everyday roles, and ends with the absence of strategy and tactics in social interaction. At the top is behavior seen in tricksters and swindlers who are willing to lie and cheat to make a profit. They turn social interaction into a zero-sum game in which there is inevitably a winner and a loser. Somewhat more ethical are politicians, who seek office by parading their virtues and accomplishments; they may be forced to take one position in response to one segment of their electorate and another position to a different segment. It is well known that in politics appearance is more important than reality, and no serious politician runs for office without a knowledgeable public relations person to present a picture that the public will like. Politicians rarely kiss babies anymore, but the idea underlying baby-kissing is alive and well: paint a picture of oneself as affable, approachable, and a person who loves children. It is no accident that the most popular president of this era is an actor.

There is also impression management when a person enters a novel role, is unsure of how to fill the role, and therefore exaggerates to establish his or her credentials. Thus, a new teacher may mention educational achievements to students, claim excessive knowledge, and refuse to admit ignorance or mistakes. This novice might take too much credit for previous work done with a mentor or claim acquaintance with those who are well known in the teacher's specialty. Students might be faced with tough discipline and demanding assignments as the teacher strives to establish a reputation consistent with the role.

Similar attempts may be seen when an adolescent male wishes to be seen as a man and therefore exaggerates any masculine characteristics. He tries to keep his voice low, avoiding any juvenile squeaks, grows a mustache or beard, and may try to demonstrate how much alcohol he can consume. He may also suggest that he has a responsible job, has attended important events (rock concerts), is sophisticated about restaurants and music, and has experimented with drugs, sex, and various living arrangements. Furthermore, the more insecure the male adolescent is about traditional masculinity— perhaps because of excessive youth or an apparently unmasculine body build—the more he tends to exaggerate his attempts to manage impressions, often to the point of caricature. Thus to demonstrate masculinity, he may curse more frequently, try riskier sports, refuse to back down from other males' challenges, challenge other males more frequently, and in general attempt to support a macho image.

Add 3 decades and there may emerge a middle-aged man who attempts to project an image of continuing youthfulness by maintaining a trim and muscled body, wearing his hair the way young men do, coloring the gray or using a hairpiece, wearing clothes styled for younger people, and demonstrating the same taste in music and dance as do younger people. Both the middle-aged man and the adolescent are being defensive in their impression management, for they are fighting against a public image they wish to deny.

Whether the impression management is assertive or defensive, it tends to be active: Grooming, clothes, and behavior are tailored to project an image that will be seen by others. There is also a kind of impression management that works passively and indirectly. It consists of flattering the other person with attention, compliments, and acquiescence. Such behavior is of course *ingratiation:* strategically and tactically responding to elicit a positive response from the other person. If you attend to my conversation, find it interesting, laugh at my jokes, and find my ideas original, surely I must regard you as bright, perceptive, and affable. I am bound to like you, not because of any specific behaviors or attributes that you have displayed but because of your reaction to my attributes. As Jones (1964) has pointed out, the flatterer must be careful not to overdo it, else the recipient may be aware of being manipulated. Most of us are delighted to receive boosts to self-esteem, however, and are unlikely to discover that we are being manipulated even when it is obvious to an observer. The ingratiator uses a familiar set of social rewards. The stimulation rewards are attention and responsivity, and the even more powerful affective rewards are deference, praise, and sympathy (affection is rarely used). These rewards are used deliberately to obtain praise or mild affection as an immediate consequence, but the ultimate motivation tends to be the economic incentives of money, goods, or perquisites. It is an unusual ingratiator who manipulates others just to be liked or respected, for these rewards often can be obtained, without strategy or tactics, in everyday social relationships. Some people may have little confidence that they will be liked for themselves and therefore resort to impression management.

Impression management tends to occur when there is a status difference, especially by subordinates who want to improve their position with superordinates. It also occurs when people first meet and tends to continue only as long as the relationship remains superficial. The impression manager is presenting a facade that is analogous to the way an actor plays a role on stage, and it is virtually impossible to maintain the pose over time. There is likely to be a revealing slip in the facade as affects and impulses break through. If the boss tells the same joke again, will the worker be able to produce a laugh that passes as spontaneous? This issue—the managing of impressions over time—is related to questions about the abilities and knowledge required to manage impressions, and relevant personality traits.

Abilities, Knowledge, and Traits

Managing impressions starts with the inhibition of spontaneous behavior. The ingratiator cannot laugh when the other person behaves in a ridiculous fashion, nor become angry when the other is insulting. The adolescent male who is trying for a macho image must suppress all traces of fear. The middle-aged man who is trying for an image of youthfulness must not reveal how tired he is or how bored he is by music preferred by juveniles. There must be excellent inhibitory control, which allows the person to plan and carry out only behavior that is consistent with the projected image.

The impression manager must also possess detailed knowledge of social contexts in order to recognize what would be appropriate social behavior, the roles being played by others, their varying statuses, and the extent to which adherence to rules is demanded. Such a person must also know others' personality traits and preferences, and therefore the kind of behaviors that might please them. Others' verbal behavior and nonverbal cues must be scrutinized and their current behavior placed in the context of knowledge about social reality. The impression manager must know which behaviors are needed to project the desired image and possess the ability to encode such behaviors. In brief, the requirements include detailed social knowledge, social skills, the ability to maintain a facade, the motivation to deceive, and the ability to improvise as situations change.

The Self-Monitoring Scale (Snyder, 1974), has been explicitly designed to assess those who stage manage their social behavior and has been found to consist of three separate factors (Briggs, Cheek, & Buss, 1980). One factor, *extraversion,* is a well-known personality trait that has been assessed previously. A second factor, called *acting,* may be related in that it taps the ability to perform:

1. I would probably make a good actor.
2. I have considered being an entertainer.
3. I have never been good at games like charades or improvisational acting. (reversed)
4. I can make impromptu speeches on topics about which I have almost no information.
5. I can look anyone in the eye and tell a lie with a straight face (if for a right end).

These items might predict who would be able to manage impressions on the assumption that the ability to perform and improvise as does a stage actor would carry over into everyday life social interactions. Some actors undoubtedly use their skills in offstage social encounters, but for others there appears to be no transfer, and the possibility remains that the items on the acting factor of the Self-Monitoring Scale may be better for selecting actors than for those who manage impressions in daily life.

The items that comprise the Other-Directness factor of this scale would appear to be a good measure of some of the tendencies underlying impression management:

1. In different situations and with different people, I often act like very different persons.
2. In order to get along and be liked, I tend to be what people expect me to be rather than anything else.
3. I'm not always the person I appear to be.
4. I guess I put on a show to impress or entertain people.
5. Even if I am not enjoying myself, I often pretend to be having a good time.
6. I may deceive people by being friendly when I really dislike them.
7. I would not change my opinion (or the way I do things) in order to please someone else or win their favor. (reversed)
8. I feel a bit awkward in company and do not show up as well as I should. (reversed)
9. When I am uncertain how to act in social situations, I look to the behavior of others for cues.
10. My behavior is usually an expression of my true inner feelings, attitudes, and beliefs. (reversed)
11. At parties and social gatherings, I do not attempt to do or say things that others will like. (reversed)

These items would seem to capture the essence of what it is to alter one's behavior to please others, and it is enlightening to examine the correlations between this subscale and other self-reports. It correlates .13 with the acting factor, a relationship so slight as to suggest that acting ability may not be at all involved in putting up a front for others. Furthermore, it correlates .37 with shyness and − .49 with self-esteem, which suggest that it is mainly socially anxious and insecure people who look to others for cues and who alter their behavior accordingly. These relationships offer the possibility that only a minority of those who present a social facade are intent on manipulating others for a social or economic gain, whereas the majority attempt to manage impressions because they are not sufficiently confident of their own spontaneous behavior or of social skills.

In light of the research by Briggs, Cheek, and Buss (1980) and by other researchers subsequently, Lennox and Wolfe (1984) suggested that the Self-Monitoring Scale lacks congruence with the concept of impression management and decided to change it. They concluded:

Our attempts to remedy the psychometric deficiencies of Snyder's Self-Monitoring Scale suggest that two of the assumptions guiding his original research were wrong: that acting ability in the theatrical-entertainment sense has much in common with the devices people use to modify their self-presentation in everyday life, and that cross-situational variability of behavior is associated with effectiveness in social interaction. (p. 1361–1362)

Their solution was to replace Snyder's original scale with a revision, which they offered in the form of two subscales that emerged from a factor analysis. The first is the Ability to Modify Self-Presentation:

1. In social situations, I have the ability to alter my behavior if I feel that something else is called for.
2. I have the ability to control how I come across to people, depending on the impression I want to give them.
3. When I feel that the image I'm portraying isn't working, I can readily change it to something that does.
4. I have trouble changing my behavior to suit different people in different situations. (reversed)
5. I have found that I can adjust my behavior to meet the requirements of any situation I find myself in.
6. Even when it might be to my advantage, I have difficulty putting up a good front. (reversed)
7. Once I know what a situation calls for, it's easy for me to regulate my actions accordingly.

The other subscale is Sensitivity to Expressive Behavior in Others:

1. I am often able to read people's true emotions correctly through their eyes.
2. In conversations, I am sensitive to even the slightest change in the facial expression of the person I'm conversing with.
3. My powers of intuition are quite good when it comes to understanding others' emotions and motives.
4. I can usually tell when others consider a joke to be in bad taste, even though they laugh convincingly.
5. I can usually tell when I've said something inappropriate by reading it in the listener's eyes.
6. If someone else is lying to me, I usually know it at once from that person's manner of expression.

Notice that the second subscale involves social perception, whereas the first involves the ability to manage impressions. The two correlate a modest

.22, which is consistent with a body of research on deception showing that deceiving others is essentially unrelated to detecting deception in others.

The last personality trait relevant to impression management is public self-consciousness, for an awareness of oneself as a social object and a concern for the impression made on others would seem to be requisites for attempting to stage manage one's own behavior. In line with this supposition is a correlation of .28 between the acting subscale and public self-consciousness.

CONTEXTS AND DIMENSIONS

The three dimensions discussed in this chapter—public self-awareness, formality, and impression management—all involve behavior that varies with the social context. Behavior at the high end of these dimensions is likely to occur when the context is public (and therefore social behavior can be observed by others) and when the relationship is superficial (strangers or casual acquaintances). In addition, people tend to manage impressions especially when economic rewards are available, whether immediately or as the eventual outcome of being liked by the other person.

Social contexts offer cues to the participants, and of special interest here is the behavior of those who are high on the trait dimensions relevant to awareness of oneself as a social object, following the rules of social behavior, and presentation of self (or ingratiation). When social behavior occurs with no observers and the relationship is one of friendship (or even more intimacy), even those high in public self-consciousness are temporarily less aware of themselves as social objects. The interactants presumably know each other well and have habituated to each other's attention, and there is no longer any need to be concerned about the impression being conveyed. Also, ingratiators and impression managers are less likely to attempt social manipulation in such relationships. And in informal contexts, there is little need for public manners, protocol, or formal dress, and issues of status wane in importance.

For a minority of people, however, the change in context may lead to little change in social behavior, for they seem to carry over their public behavior into private settings. Thus, some wives are modest about their bodies even with their husbands, and some adolescents think that they are the center of attention at the family dining table. Some men are so formal that they wish to be called sir by their children even in the privacy of the home, and some faculty members are so status conscious that they wish to be addressed by their title even when having an after-hours drink. Some ingratiators have the habit so strongly ingrained that they have trouble turning off the flattery even when they are already liked and there is no possibility of further gain.

The Stage Metaphor

The three dimensions discussed in this chapter may be related to the metaphor of being on the stage of a theater (Goffman, 1959). When actors are on stage, every aspect of their appearance and performance is observed closely by the audience. When on stage, they are conspicuous and therefore have a keen sense of themselves as social objects, the stage parallel of public self-awareness.

During the play, actors read the lines as they were written, follow the script, stay in character, respond to cues and supply cues to other actors, and enter and leave the stage on cue. They also obey unwritten rules of stagecraft: Do not turn your back on the audience when speaking, do not block the view of another actor or talk while another actor is talking, do not look directly at the audience, and keep the play going even if another actor falters. Such rules tend to maintain harmony within the troupe and lead to good performances. Similarly, in everyday life the rules of social behavior promote harmony and allow people to play the social roles they have adopted or the ones that have been assigned to them; formal behavior is socially adaptive.

Before a play opens, actors rehearse their lines and actions, as they plan to create the impression of a character on stage. They select some aspects of their own personality, exaggerate some aspects, and add new responses to their repertoire. Dress and grooming are also appropriate for the goal of conveying the personality of a particular character to the audience. Similarly, in everyday life those who would manage impressions rehearse, plan, and feign behaviors that will convey specific images to others. They are not merely following rules but actively manipulating their own behavior or the behaviors of others (ingratiation). In a sense, they are always on stage.

The stage metaphor is apt for the high ends of the dimensions of public self-awareness, formality, and impression management, but there is another aspect of the metaphor that should not be ignored (Buss & Briggs, 1984). Actors leave the stage, remove their costumes, and resume the typical behavior of everyday life when they are not necessarily the center of attention, closely following the rules of stagecraft, or creating a role. The low ends of the three dimensions are analogous to offstage behavior. People who are low in public self-consciousness rarely feel conspicuous and are relatively unconcerned about the impression they might make on others. Such women do not dress up to do grocery shopping, and they cannot be bothered with the latest hair or dress style. Those low in public self-conscious tend to be unaware of how they are perceived by others and may be surprised when they are told.

The behavior of informal people was spelled out earlier, and it needs to be added that some of them may rebel against social conventions. The rebels are likely to be young people who refuse to meet the standards for hair length, appropriate clothes, or attention to status; in the 1960s many young people delighted in flouting authority by calling the police "pigs."

There is no particular name for people at the low end of the impression management dimension, although they can be easily described. Their social behavior is open and straightforward, and they dislike seeing people manipulated. Their responses are spontaneous and unrehearsed, and therefore reflect the impulses of the moment, longstanding habits, and personality traits. Thus they are less likely to vary in social behavior from one context to another.

The various behaviors at the bottoms of the three dimensions appear to be related, and we should not be surprised to find that the person who does not manipulate is also informal and low in public self-consciousness. Such a person may be called *expressive* in the sense that individual tendencies tend to appear in social behavior with less of the restraint that limits such behavior in other people. Thus when a social role is being played—say, that of a teacher—more of an expressive's personality goes into the role than does when the role is played by those at the high end of any of the three dimensions. Such a person might have difficulty fitting in to a particular niche in society and would have to seek one that would fit the personality already in place. In terms of the stage metaphor, casting would be crucial for an expressive, but those at the high end of the three dimensions might more easily fit into social roles assigned to them.

As this discussion implies, the three dimensions tend to be distinct at the high end. It is relatively easy to separate public self-conscious behavior from formal behavior, and formal behavior from impression management. The three dimensions, however, appear to converge at the lower end. Unself-conscious behavior is likely to be similar to informal behavior, which is not very different from open, spontaneous behavior.

The onstage-offstage metaphor may be especially apt in relation to social rewards, which may be delivered spontaneously, routinely in the course of following rules, or to create an impression. In a conversation the listener may hang on the speaker's words and gestures because they are so interesting, because it is polite to pay attention, or because by pretending to be fascinated the listener will be viewed by the speaker as a sensitive and intelligent person. When the listener smiles or laughs in response to the speaker, it may be a spontaneous affective reaction, a smile because one is supposed to smile, or the kind of laughter one hears when the boss tells a joke for the second time. Praise may be offered for an excellent performance, because it is good manners to do so (the dinner was terrible, but the guest says it was delicious), or because flattery is such a successful technique of ingratiation. Sympathy may be preferred because the reacting person is moved by the other's plight, because it is nothing more than good manners to offer condolence, or because one can get into the other's good graces by feigning sympathy. Affection tends to be a genuine emotion, for it is not dictated by the rules of social behavior, and it is difficult to feign (and is used for manipulation only by those at the extreme end of the impression-management dimension).

Recall that social rewards are dimensional and can be aversive if they are insufficient or excessive (stimulation rewards) or if their bipolar opposites occur (affective rewards). There is obviously no payoff for shunning others, being explicitly inattentive or responsive, being critical or unsympathetic, or showing dislike. Yet, these responses occur regularly in social interaction, weakening friendships and disrupting relationships. It is possible to inhibit such behavior for a while, being polite, ingratiating or even manipulative, but only a person with consummate acting skills would be able to maintain the facade over time. As the minutes or hours pass, the smile becomes fixed, the laughter becomes forced, attention wanders, and it may be difficult to suppress the urge to tell the other that he or she is boring, incorrect, a poor performer, or irritating. Anyone who has been socialized is capable of a facade of good manners, white lies, ingratiation, and pretense, but such behavior is limited not only over time but over the course of a relationship. Furthermore, there is a minority of people, called *expressives,* whose behavior—even at the start of a relationship—is spontaneous, unrehearsed, relatively uninhibited, and consistent with their enduring dispositions. They represent the offstage part of the drama metaphor, in which there is little concern for costumes, facades, and the rigid codes that govern social behavior.

NOTES

Deception

Modern research on deception dates back to the early work of Ekman and Friesen (1969), who focused on nonverbal cues as the major means of detecting lying and covering up. These two investigators and their colleagues eventually moved toward the study of emotions, and currently the most active group of students of deception is at the University of Virginia under the leadership of Bella DePaulo. The most recent comprehensive review of research on deception may be found in DePaulo, Stone, and

Lassiter (1985a). Among other things, they summarized developmental research, which revealed that:

> first graders cannot successfully tell a lie. When they attempt to do so, their underlying affect leaks out, and the fact that they are lying is obvious to their peers. Third graders have trouble, too, in much the same way—their true feelings leak. There seems to be notable improvement by fourth and fifth grade. These children can fool their peers and adult strangers, and sometimes they can even fool their parents. There is some evidence that between the ages of five and twelve, children become increasingly adept at hiding their deception facially. At all of these ages, however, children's voice tones readily reveal to others when they are lying and when they are telling the truth. (p. 358)

These authors suggest that children can best practice the arts of deception at play, for in almost every game it is advantageous to conceal one's intentions to practice deceit. And of course, deception is useful in avoiding punishment in real life situations.

DePaulo et al. (1985a) also report a developmental sequence in the strategies used to deceive. Young children do not employ strategy and are found out. Older children and young adolescents attempt to simulate the affect they are supposed to have, and they are more successful at deception. College students use the strategy of exaggeration or "hamming," and they are the most successful deceivers.

Recently, these authors studied the impact of motivation in deception (DePaulo, Stone, & Lassiter, 1985b). Paradoxically, as motivation to lie increased, the deception became more detectable, especially in nonverbal behavior. The explanation offered is that strongly motivated deceivers focus on nonverbal channels in an attempt to control leakage. This is not only a difficult task, but the attention to these channels may disrupt the free flow of behavior, thereby alerting observers to deception. This research also documented the common-sense notion that when ingratiation is attempted, lying is more likely to be detected, probably because observers tend to be more suspicious.

The verbal channel has not been neglected; Siegman and Reynolds (1983) investigated verbal fluency in relation to self-monitoring (Snyder, 1974). They found only minimal support for the total self-monitoring score being a determinant of deception in the verbal channel, but the extraversion subscale (Briggs, Cheek, & Buss, 1980) was significantly correlated with deception. In attempting to explain why, Siegman and Reynolds emphasized the face-to-face nature of their paradigm: "Perhaps extraverted individuals, being socially secure and at ease, are relatively less upset than introverts at having to lie to someone's face and hence are better able to control their expressive behavior. Moreover, the extravert's expressive skills may be helpful in regulating expressive behavior in social situations" (p. 1331). The acting subscale was also correlated with deception, but the relationships were not as strong as those for extraversion. When the acting and extraversion scores were combined, the correlations for the three measures of deception were .46, .51, and .63. This study is important in that, unlike most of the deception research, it is close to real life. The subjects had cheated on a laboratory task and were given the opportunity to lie. In this context, the correlations between deception and the two subscales of self-monitoring are impressive.

Self-Presentation

The pioneer in this area is Erving Goffman, who coined the term "self-presentation" in his book, The Presentation of Self in Everyday Life (1959): "I shall consider the way in which the individual in ordinary work situations presents himself and his activity to others, the ways in which he guides and controls the impression they form of him, and the kinds of things he may and may not do while sustaining his performance before them" (Preface). Goffman's theatrical metaphor was apt and therefore embraced by many psychologists, who may have forgotten that as a sociologist, Goffman was unconcerned with psychological issues: "I assume that the proper study of interaction is not the individual and his psychology, but rather the syntactical relations among the acts of different persons mutually present to one another. . . . A psychology is necessarily involved, but one stripped and cramped to suit the sociological study of conversation, track meets, banquets, jury trials, and street loitering" (pp. 2–3). Notice that all but one of his examples deal with public and sometimes formal social contexts rather than informal, interpersonal situations.

One of the foremost theorists and researchers in self-presentation is James Tedeschi, who recently summarized his approach (Tedeschi & Norman, 1985). He distinguished between defensive and assertive self-presentation. Defensive social behavior occurs when a person is trying to escape from negative attributions by others, whether realistic or not. "Assertive impression management refers to those behaviors initiated by the actor to establish particular identities or attributes in the eyes of another" (p. 295). A second distinction focuses on the time frame of goals. Tactical impression management has short-term goals, usually in the immediate situations, whereas the strategic variety attempts to establish enduring identities.

Crosscutting the two distinctions yields a fourfold classification scheme that, it is claimed, can account for extraordinary diversity of social behavior. Thus strategic-assertive self-presentation is assumed to underlie or to be involved in attraction, esteem, prestige, status, credibility, and trustworthiness, and tactical-defensive self-presentation includes self-handicapping and prosocial behavior.

Another important theorist and researcher in self-presentation is Schlenker (1980), whose book on impression management was one of the early general statements of the position by a psychologist. In extending the concept beyond social interaction, he wrote "there is nothing intrinsic to the concept of impression management that dictates that is must be directed toward only a real audience. Imagined audiences, which range from the generalized other to specific significant others . . . can be conjured. These are often played to with more gusto than the immediate real audiences people encounter" (p. 306). Thus self-presentation can occur even when no one else is present. Another extension was suggested by Snyder (1979) who believes that even when people are just being themselves and allowing others to see them without any facade, they are self-presenting themselves "as they really are." Furthermore, Baumeister (1982) assumes that people manage impressions to validate their own identities to themselves. If these various extrapolations are combined with Tedeschi's expansion, self-presentation behavior becomes more or less equivalent to not only social behavior but also with thoughts and actions that occur when no one else is present.

If self-presentation were so pervasive, it would not be necessary to specify the conditions under which it occurs or the personality traits with which it might be linked. The position taken in this book is of course different. Here it is assumed that in many social contexts people tend to act on momentary impulses, to express their emotions, or to act in accord with enduring personality dispositions. It then becomes necessary to specify the conditions under which self-presentation is likely to occur and the personality traits that facilitate its occurrence, as was done earlier in the chapter.

It also appears necessary to distinguish between two of the behaviors that tend to be labelled *impression management*. The first class includes pretense and ingratiation. The second consists of formal behavior: observing the implicit rules of social interaction. The differences between these two classes of behavior, neglected in theories of self-presentation, were presented earlier in the chapter. Formality has been studied extensively in cultural anthropology and sociology, fields that have focused on status, forms of address, appropriateness of demeanor and clothing, and the rituals specific to particular collectives, social classes, and societies. The psychological study of formality, however, has been neglected, and there is no published personality measure of the trait of formality. The lack of interest by psychologists may be due to the separation between psychology and related social sciences or to the general neglect of the stylistic aspects of behavior (see chapter 8).

Self-Awareness and Self-Consciousness

Fenigstein (1979) manipulated shunning by having college women ignored by two female confederates. Subjects high in public self-consciousness were much more upset and avoided subsequent interaction more than did those low in this trait. In a study on allocation of reward, public self-consciousness made subjects sensitive to external (social) standards, whereas private self-consciousness made them sensitive to internal (personal) standards (Kernis & Reis, 1984). Public self-consciousness should make people aware of how their behavior is viewed by others. Tobey and Tunnell (1981) videotaped college women and asked them to predict their impressions on potential viewers of the tapes. Those high in public self-consciousness (and those high in the acting factor of the self-monitoring scale) predicted more successfully than those low on the trait.

The literature on public and private self-consciousness has been reviewed extensively elsewhere (Buss, 1980; Carver & Scheier, 1981), so the topic need not be pursued here any further, especially because the distinction between the two traits is widely acknowledged (see also the Appendix). There is less agreement, however, about whether public and private self-awareness can be differentiated, which makes research by Froming, Walker, and Lopyan (1982) especially appropriate. Subjects were pretested on their attitudes toward the use of punishment in the laboratory. One sample opposed punishment but believed that most people favored its use for research purposes. They were allowed the opportunity to punish other ostensible subjects with electric shock under one of three conditions: A small mirror was in front of the subject (private self-awareness), an evaluative audience was watching (public self-awareness), or a control condition. Private self-awareness was expected to direct attention to personal attitudes (less shock than control), and public self-awareness was expected to direct attention to social or public attitudes (more shock than control); these hypotheses were confirmed. Another sample of subjects favored using punishment for research purposes but believed that most people opposed it. The results for them were precisely the opposite of those for the first sample. Thus a private self-awareness manipulation induced a change in behavior opposite to that induced by public self-awareness, and then these findings were reversed by appropriate selection of subjects. This research makes it clear that the two transient states of self-awareness are distinct.

7 Social Anxiety

Social anxiety is discomfort in the presence of others. Its most observable aspect is the relative absence of normal social behavior, specifically, reticence, inhibition of speech and gestures, and a reluctance to become involved in conversation. When the discomfort is no longer bearable, the socially anxious person simply withdraws. Acute social anxiety may be seen in hand tremors, speech hesitations, stuttering, and awkward gestures or speech. Such behavior may appear in dyadic interaction or when there is an audience. The personality trait can be measured by a social anxiety scale, which emerged as one of the factors of the Self-Consciousness Inventory (Fenigstein, Scheier, & Buss, 1975):

1. It takes me time to overcome my shyness in new situations.
2. I have trouble working when someone is watching me.
3. I get embarrassed very easily.
4. I feel anxious when I speak in front of a group.
5. Large groups make me nervous.

Notice that the items refer to discomfort both in dyadic interaction (shyness and embarrassment) and in front of an audience (audience anxiety). Two words in these items have an important implication. *Embarrassment* implies the presence of public self-consciousness, whereas *anxiety* suggests the presence of fear. This distinction is crucial to an understanding of shyness, which is assumed to consist of two related phenoma: fearful and self-conscious shyness (Buss, 1985).

FEARFUL SHYNESS

Shyness refers to inhibition of normally expected social behavior when with one or several other people, normally in a conversation. *Fearful shyness,* as its name suggests, is accompanied by anxiety that varies from wariness to panic. It appears during the first year of life. For the first 6 months or so, infants welcome strangers and are curious about them. Subsequently, their curiosity is opposed by a fear of social novelty, which is called *stranger anxiety* or *wariness.* Infants may look like they are going to cry or may actually cry, they may attempt to hide behind their mothers or seek their mothers' comfort, and their heart rates are usually accelerated. Stranger anxiety is more likely to occur in infants who are high in the temperament of emotionality, especially those who are cared for exclusively by their mothers. Such anxiety is less likely to occur in infants who are low in emotionality, high in sociability (which may overcome social inhibition), and have many caretakers. Even among infants who have acute stranger anxiety, the reaction gradually wanes as the months pass and they become habituated to strangers and to other kinds of social novelty. For a minority, however, novel social contexts continue to elicit fearful shyness.

Older children tend not to cry or to run for mother and instead manifest the inhibition and disorganization of social behavior just described. At this age, a cognitive component has been added, and they may worry about future interactions and plan to avoid them when possible. Such fearful shyness is different from nonsocial fears in the object of worry, but the autonomic component is the same as in any fear: activation of the sympathetic nervous system. Thus, the essential difference between such shyness and other fears is that fearful shyness is exclusively social.

Determinants

One cause of fearful shyness, already mentioned, is social novelty. Fear of strangers occurs not only in humans but in most animal species. Prudence would seem to be adaptive. Approaching strangers may have catastrophic consequences, and parents warn children not to accept rides or gifts from people they do not know. The negative side of caution is the difficulty of making new friends, which is less important adaptively than avoiding potential danger.

A related cause is intrusiveness. Infants tend to become frightened when a stranger approaches too quickly and appears to loom before them, and adults become edgy when another person comes too close (unless it is an intimate). There are spatial zones surrounding us, which we do not like to be penetrated except by very good friends or members of the family (Hall, 1966), and spatial intrusion tends to elicit a strong avoidance reaction.

Children are increasingly subjected to social evaluation. Typical criteria are attractiveness, friendliness, modesty, and manners, as well as social behavior appropriate to their age. Praise is a powerful social reward, and acceptance and liking are desired by everyone. When children or adults are criticized or rejected, they are likely to become upset and socially cautious. When attempting to make friends, they may be inhibited in their social behavior and even fearful of rejection. If they have been punished by parents or other socializing agents for breaking the explicit or implicit rules of social interaction, children may worry about the outcome on subsequence occasions.

The determinants mentioned so far—novelty, intrusiveness, and evaluation—may lead not only to transient fearful shyness but also to the disposition to be shy. The trait of shyness may also originate in other personality dispositions. When children are regularly punished in social contexts, they are likely to develop fearful shyness. The children especially susceptible to such conditioning are those high in fearfulness, which differentiates from the primordial emotionality. Fearfulness is heritable and starts early in life (Buss & Plomin, 1984). It correlates .50 with shyness, and there may be a logical basis for concluding the former causes the latter. Shyness refers to discomfort and inhibition only in social contexts, whereas fear occurs in both social and nonsocial contexts. Thus a fearful person is likely to be afraid of not only social contexts but also airplanes, deep water, hospitals, snakes, insects, and a variety of other potentially dangerous stimuli. Shy people are not necessarily afraid of nonsocial stimuli. We expect a majority of fearful people to be shy, but only a minority of shy people would be nonsocially fearful. Thus, as the broader category of behavior, fear is assumed to be a cause of shyness rather than shyness being a cause of fear.

Once the tendency to become shy is established by fearfulness, it may be maintained by being low in the temperament of sociability. Unsociable children, by definition, are weaker in motivation to be with others and less rewarded by their company. They are likely to avoid others, make fewer friends, shrink from strangers, and leave social interactions more quickly because the rewards are insufficient to tolerate the aversiveness present in most such interactions. As a consequence, there is little opportunity to habituate to novelty and to allow fear to extinguish. Thus if there is any tendency to be fearful of social contexts, low sociability tends to strengthen this fear.

It may be argued that shyness is nothing but low sociability, which would make the foregoing argument true by definition. Most extant extraversion questionnaires include shyness and sociability items, and earlier sociability questionnaires had shyness items, including the previous measure of sociability temperament (Buss & Plomin, 1975). Subsequently, sociability and shyness were defined and assessed separately to determine their relationship (Cheek & Buss, 1981). *Sociability* was defined as the tendency to affiliate with others and to prefer to be with them. *Shyness* was defined as the following reactions when with others: tension, feelings of awkwardness or discomfort, and inhibition of social behavior. Items were constructed that assessed either sociability or shyness as just defined. The questionnaire, consisting of 14 items, was administered to 912 college men and women (there were no gender differences). A factor analysis yielded separate factors for sociability and shyness, with only one of the sociability items having a significant factor loading on the shyness scale. (The items are listed in the Appendix.)

The shyness and sociability measures correlated −.30, which means that sociable people tend to be unshy and unsociable people tend to be shy. The size of the correlation, however, suggests that this linkage is not strong and that there are sizable minorities who are both sociable and shy or both unsociable and unshy. Fearfulness correlated a nonsignificant −.09 with sociability but a highly significant .50 with shyness. Self-esteem correlated .18 with sociability and −.51 with shyness.

Thus, shyness and sociability may be regarded as separate personality traits. This conclusion is based on self-reports, and it was important to demonstrate that these two traits might each affect social behavior. Accordingly, in the same study, college women who were high or low on either trait were selected, yielding four groups of subjects: shy–sociable, unshy–sociable, shy–unsociable, and unshy–unsociable. Pairs of women who were matched on both traits were allowed to get to know one another in a bogus waiting room situation, and they were surreptitiously videotaped. Shy subjects were more tense than unshy subjects and reported afterward that they were more inhibited, but the trait of sociability also made a difference in their observed behavior. Most of the differences between shy and unshy subjects were caused by the behavior of the shy–sociable subjects: they spent less time talking, averted their gaze more, touched themselves more (nervously), and observers judged them to be more tense than the other three groups. Thus, sociable behavior was determined not only by the trait of shyness but also by the trait of sociability. Although the traits are related, they are separate enough for shyness to be something more than low sociability.

SELF–CONSCIOUS SHYNESS

Self-conscious shyness is regarded as the extreme of public self-awareness: when awareness of oneself as a social object is so acute that it is experienced as feelings of awkwardness or discomfort. At such times one feels psychologically naked and excessively exposed to the scrutiny of others. There typically is an associated desire to sink out of sight and to escape from the prying eyes of others. When this feeling is especially intense, it becomes embarrassment, a reaction that is not only experienced but observable because of the blushing that usually accompanies it.

So far as is known, we are the only species that blushes; furthermore, infants do not blush. It is not a lack of the vascular bed in the cheeks of the face, which fill up and redden. Human infants, for example, can become flushed when they cry or protest any discomfort. Rather, infants and members of other species do not blush in circumstances under which adult humans would blush; possibly because they do not have any sense of themselves as social objects. Thus blushing, a clear sign of the presence of embarrassment, would appear to be a marker that establishes the presence of a social self.

Testing this hypothesis requires a developmental study of embarrassment. There are ethical and practical problems to studying embarrassment in young children, for it would not be proper to induce it and the response appears infrequently. Therefore, parents were asked about their children's embarrassment (Buss, Iscoe, & Buss, 1979). Parents of kindergarten, nursery, and elementary school children were sent a questionnaire that inquired about blushing or any other signs of embarrassment in the children during the past 6 months, an interval that would not strain memory. The frequencies of embarrassment for appropriate age groups were: 3 and 4 years, 26%; 5 years, 59%; and 6 years, 73%. Thereafter, the percentage was relatively stable throughout the remainder of childhood. Although a minority of children were reported to be embarrassed at 3 and 4 years of age, the big jump in frequency was at 5 years. Thus at roughly the fifth or sixth year of life socialization training has rendered children susceptible to embarrassment: they are capable of public self-awareness and therefore of self-conscious shyness.

Determinants

Paradoxically, one cause of self-conscious shyness is a social reward, attention from others. This reward is a dimension that ranges from insufficient to excessive attention, the reinforcing part of the dimension being the middle. Both extremes of the dimension can result in acute awareness of oneself as a social object. Few people enjoy being stared at, especially by strangers. Envision someone arriving late at a party, only to find that everyone has stopped talking to look at the latest arrival. Under laboratory conditions, being stared at for only 2 minutes is sufficient to cause physiological arousal and reported feelings of discomfort and embarrassment (Strom & Buck, 1979). Even close scrutiny of friends can cause discomfort and feelings of being exposed and vulnerable. Presumably, this association between being observed and feeling defenseless may be traced back to parental scrutiny. When parents attend to their children, it may be to compliment them, but most of the time it is to point out mistakes and failures: sloppiness, bad manners, inappropriate dress, and generally the poor impression the children might make on others. This link between being observed closely and a negative public image would tend to make older children and adults self-consciously shy whenever they were under scrutiny.

A related cause is being conspicuously different from others. Americans wandering down a street in China must be aware of nationality differences in facial characteristics and dress. There are also occasions that mark one's social uniqueness: a small boy in a men's locker room or a woman dressed casually who discovers that everyone else is in evening clothes.

Perhaps the most common cause of embarrassment is a breach of privacy, when the distinction between public and private is shattered. We strongly socialize a firm line between what is allowed to be observed and what must be unobserved. Bodily modesty is important here, not only in what is allowed in clothing but also in what is exposed during elimination or in sexual behavior, and the latter acts themselves are, by common consent, supposed to be private. When a woman opens a bathroom door to discover a man partly unclothed, both are embarrassed.

There is another kind of public–private distinction, that between covert feelings and overt behavior (discussed in the last chapter). Most people have tender feelings or vaulting ambitions that they share with no one except perhaps one or two intimate friends or family members. When an adolescent's crush is inadvertently revealed to others, he or she is likely to blush. Even teasing about being the object of another's crush can cause embarrassment. Such leakage may explain why overpraise can lead to embarrassment. When college students were told by an accomplice that they were more attractive and sensitive to others than they had believed, they tended to blush (L. Buss, 1984). One way to account for this finding is to assume that overpraise confronts the recipient with the possibility that others will believe that he or she is conceited, thereby exposing self-evaluations that were supposed to be private. Although this explanation is speculative, it does parallel the observed results of teasing about crushes, and it is difficult to arrive at any other explanation of this paradoxical effect of overpraise.

Formal situations also supply a context in which self-conscious shyness is likely to occur. Recall that formality is defined by more complete and detailed rules, as well as an expectation of closer adherence to these rules. In the face of such detail and specificity, mistakes are more likely, causing embarrassment. Furthermore, when one has only incomplete knowledge of the rules, it may be best to be cautious and inhibited in social behavior— that is, shy. Some of the most significant rules of social behavior deal with status, and when status considerations are important, those of subordinate status tend to inhibit spontaneous behavior. They may feel self-conscious about the status differential, especially when the subordinate occupies an exalted position: the president, the pope, a Nobel prizewinner, or an international movie star. Formal situations are usually public: a restaurant rather than one's own dining room or a church service rather than a private confessional. The more public the context, the more the participants feel observed and therefore self-consciously shy.

The last determinant of transient self-conscious shyness is the laughter of others. The laughter may be goodhumored and spontaneous in response to a minor social miscue or it may be derisive, taking a nasty turn toward ridicule and teasing. The object of this hilarity tends to be doubly embarrassed: because of being laughed at and also because of an awareness of having made a social mistake.

Self-conscious shyness is not only a transient reaction but also a personality disposition. One cause of such shyness may be a history of being teased and ridiculed, but there are also several personality determinants. One is public self-consciousness, by definition. Another is a lack of social skills, for anyone who does not possess the knowledge and available responses needed for social interaction is likely to be subject to repeated feelings of acute self-consciousness. A third determinant is self-esteem. Those who are low in self-esteem are likely to believe that others are aware of their real or imagined deficiencies. Feelings of inferiority tend to make one think that others are continually observing and perhaps even laughing, which usually elicit acute public self-awareness.

There are data bearing on two of these hypotheses. Shyness has been found to correlate .26 with public self-consciousness and −.51 with self-esteem (Cheek & Buss, 1981). Correlation does not imply causation, however, and there is no logical basis for suggesting that either of these traits causes shyness any more than shyness causing these traits. To compound the problem of interpretation, no measure of shyness distinguishes between self-conscious and fearful shyness, and until such a differentiation is made in a trait measure of shyness, the aforementioned correlations offer only highly tentative support for the explanation.

FEARFUL VERSUS SELF–CONSCIOUS SHYNESS

The two kinds of shyness are compared in Table 7.1. The emotional reaction in fearful shyness is of course fear, sometimes accompanied by worry, and in self-conscious shyness it is acute public self-awareness, sometimes accompanied by embarrassment. Fearful shyness occurs in animals and human infants, for this kind of shyness requires nothing more than a sensory self. Self-conscious shyness requires an advanced, cognitive self and is therefore seen only in human older children and adults. Among humans, fearful shyness can appear during the first year of life, but self-conscious shyness must await the development of a cognitive self and therefore occurs during the fifth year, though some precocious children may display it earlier.

Fearful shyness may be elicited by social novelty, physical intrusion, or social evaluation. If the novelty consists of a new group of people, it may induce a feeling of conspicuousness and therefore self-conscious shyness. And social evaluation may occur in a manner that makes the recipient feel scrutinized. Thus both novelty and social evaluation, although direct causes of fearful shyness, may also be the indirect causes of self-conscious shyness.

The immediate causes of self-conscious shyness appear to be the out-

TABLE 7.1
Fearful versus Self-Conscious Shyness

	Fearful	*Self-Conscious*
Affective reaction	Fear (worry)	Public self-awareness, embarrassment
Autonomic reactivity	Sympathetic	Parasympathetic (if any)
Present in	Animals, humans	Older human children, adults
Necessary self	Sensory	Cognitive
First appearance	First year	Fifth year
Causes of the transient reaction	Novelty Physical intrusion Social evaluation[a]	Being observed Psychological intrusion Being different (feeling conspicuous) Breach of privacy Formality
Dispositional causes of the trait	Fearfulness Sociability (low)	Public self-consciousness Social skills (lacking) Self-esteem (low)

[a]See section on Dating and Interviewing.

come of socialization training in which children are taught to become aware of themselves as social objects. After such training, self-conscious shyness can be induced by the close observation of others, being conspicuously different from others, and formal situations. Breaches of privacy, especially those involving modesty, are likely to cause embarrassment. There is also a self-induced cause of embarrassment: when a person makes a silly social mistake (i.e., refers to a man's wife as his daughter) or is clumsy (i.e., knocking coffee into someone's lap).

Shyness is also a personality trait, referring to people who tend to be especially uncomfortable with strangers and may even feel awkward with friends. Presumably, this disposition could be separated into two different components, although so far this has not been accomplished. If it were, fearful shyness would be linked with the temperaments of fearfulness (almost by definition) and low sociability. This linkage would seem to be causal, for the temperaments are heritable. Self-conscious shyness would be linked with public self-consciousness, by definition, and with the trait of self-esteem.

Shy people thus represent a mixture of fearful and self-conscious shyness. Fear is a more powerful emotion than embarrassment (the extreme of public self-consciousness). The sympathetic activity of the autonomic nervous system that occurs in fear tends to prime the person for emergency action, whereas the parasympathetic activity that occurs in embarrassment represents only a slight arousal. It follows that fearful shyness is more intense and leads to greater social avoidance than self-conscious shyness. Thus, in social phobics it is fear that predominates, and the treatment of choice would seem to be the same as in nonsocial fears: systematic desensitization, which replaces the arousal reaction with tranquility. Those who are self-consciously shy, in this framework, are not sufficiently autonomically reactive to become social phobics. There is less need for therapy, and it would suffice to train them either to habituate to receiving attention or to develop ways of shifting attention from themselves.

A lack of social skills is also a dispositional determinant of self-conscious shyness. Anyone with insufficient knowledge about social situations and few social responses is likely to feel awkward and uncomfortable when with others. There are adults who are unsure of how to ask another person to come to the house for a visit, how to respond to praise, how to ask for a date, or how to turn down a date. Lacking social skills, such people tend to be self-consciously shy.

Dating and Interviewing

A first date with a member of the opposite sex may produce a special kind of shyness, variously called *heterosocial anxiety, heterosexual dating anxiety,* and *dating anxiety*. Each member of the pair desires to be liked and perhaps even admired by the other, and therefore each attempts to look attractive and to behave in a way that will interest the other and elicit approval. This situation forces each member to be aware of the implicit evaluation being made by the other. The focus of the evaluation is those aspects of the self that are open to observation: appearance, manners, speech, gestures, and social behavior generally. This acknowledged but implicit focus, inevitably makes each member keenly aware of the self as a social object. As a result, any shyness that occurs is tilted toward the self-conscious type of social anxiety.

These remarks would seem to contradict those made earlier and summarized in Table 7.1, in which social evaluation is listed as an immediate cause of fearful shyness. The difference lies in the nature of the evaluation. If it is the public self that is under examination and the outcome will be an acceptance or rejection of oneself, the social anxiety will be self-conscious shyness. If it is aspects of one's nonsocial self—talents, skills, background knowledge, or experience—that are being evaluated, the anxiety tends to be a fear of failing: not self-conscious shyness but fearful shyness.

The best example of such evaluations occuring in a social context is a job interview. The interviewer may have some interest in the other's social self, but the major focus will be on the applicant's job qualifications. If the interviewee is rejected for the position, it is likely to be because of a lack of qualifications for the position. Although personal aspects may play a role in such a decision, the applicant knows that the evaluation is not of the self as a whole but only of those aspects relevant to the job. Therefore, for most people, any negative affect that occurs during the interview is likely to be a fear of failing. The evaluation occurs in a social setting, hence it is a social anxiety—in this instance, fearful shyness. If the evaluation were in a nonsocial setting—taking a civil service examination, for example—any negative affect would properly be labelled *evaluation anxiety*.

Thus, in social contexts when the evaluation focuses on the nonsocial aspects of the person, fearful shyness is likely (as in a job interview). When the evaluation focuses on the observable aspects of the self, self-conscious shyness is likely (as in dating). These comments require an amendment to Table 7.1: Social evaluation can elicit either fearful or conscious shyness. Social evaluation was restricted to the fearful shyness column in the interest of simplicity; outside of dating, most instances of evaluation involve the nonsocial aspects of the person being evaluated.

SPEECH ANXIETY

Speech anxiety is a good example of the mixture between the fear and public self-awareness components of social anxiety. The speaker is the center of attention and under constant observation, hence public self-awareness tends to be intense; and the speaker is engaging in a performance that is explicitly evaluated by the audience, hence the fear component may also be intense. This fear component will be called *performance anxiety*.

The very conspicuousness of the speaker makes it easy to list the observable behavior of those who are speech anxious (Mulac & Sherman, 1974):

1. Verbal fluency—hunting for words, pauses filled by "Ah" and "Um," and stuttering.
2. Voice—quavery, tense, monotonous, excessively fast or slow.
3. Facial expressions—little eye contact, blinking, grimaces, and twitches.
4. Arms and hands—rigid, tense, motionless, or fidgety.
5. Body—swaying, rocking, pacing, and shuffling of feet.

Anyone who displayed such behaviors would receive a failing mark for the performance but might still be liked as a person because of attractiveness, grooming, politeness, and perhaps warmth. Although it is difficult to be appealing to an audience if one has stage fright, it does happen. In the mirror image outcome, a speaker can be seen as an excellent performer—at ease, interesting, and offering a well-paced, informative talk—but also as being unattractive, poorly groomed, impolite, and perhaps even cold. The audience may like both the performance and the person or may like neither. The most interesting outcomes in the present context are the first two—liking the performance but not the person, or the opposite—for they demonstrate the value of separating these two components and by implication, separating speech anxiety into acute public self-awareness and performance anxiety.

Immediate Causes

The determinants of transient speech anxiety may be placed in a time framework that starts with the interval preceding the performance. Just before the speech, dread and apprehension are greatest, as speakers anticipate possible failure and worry that they will perform poorly. There is no scrutiny by anyone, so there is no reason for public self-awareness, but performance anxiety is high.

The second time interval consists of the first several minutes of the talk, just after the speaker has been introduced and faces the audience. These are the moments of closest observation by the audience and greatest awareness of this attention by the speaker, the result being a peak of the feeling of conspicuousness. Accompanying this public self-awareness is intense performance anxiety, which is caused by novelty. Such novelty may take several forms: the role of speaker, the unfamiliarity of the audience, the lack of experience with a microphone when one is used, and the strangeness of the setting. The less familiar the setting, the greater the performance anxiety, especially for novice speakers who have so little experience that almost any environment is novel, especially the perspective of seeing the audience from the front of the room. Even experienced speakers may have a moment of panic when starting to speak in a strange room, in a new town, or in the context of novel audiovisual equipment. Some teachers with many years of experience and therefore having minimal speech anxiety may have a moment or two of panic when speaking in a new room, and some teachers have performance anxiety only on the first day of each new school year.

The last time interval consists of the remainder of the talk. For most people, it is easy to habituate to the novel setting, role, and audience; therefore fear tends to wane. As the speaker starts concentrating on the topic at hand and sampling the audience's reactions, attention is drawn away from the self, and public self-awareness wanes. The speaker is increasingly freed of the constraints of performance anxiety and acute self-focus, and increasing attention to the performance improves it and puts the speaker more at ease. Of course, if the speaker makes a mistake or the audience reacts negatively by not paying attention or talking, speech anxiety quickly returns.

This temporal framework may help to understand the mechanisms by which speech anxiety diminishes over months and years. The first diminution in anxiety occurs for the time segment that starts a few minutes after its beginning, the last segment in this time framework. There are teachers, for instance, who are scared before and just at the beginning of a lecture but are calm once it gets under way. This drop in distress occurs presumably because during this time period there is the least experience of strangeness (from novelty) or conspicuousness.

Now consider the first few minutes of the talk, when conspicuousness and novelty are at a peak. Over months and years, these feelings habituate, aided by tricks of the trade acquired by experienced teachers or speakers. Thus at the beginning of a lecture, the teacher might direct the attention of the audience to a slide, to the blackboard, or to a member of the audience, thereby avoiding feeling conspicuous. And with the passage of time, novelty of role, setting, and audience all dissipate thereby removing any immediate reason for performance anxiety.

The last component of speech anxiety to vanish is the worry component that occurs prior to the speech, especially the few minutes preceding it. Long after people have habituated to stage fright while in front of an audience, they may still be apprehensive before starting to perform. What they lack is the confidence that comes with repeated successes at the endeavor. Those who feel unprepared or who have not been especially successful are likely to have strong performance anxiety, perhaps with good reason.

It has been said by teachers and especially by stage performers that stage fright prior to going onstage is necessary for a good performance, the implicit assumption being that such fear somehow provides the motivation for doing a better job. A related assumption is that the absence of some kind of arousal leads to a performance that lacks energy and vivacity. It cannot be denied that many people are aroused before they go onstage, and this arousal might facilitate their performance, but there is more than one kind of arousal. In this instance, there may be a confusion between speech anxiety and excitement. The fear reaction is marked by worry and discomfort. The excitement reaction, in contrast, involves no discomfort or any other negative experience. Consider watching a suspense movie and being caught up in the adventures of the protagonists; eagerly awaiting a telephone call that announces the winner of a contest; or getting ready to run a race or play a game of poker. These events illustrate the excitement of suspense while being a spectator or while preparing for a contest the outcome of which is in doubt. We participate in such events (or act as an audience) because of the pleasurable arousal generated by the indeterminacy of the outcome, especially when the outcome cannot be too negative in its impact. We are gripped by excitement as the event is about to unfold.

Just before speakers are about to face the audience to give, say a colloquium, they are aroused. If they are not speech anxious and have had prior successes, the arousal may be neutral or even pleasant. The excitement they feel is similar to that experienced by runners just before a race, and many race horses behave as though they were excited by the anticipation of racing. Thus there may be no anxiety at all, just the rush of arousal that occurs immediately before an impending event.

This distinction between excitement and anxiety bears on the common-sense notion that stage fright is a necessary condition for a good performance. This notion appears to be incorrect, for stage fright tends to inhibit and disorganize a performance. It causes speakers to become stiff, forget the speech, stammer, shake, and perhaps even freeze into immobility. Excitement, which is neutral or positive in affect, can make a speaker more lively, spontaneous, and perhaps even larger than life. Thus to get "up" for a performance, the condition should be excitement, not speech anxiety. When people suggest that stage fright is necessary for a good performance, they are confusing two different kinds of arousal. Excitement may be helpful, but anxiety can only be detrimental.

Personality Traits

There are several published questionnaires that assess speech anxiety, but they tend to include other kinds of items, for example, items concerning extraversion or shyness. There is a 6-item scale that refers solely to speech anxiety (Slivken & Buss, 1984):

1. I always avoid speaking in public if possible.
2. Although I do OK with friends, I am at a loss for words in front of an audience.
3. I feel extremely self-conscious while I am speaking in front of a group.
4. I feel very relaxed just before I speak in front of a group. (reversed)
5. I tend to make mistakes and do poorly when speaking before a group.
6. I am afraid to express myself in a group.

Notice that the various aspects of speech anxiety are sampled in this questionnaire: avoidance, prior anxiety, self-consciousness, tension, and disorganization while speaking. Despite this diversity, the items cluster together (alpha = .82).

Several personality traits are likely to lead to speech anxiety. Just before or during the speech, there is often anxiety, and therefore the trait of fearfulness is a likely dispositional determinant. During the performance, there is often considerable public self-awareness, and therefore a person high in public self-consciousness should be predisposed toward speech anxiety. A major dispositional determinant is the trait of shyness. It seems likely that anyone who is shy would tend to have speech anxiety, but not everyone who is high in speech anxiety is likely to be shy. There are many unshy people who fear public speaking, perhaps because they have had little experience, have had bad experiences, or simply lack the requisite skills. Those who are shy, but who are relaxed public speakers are rare. They tend to be a minority of actors, teachers, politicians—all vocations that require public speaking—who manage to overcome their speech anxiety because it is crucial to do so, but who remain shy in their everyday social interactions.

SHYNESS VERSUS SPEECH ANXIETY

Shyness and speech anxiety are similar in several respects. Fear and public self-awareness occur in both, and in both there is discomfort and a tendency to escape from or avoid the social contexts in which this discomfort occurs, hence the reason for calling the two reactions *social anxiety*. The two reactions are also different in several ways, and this section focuses on the contrasts.

Shyness occurs in personal interactions involving just a few people, often only two. Any of the interactants may become conspicuous for the reasons discussed earlier, but this usually does not occur. Furthermore, the conversation proceeds back and forth, as each person takes turns at being the speaker and then the audience. Speech anxiety occurs in more formal and more public contexts in which typically there are many people who comprise the audience. They focus on the speaker who is extremely conspicuous and who does virtually all the talking.

Social interaction occurs much of the time in everyday life, so novelty is less of an issue for shyness, although people are exposed to novel contexts and to strangers. Evaluation tends to be moderate in social interaction, and it is rarely explicit; when it occurs, the focus in social interaction is likely to be on the person rather than on the performance. For most people, the occasions that demand public speaking are rare and therefore novel. Evaluation is everpresent and almost always explicit, and the focus of the evaluation tends to be on the performance component. As a result, the speaker tends to be afraid of giving a poor performance and therefore failing, whereas the social interactant tends to be self-consciously concerned about rejection of the public aspects of the self.

These various contrasts are summarized in Table 7.2. The bottom line of the table warrants further discussion. Let us narrow the focus to only the fear aspects of shyness and speech anxiety. Given this focus, the fear in shyness is of being unable to hold up one's end of the conversation or of appearing stupid or unattractive to the other person, whereas the fear in speech anxiety centers mainly on the failure to give an organized, flowing, and interesting speech. In both kinds of social anxiety the fear is related to an evaluation process, whether explicit or implicit, and therefore, speech anxiety and shyness may be grouped under the heading of evaluation anxiety that occurs in a social context. Not all evaluation takes place in a social situation, however. Test anxiety occurs when individuals take tests in isolation, though they may be in the same room. Test anxiety and social evaluation anxiety may be grouped under the heading of *evaluation anxiety*. There are also fears that are unrelated to evaluation—fear of high places, airplanes, or hospitals, for example. These phobias may be grouped with evaluation anxiety under the most general heading of all: *fear*. In brief,

TABLE 7.2
Shyness versus Speech Anxiety

	Shyness	*Speech Anxiety*
Conspicuous	Sometimes	Always
Public self-awareness	Moderate to intense	Intense
Novelty	Moderate	Intense
Evaluation	Implicit	Explicit
Performance component	Little	Much
Fear	Usually mild	More intense
Content of fear	Of rejection	Of failure

when only the fear aspects of shyness and speech anxiety are considered, they are specific reactions (or personality traits) that belong to the broader category of social anxiety, and the progression continues to the superordinate categories of first evaluation anxiety and then fear.

ATTENTION FROM OTHERS

Attention from others may be regarded as a dimension that starts with being ignored, progresses to the rewarding middle, and ends with excessive attention (see chapter 2). Socially anxious people require little attention, and as observation from others increases, it soon becomes aversive. Those who are not socially anxious require a moderate amount of attention, become upset when ignored, and may become uncomfortable under intense scrutiny. And there are those who become extremely upset when ignored and seem never to get enough attention. These three types of people represent particular points on a dimension of reactions to social attention.

Reactions to Social Attention

At the low end are those who tend to avoid attention from others: the socially anxious people who have been the focus of this chapter. There are also people who have a strong need for privacy and therefore avoid the spotlight; the majority are likely to be shy, but a minority may be unshy but prize their privacy.

Moving up the dimension, we find people who neither avoid attention nor seek it. Presumably, they are low in sociability and therefore have no strong need for this particular stimulation reward. At the same time, they do not find attention aversive and respond appropriately when they are in the spotlight.

Further along the dimension are those who do not seek attention but nevertheless receive it. Those who are sociable and unshy (extraverts) tend to initiate conversations, do much of the talking, sometimes interrupt others, and in general express their thoughts and feelings. Such social assertiveness tends to make them the focus of attention, but presumably they act this way not to receive attention but merely to express themselves. The attention is a byproduct of social assertiveness. Similarly, charismatic people may do little deliberately to achieve or capture other's attention, but somehow people cannot help but be drawn to this minority of people who act as social magnets.

Next are those who seek attention but only as a means to another end. To do their job, teachers need to ensure that students are watching and listening. To sell, a salesperson must get the customer to listen. Television announcers who are advertising products must get potential customers to watch them. Politicians who are running for office must be noticed so that voters can see what they look like and perhaps even learn about their platform. Anyone who attempts to be a leader must capture the attention of followers. Vocations that are highly public inevitably involve audiences. Professional athletes make a living by performing in front of large audiences; so do musicians, actors, and clowns. Thus in particular vocational roles, attention is required because information must be communicated or because the vocation involves performance. It is possible, of course, that the vocational role might spill over into everyday personal interactions. Thus the actor who is accustomed to occupying center stage may need to be in the spotlight even when offstage and just talking with friends. Some teachers tend to lecture to others long after they have left the classroom. Politicians, especially, may have difficulty in separating the vocation from the person, so strong is the habit of seeking out the public's eye.

Further along the dimension are a set of borderline cases, all involving physical attractiveness. There are women who take off their clothes or engage in "exotic dances" to entertain men. These strippers earn their living this way, but their performance appears to go beyond the instrumental use of attention, for the audience is made aware of what are ordinarily private aspects of persons. Similarly, models of both sexes earn money by posing for advertisements, but they are selected for this vocation because of their physical attractiveness. The point is that they start out with natural beauty, which is sufficient to capture others' attention, and then use these physical attributes to earn money. There is of course nothing wrong with earning money in this way, but it would appear to go slightly beyond using attention instrumentally. The case may be stronger for women to enter amateur beauty contests, which afford an opportunity to display their faces and bodies. It is true that some of these women hope eventually to go on to a career in modeling or acting, but the majority appear to be parading their obvious physical assets for others to admire. The same motivation may hold for bodybuilders, who are not only at least moderately narcissistic but who also wish to display their bodies to others. The common theme running through all these examples is the presentation of physical attributes that are valued in our society. These attributes are used to seize the attention of others and must therefore be regarded as exhibitionistic. However, the vocations and the amateur contests are all socially approved ways of displaying physical attributes, for such beauty is universally admired. This class of people represents a more or less socially approved exhibitionism, hence their designation as borderline cases.

The unequivocal instances of exhibitionism are marked by socially inappropriate and immature behavior. Young children may become jealous when a sibling—the baby of the family, for example—is receiving the attention that they once had. To regain parental attention they may throw a temper tantrum, curse, engage in mischievous behavior, and generally regress to early modes of behavior. We are not surprised to observe such behavior in children, who are still being taught to share attention and yield the floor to others. We are surprised when we see such behavior in adults. There are stage performers who upstage their fellow actors, mugging when the other actors are speaking. On interview shows, they interrupt when another celebrity is being interviewed. In everyday social interaction, exhibitionists pout when they are ignored and may go to great lengths to capture the attention of others. They may wear outlandish clothes, cut or dye their hair so that it cannot escape notice, or deliberately appear overdressed or underdressed. At a televised football game, an exhibitionist may dash across the field so as to be seen by everyone, not caring that the game is disrupted. Some years back, there was a fad of "flashing," that is, suddenly appearing onstage naked at a formal occasion such as the Academy Awards. Later, young men tried "streaking" across the campus in the nude. Some of these acts occur partly because they require daring, but long after the fad has disappeared, exhibitionists may be tempted to try such behavior; in their attempts to be in the spotlight, anything goes. The current group of punkers may represent an amalgamation of rebellion and exhibitionism. The rebellion is demonstrated by the refusal to wear "normal" clothes or hair styles. The exhibitionism is revealed by hair colors, hair styles, and clothes so striking that they must attract notice.

In brief, people may be aligned along a dimension that varies in the extent to which they seek attention. Such attention in its social extreme, in the form of fame, is almost universally sought, and a minimum of attention from others is necessary for social interaction. Nevertheless, people differ considerably in their motivation to achieve this social reward and in whether it is intrinsic or instrumental. At one extreme of the dimension are the socially anxious, who avoid attention because it brings discomfort. At the other extreme are the exhibitionists who seem to be insatiable in their need for attention and prize it as an end in itself.

We can only speculate about the origins of exhibitionism. Some children may be deprived of attention and therefore may continually seek it. Attention from parents and later from siblings and friends may be so scarce that an excessive need is built up and carried forward to adulthood. Other children may receive so much attention that a strong expectation (or habit) is established. The reward may become so potent that they will try any means, including inappropriate and immature behavior, to achieve the reward. Some children may learn to associate attention from others with self-esteem, so that their feelings of self-worth depend to some extent on being the center of attention. As adults, maintenance of their self-esteem may require excessive attention-getting.

A final issue concerns what happens to performance when people are the focus of hundreds or thousands of people, the best example being sports events. Some athletes freeze in front of a large audience, especially when the contest is close and the outcome is on the line. It is a reasonable guess that such athletes have stage fright. Others seem to rise to the occasion, producing their best effort when thousands are watching and the next few minutes will settle the outcome. For them the stress of the occasion acts as an intensifier of motivation, bringing forth their optimal performance. Of course, there are some people who find being in the spotlight not stressful but rewarding, and among those who meet the challenge of playing well before crowds are those we label *exhibitionists.*

NOTES

Social anxiety belongs not only to the discipline of psychology but also to communication. Specialists in the latter field started out with an obvious interest in speech anxiety and then broadened their purview to include the discomfort that occurs in a variety of social contexts. Their views are summarized by Daly and McCroskey (1984) and by Richmond (1983). Speech anxiety occurs only in the limited context of performing before an audience, whereas shyness can occur in many social situations, which may be why psychologists have focused more on shyness. A variety of approaches, measures, and findings are summarized by Jones, Cheek, and Briggs (1985).

The self-presentation approach has been used by Schlenker and Leary (1982) to account for social anxiety, which they define as "anxiety resulting from the prospect or presence of personal evaluation in real or imagined social situations" (p. 642). The basic assumption in the self-presentation approach is that all people are motivated to make a good impression. Socially anxious people try to manage specific impressions in particular situations but believe that they will fail and obtain negative reactions from others. The emphasis is on cognitions, the assumption being that individuals continually examine their behavior in relation to prior expectations. When the behavior falls below expectations, the resultant negative affect motivates attempts to escape. If they cannot escape, they become mired in self-preoccupation, as they obsess about their social failure. This approach, which has also been applied specifically to shyness (Leary & Schlenker, 1981), does not differentiate between speech anxiety and shyness, for the same cognitive mechanisms are assumed to occur in any kind of social anxiety. These mechanisms consist of cognitions about the self in social interaction, and self-attention is held to be crucial. In this framework there is apparently no room for a fear component in social anxiety.

An emphasis on cognitions leads naturally to examining the attributions of socially anxious people. Teglasi and Hoffman (1982) had shy and unshy subjects complete an attribution questionnaire, which also inquired about affective reactions to the social situations. The shy subjects reported that positive outcomes were less likely and negative outcomes more likely for them, they expressed less positive affect when the outcome was positive, and their attributions were generally self-defeating.

Brodt and Zimbardo (1981) reported that having shy subjects misattribute their arousal to noise was successful in causing them to lose their shyness. Analysis of their findings revealed, however, that their data did not sustain their conclusions (Slivken & Buss, 1984). Furthermore, the latter authors found that misattribution has no impact on speech anxiety, but the trait of speech anxiety significantly determined behavior in the laboratory. This result is consistent with the failure of misattribution to alter the behavior of speech anxious subjects in an earlier study (Singerman, Borkovec, & Baron, 1976). In discussing the use of misattribution as a therapy, Teglasi and Hoffman (1982) suggested that there is little basis for assuming that attributions are the cause of the social anxiety rather than the consequence of it: "When attribution is the symptom, rather than the cause of the problem, focusing on attribution as the key to intervention may be counterproductive. Thus, directly changing attributions in interpersonal situations where there is ample evidence to justify the attribution may not be justified" (p. 384). By implication, if the discomfort can be reduced or the social behavior changed, attributions will also change, for they rest on the valid perceptions of socially anxious people. This issue here may involve the potency of personality traits. Misattribution has been found to be effective for unselected subjects, but it cannot override the influence of strong personality traits on behavior.

One way to study shyness is to observe shy people during the process of becoming acquainted with strangers. Pilkonis (1977) used accomplices to meet with shy subjects, who were observed to be less willing to speak or to break the silence. Cheek and Buss (1981) studied dyads composed of real subjects and found that shy subjects talked less and averted gaze more than unshy subjects. Thus, the trait of shyness is not merely a convenient label that can be altered by a cognitive manipulation but a strong personality disposition.

An older shyness questionnaire (Watson & Friend, 1969) contains 14 true and 14 false items. Though its shyness items appear to be on target—typical example, "Being introduced to people makes me tense and nervous"—it also contains sociability items such as these: "I try to avoid situations which force me to be sociable" and "If the chance comes to meet new people, I often take it" (reversed). Clearly, we need a measure of shyness unconfounded by sociability, which may be why this questionnaire is little used in current research.

The literature on dating anxiety, too extensive to review here, is dominated by attempts at therapeutic intervention, largely by means of behavior modification. In this therapeutic context, anxiety about interacting with a member of the opposite sex is treated like any other fear, and an attempt is made to desensitize the fear by linking a relaxation response to the anxiety-provoking situation. This variety of social anxiety, like the more general reaction of shyness, peaks in adolescence, but it occurs in older adults. The trait may so strongly inhibit behavior that in severe cases, people are unable to act on their strong motivation to meet members of the opposite sex and become frustrated and depressed. It would be of interest to determine whether such extreme behavior is caused by public self-consciousness or fear.

8 Style

Style is roughly equivalent to the manner in which responses are delivered rather than to the content of responses: the how, not the what of behavior. Thus, one kind of greeting behavior is the handshake (content), which may be delivered with a firm, strong clasp or with a hand as limp as a dead fish (style). In this example, style can be easily distinguished from content, but for some interpersonal behaviors the distinction can become blurred, an issue discussed later. This example also represents the exposition in that it offers extremes, which provide the clearest and most dramatic illustrations of the stylistic dimension.

Not all style occurs in the context of social behavior, and the focus here is on interpersonal style. Some borderline examples are included: one may walk alone, with someone, or toward someone. Thus, walking is sometimes interpersonal and sometimes impersonal, and in this and other instances, the exposition of interpersonal style may occasionally spill over into impersonal style.

ELEMENTS OF MOVEMENT

Style may be analyzed at several levels, the most basic being the physical elements of movement. Behavioral movement may be aligned on an anatomical dimension of large to small: whole body movements, gestures made with the arms or hands, head movements, facial expressions, and voice or speech. This sequence is followed throughout, although any of the segments are omitted when they are irrelevant.

Displacement

One basic element of style is displacement, the amount of space taken by the movement. The most frequent whole body movement is walking, which varies considerably in length of stride. Taller people obviously take larger steps than shorter people, but even among those of the same height, length of stride varies. Some people take long steps, which causes the body to bob up and down and sometimes gives the impression of a vigor that has been stereotyped as masculine. Others take such short steps that their walk appears mincing and may therefore fulfill a feminine stereotype. Some people walk with their arms swinging forward to traverse a relatively large distance, whereas others hardly move their arms at all.

Vertical displacement also occurs when walkers lift their heels early in the stride, causing them to rise up on the balls of the feet and offering the impression of youthful exuberance or awkwardness. At the opposite extreme, there is no vertical displacement, the feet never leaving the ground; this shuffling walk marks fatigue or the worn out style of old age.

There are two kinds of lateral displacement. One is the side-to-side rocking of the body, especially noticeable in the swaying of the shoulders, a rolling gait helpful in navigating over unsteady surfaces and therefore associated with sailors. The other is a twisting walk in which the pelvis rotates. Seen mainly in women, such hip movements are considered sexually attractive or provocative by many men. Even those with narrower hips, however, can manage to swing them, and this kind of displacement should not be attributed solely to anatomy.

Although most gestures are made with the arms and hands, a few involve only the shoulders. When people shrug, either unilaterally or bilaterally, they vary in the amplitude of the movement. Some raise the shoulders imperceptibly, but others have a large displacement in what is an elaborate or dramatic shrug.

An important measure of gestural displacement is the distance of the elbows from the body. In pointing, for example, the arm may be fully extended, or the elbow may be kept close to the body in an economical gesture. It is an anatomical truism that the more the arms are extended, the larger is the displacement of the gesture. Thus, one can wave with the hand kept close to the body or with the arm extended and moving up and down. There are variations in the space traversed when people make rotating or sweeping gestures. Handshakes can also involve a large or small vertical displacement: some people give a minimal tug and others pump the hand up and down.

Movements of the head are seen mainly in nods and shakes. Some people barely move their heads when nodding assent, whereas others move their heads some distance forward. Similarly, the rotation in the headshake may be large or small. Displacement of the head is a minor stylistic issue, and these observations are included only for completeness.

The displacements that occur in facial expressions are small but important. The eyebrows often rise, usually as an expression of surprise, interest, or recognition of an acquaintance, and like the other expressions being discussed, there are marked individual differences. Some people barely raise the eyebrows, whereas others lift them almost as if trying to reach the hairline. Similarly, when the eyes widen in surprise or in fear, they may open just a little or so much that there is a large area of white showing. Although less noticed, the nostrils occasionally dilate, usually in a strong expression of emotion, and there are individual variations in the extent of dilation. When the mouth opens, it is part of the expressions of surprise, laughing, or smiling. When people are surprised or merry, the mouth may open just a little or so wide that the gums are exposed. When people laugh, the mouth may be closed, the corners spread just a little, or spread in a wide smile.

We are bilaterally symmetrical organisms, who usually respond approximately symmetrically much of the time, the most common exception being when the hands are used. Aside from gestures, however, there may be asymmetry of displacement of the body, head, and face. During walking, the body may tilt to one side instead of being erect. One shoulder may be carried higher than the other, and when shrugging occurs, it may be asymmetrical. The head may be cocked to one side, which may give the person a quizzical expression. When the eyebrows are raised, one tends to be higher than the other, and the expression is altered when only one eyebrow is raised. And the smile may be wider on one side of the face than on the other, presenting what has been called a "crooked smile."

There are also tilts that deviate in the degree of lean away from the vertical. When walking, a person's body may lean forward, giving the impression of determination or a business-like attitude, or it may lean backward, which causes the arms to swing more. These asymmetries, like all the stylistic behavior being discussed, are assumed to be reliable and consistent features of each person's nonverbal behavior. As such they comprise interesting individual differences and may be linked to personality traits defined by content.

Vigor

Vigorous responses are those involving a greater expenditure of energy. Thus in walking, the push off the ground may be strong, leading quickly to the next stride, or it can be weak, producing what is observed as a feeble walk. When the foot strikes the ground, it may do so as softly as a ballerina landing after a jump or as firmly as a small person trying to make the floor shake. Some people tread lightly, and others pound the floor and therefore never surprise anyone at their arrival.

When an object is picked up, it can be lifted gently or hauled up quickly. A door can be pushed softly or thrust open violently, and an elevator button can be touched or punched. When a fist is made, the fingers can cling together loosely or can be clenched. When making an emphatic point, the person can pound the fist forcefully on the table or hit it lightly. And as mentioned earlier, hands can be shaken firmly or limply.

When gesturing is accomplished with the head, it takes the form of either nods or shakes. The nod may be made quickly to suggest a firm and definite affirmative or it may be made slowly to suggest vague acquiescence or ambivalence. The shake can be made quickly to indicate a definite No or slowly to suggest the kind of negation that is expressed verbally as "We just don't do that kind of thing here."

Variations in vocal vigor are especially noticeable. Some people speak so softly that listeners may have to strain just to understand, whereas other speakers may boom so loudly that listeners have to back away. There may be another aspect of vigor that is difficult to specify precisely. Some people possess a voice so penetrating that even when we equate it for loudness, it seems to be heard at some distance, whereas others possess a voice that seems not to carry even when its loudness is sufficient. Thus the psychological dimension of intensity, as it applies to the voice, may be based not only on loudness but also on penetration.

Vigor is also an important aspect of the voice when it is raised in emotion. The point to remember whenever style involves an emotional response is that variations in the intensity of the emotion are not considered because they involve content, not style. Thus, when individual differences in stylistic aspects of emotions are being discussed, it is implicitly assumed that intensity of emotion has been equated across individuals. When people are happy, their laughs may vary from petite giggles to booming explosions. When people are sad, their crying may vary from muffled sobs to penetrating wails. And in anger, voices may vary from mild whimpers to furious roars (again, assuming an equal intensity of rage).

Tempo

Tempo refers to both the rate of making repeated responses and how quickly individual responses are made; the longer the duration of a response, the slower is its tempo. Some people walk briskly, whereas others just stroll down the street. Some people dash up stairs and gallop down, whereas others climb at a slow pace and descend in stately fashion. Whole body movements also vary in tempo in such activities as sitting and rising, entering or leaving a car or elevator, and moving objects from one room to another.

Gestures can be made quickly or held for a while. In a handshake, the hand can be grasped and released or held for a number of seconds. When the hand is waved at another person, it can move fast or slow, and when the hand is used to urge another person to come closer, the gesture can be swift or leisurely.

The major head movement involving tempo is turning to look at or listen to another person, which can be accomplished quickly or slowly. Eyeblinks can occur as quickly as the metaphor implies or so slowly as to imply drowsiness. The eyes can move quickly from one person to another, but they may also linger or even stare. A smile can end quickly, remain fixed, or gradually fade.

In interpersonal terms, speech is undoubtedly the domain in which tempo is most noticed. The rate of speech may be so fast that syllables are omitted and the listener has trouble deciphering it. It may be drawled so slowly that each syllable is stretched out, and the listener wonders if the sentence will ever end. Speech may be delivered in staccato bursts, with hardly a moment of pausing for breath, or it may be spoken at a deliberate pace, with time out for lingering sighs. Speech tempo is well known to vary with the regions of the country, but even within a region there are marked individual differences; some New Yorkers speak slowly, and some Texans speak quickly.

Suddenness

Suddenness refers to the latency of responses, the time between the stimulus to action and the onset of action. Thus, when the elevator arrives, some people enter immediately and others linger in the hall before entering. When told that the doctor is available, some people rise at once from the waiting room chair and others take their time about getting up. When asked for directions, one can point immediately or can delay in doing so. When a friend waves, the return wave can be immediate and responsive or delayed and offhand.

Affective responses also vary in suddenness. When greeting a friend or finding something amusing, some people are quick to smile and others smile so gradually that it may appear unspontaneous. In initiating a conversation, a person can start immediately, perhaps even before the listener is ready or can delay so long that the listener becomes impatient. Some speakers are so eager to start that they tend to interrupt the other's speech, but others are so hesitant that they may miss the opportunity to talk when it is available.

Both suddenness and tempo involve time, but their similarity ends there. Tempo refers to both the duration of an individual response and the rate of responding (the number of gestures made during a 10-second period). Suddenness refers to how long it takes the person to initiate the response. It is likely that most people with a fast tempo also tend to respond with a quick duration and rapid rate. That the two dimensions are probably correlated does not deny, however, that it is worthwhile to keep the concepts separate and to measure them independently. Indeed, two kinds of people might be of special interest: those with a fast tempo who are slow to initiate a response and those with a slow tempo who initiate a response quickly.

Although suddenness and tempo both involve time, the other two physical dimensions of style concern vigor, either directly or in the form of displacement. Examples of the four physical dimensions are presented in Table 8.1. People high in the temperament of activity (Buss & Plomin, 1975) are expected to occupy the high end of all four dimensions.

PSYCHOLOGICAL DIMENSIONS

The elements of movement are easily observed and recorded, as may be seen in the numerous examples of everyday behavior that have already been cited. The psychological dimensions of style include not only elements of movement but also aspects of behavior that cannot be easily aligned along the physical dimensions of space or time. To cite just one example of the latter, gracefulness of gestures cannot easily be recorded along physical dimensions but requires the judgment of observers. The psychological dimensions of style vary in the mix of behaviors that can be objectively recorded and those that require the judgment of observers. The sequence proceeds from a stylistic dimension derived

TABLE 8.1
Physicial Dimensions of Style

Dimension	Example
Displacement	Breadth of gestures
Vigor	Loudness of voice
Tempo	Speed of speech
Suddenness	Quickness of smiling

mainly from elements of movement to dimensions for which these elements are minor.

Animated-Lethargic

This dimension consists of all four elements of movement: displacement, vigor, tempo, and suddenness. Animated people walk briskly, tend to dash for the elevator, and sit and rise quickly. Their handshakes are vigorous, and they wave suddenly and rapidly. When signalling agreement, their heads bob up and down; when signalling disagreement, their heads rotate like a top. Laughing is accompanied by the head being thrown back. Affective expressions appear suddenly and disappear just as fast. The smile tends to be broad and the eyes bright, as the person appears to be beaming. The laugh is explosive, and the voice carries. Animated people speak rapidly, hardly pausing for breath, and the pace may be staccato.

At the other end of the dimension, lethargic people tend to have a dawdling gait, and their progress on stairs is gradual. Their movements tend to be deliberate and sluggish, and they will not rush to catch an elevator. When shaking hands, their grips are often slack, and their hand waves tend to be feeble. Their head nods and shakes are slow and barely perceptible. Their smiles and frowns appear slowly and linger, and their smiles and eyes are not bright. Their laughs tend to be chuckles and their voices, faint. In general, their levels of activity are sufficiently slow to give the impression of drowsiness.

The two ends of the animated-lethargic dimension may appear so extreme as to be caricatures, but these opposite styles may be observed in the population, however rarely. The excesses of style are being emphasized because they are relatively easy to describe, and nail down the dimensions. The majority of the population occupy the moderate segments of these dimensions, and their behavior is neither as consistent nor as obvious.

Sprightly-Ponderous

This dimension overlaps animated-lethargic, but is different in its focus on lightness and heaviness. The walks of animated people are bouncy and on the balls of their feet, as they seem hardly to touch the ground, and among the young it is characterized by skipping or hopping. Their movements are airy and apparently without effort. Their gestures are brief and occupy little space. Head movements tend to be darting, as are glances, and voices tend to be high and speech rates, rapid.

The walk of ponderous people is leaden, as they appear to drag themselves forward. They rise from a chair with apparent effort and subside into a chair with relief. They appear to be weighted down, which makes all their movements appear laborious. Their hand and arm gestures are slow and when completed, the arms seem to fall to the side of the body without any resistance to gravity. Eyes tend to be hooded, giving the appearance of drowsiness. Voices tend to be low pitched and in men, rumbling. Speech is slow and tends to be interspersed with sighs.

The two extremes are undoubtedly associated with body build: cats are sprightly, elephants are ponderous. People with massive bodies, especially the obese, necessarily make labored movements that appear unwieldy. Those who are slight of build tend to tread lightly and move with little effort. There are exceptions, however, and the movement style of some people belies their body build. Moreover, most of the population is at neither extreme of body build, and there are marked variations along the sprightly-ponderous dimension among people of the same body build.

Expressiveness

Expressiveness is a combination of two closely related dimensions: emphatic–mild and dramatic–bland. People who are emphatic or dramatic tend to have movements that may be exaggerated, sometimes to the point of caricature; there is considerable displacement, vigor, tempo, and suddenness. Expressiveness also involves making stylistic responses more frequently and using a greater range of expressions. Those at the low end of this dimension display fewer expressions, have a constricted range of expressions, and their expressions tend to be seen as dull and lifeless. It follows that the dimension can best be described by focusing on those who are at the high end.

Expressiveness tends not to be seen in body movements. The exceptions are the swaggering walk observed in some men and the provocative hipswinging seen in some women. Gestures, however, furnish an appropriate stage for dramatic expressions, which are at the high end of displacement, vigor, tempo, and suddenness. The shrug is elaborate and the wave of greeting, effusive. The expressive person may make a fist, bang on the table to make a point, wave a dismissal, supplicate with the hands or use them to cut off the other person's speech, or shake a finger at someone. The hands may be used as a substitute for speech or they may "conduct" speech, the gestures keeping time and dramatizing the inflections of speech. The hands also may be used to cover the face, a theatrical gesture rarely made by men.

Affirmatives and negatives are signalled with vigorous head movements, though occasionally the movements are made very slowly for greater impact. The face is of course a major arena for expressiveness. The eyebrows of expressive people tend to be raised and lowered more often, and the height of the rise is greater. The brows may be arched, templed, furrowed, or beetled, as the face mirrors or even exaggerates transient feelings. The eyes may open wide to show a large amount of white or may close down to slits. Others are watched with a stare, with the eyes fluttering, or with sidelong glances. Variations in nose movements range from pinched to flared, and there tend to be sniffs and snorts. The mouth produces smiles that vary from a smirk to a dazzling show of teeth, but it may tighten into grimness; the lips may also curl or sneer.

The voice ranges from whispering to shouting and from low-pitched to high-pitched. It may be resonant or muffled, modulated or harsh, strong or quavery, and quiet or shrill. The expressive person is not restricted to a single kind of laugh but fluctuates between the hearty laugh and the giggle, the explosive laugh and the snicker, the loud guffaw and the insipid chuckle.

The speech is inflected, as the voice changes in loudness and pitch during the course of a sentence. Such variations introduce emphasis or drama into the vocal performance. Thus, a word or phrase at the end of the sentence may be uttered loudly or especially softly, or it may be drawn out for effect. There may be meaningful pauses or hurried sentences. There is no implication here that these various styles are deliberate, although they may be if the person engages regularly in pretense; rather, the styles tend to be habitual and are delivered spontaneously. To repeat, expressiveness involves not only a greater range of responses along the dimensions just outlined (vigor, tempo, and so on), but also a tendency to respond at the upper end of these dimensions. Thus, the expressive person may be characterized as dramatic and emphatic, whereas the nonexpressive person may be characterized as bland and mild. These are descriptions of style, however, and they do not imply that the person who is bland stylistically is necessarily unemotional or that the dramatic person is necessarily emotional. The assumption here is that two people who are roughly equal in the intensity of any current feelings may express them differently; it is these expressions that constitute the domain of style.

Precision

When gestures are made, they may be exact or loose. Thus, when a person is asked for directions, he or she may point precisely to a particular place or may indicate with merely a vague wave. Also a precise gesture usually starts abruptly and ends quickly, whereas at the other end of the dimension, the gesture starts slowly and just fades away.

Precision also includes focus, the opposite of the dimension being diffuse. Thus, a listener may attend closely or may appear to be distracted, and gaze may remain fixed on the speaker, in contrast to the gaze's wandering or being averted. Similarly, a speaker may focus directly on the listener or may allow attention to drift. Whatever expressions appear on the face, they can vary along the precision (focus) dimension: from concentrated to vague and from explicit to ambiguous.

Focus and precision also may be seen in speech. The words may be delivered with exact enunciation or they may be slurred; they may be clipped and bitten off or drawled and just fade away. The voice may be clear and penetrating or it may be murky and soft. Concerning the language itself, it may be explicit or ambiguous, concise or verbose, but this is a borderline case that may spill over into content.

The precise and focused style tends to make the person appear intense, for responses are delivered directly and in a concentrated fashion to the other person. The vague and unfocused style tends to make the person seem milder and less intrusive. We usually understand in exact terms the behavior of a precise person, but the behavior of an unfocused person tends to be ambiguous. These comments apply only to style, of course, and it is possible that a person may be vague in the way responses are delivered but precise in the content of the responses, or diffuse in style but concentrated in content. Can style be so divorced from content? The immediate answer would seem to be No, but the issue requires a more extended discussion, which occurs later.

Skill

The most evaluative aspect of style is the skillfulness of movements. It is easiest to describe the bipolar extremes here, and therefore the emphasis again is on dichotomies, although most of us fall in the moderate, middle segments of each dimension.

Walking is an obvious place to start. Some people seem to glide over the ground with the grace of a ballerina, whereas others stumble almost as if drunk. At one end of skill is a gait that is lithe and nimble; at the other end it is shambling and lurching. The walker may move with a light and balanced pace or stagger and flounder with each step. When bending to pick up an object, the person may make a smooth, deft movement or a clumsy, awkward one. The rise from a chair can be facile or labored.

When carrying objects or making the gestures that accompany speech, the movements can be supple and flowing or stiff and jerky. A cigarette can be lit and smoked with elegance or with the ill-at-ease movements of a first-time smoker. Some people shake hands gracefully; others, awkwardly. Perhaps of all the aspects of style, the skillfullness of gestures may be the most consistent, some people being generally dexterous and others, universally clumsy.

Speech, the most interpersonal of all stylistic behavior, is a domain that most easily reveals variations in skill. At one end there is speech that flows and follows a rhythmic pace; at the other extreme is sputtering, choppy speech that is interrupted with excessive pauses or such nonwords as *ah* and *um*. Words can be enunciated or slurred; they can be distinct or blurred. The speech may be a dull monotone, or the words can be inflected to accentuate meanings. Two aspects of skill would appear to be distinct, for a speaker can be eloquent or inarticulate but also can be concise or verbose.

There is another aspect of style that may be seen as separable from skill but is so close that it is included here: tense versus relaxed. The body is carried with a stiffness characteristic of coiled spring or with a relaxed suppleness. The shoulders may be hunched in a huddled position or held squarely. The muscles of the arms may be contracted, perhaps even in a position of holding oneself, or they may be extended freely so that gestures can be made. The fist can be clenched or the hand relaxed; the hands may be tightly clasped or held apart lightly. The head may be held rigidly at attention or relaxed so that it can move freely. The face may contain an almost perpetually strained expression or remain in repose. The eyes may be screwed up as if straining to see or relaxed and available for expressions. The nose may be pinched, the teeth clenched, and the jaw set, or all three may be relaxed. The voice may be strained and hoarse as the words are pushed out with great effort, or it may be smooth and modulated. Thus, there are many movements and expressions that vary along the tense-relaxed dimension, and these are related to skill, for it is difficult to be graceful and dexterous when one is tense and strained. Skilled actions require that a person be relaxed, although a relaxed attitude is certainly no guarantee of skill.

Formality

This dimension, the bipolar formal–informal, contains elements of dimensions already described, particularly dramatic–bland and precision. Formality also involves behavior that may be described along the dimensions of serious–playful, controlled–spontaneous, and disciplined–casual.

At the formal extreme, the body is usually held erect in something like military bearing, whether standing or seated. Bodily movements are firm, controlled, and careful. The stride is brisk but not hurried, and there is no bouncing or lolling. At the informal end, walking may be hurried, or the person may bounce, skip, hop, spin, or prance. The body may slump, and when seated, the person may throw a leg over the arm of the chair or turn the chair around and sit on it backward. Such movements tend to be spontaneous and make no allowance for the impression they make on any observer.

Formal gestures emphasize precision and suggest an awareness of the social nature of the context. Thus the handshake is crisp, the grip is firm, and there is no pumping of the other person's hand. Self-directed gestures that might be acceptable in isolation are avoided, and there is no nail-cleaning or scratching of oneself. Informal gestures are more playful or dramatic. The handshake may involve pumping up and down, and the arm gestures may be expansive, exuberant, and perhaps even histrionic. The hands may be used to exaggerate, to caricature, or to make playful gestures.

The formal face is serious and dignified in mien. The brows are straight and usually not elevated, the eyes look ahead, and the jaw is firm; silly expressions are avoided. The informal face may contain a series of playful elements. The eyebrows may waggle, the eyes may wink, roll, or deliver sidelong glances. The smile may be broad or even may be a smirk, and a playface may suggest that mischief is afoot.

The formal voice is modulated and certainly not too loud, and speech is grammatically correct, distinct, and perhaps even militarily clipped. The informal voice may be heard to giggle or laugh raucously. Speech may be slurred, ungrammatical, and filled with slang. The delivery may be dramatic, perhaps to the extreme of being histrionic.

Stylistically, the formal–informal dimension spills over into clothes and grooming, and despite these issues not being strictly interpersonal, they are worth brief mention. Formal clothes and grooming are neat, careful, and conventional; formal clothes are likely to be simple, tailored, "correct," and thus never flashy or immodest. The informal style is likely to be on the sloppy side, perhaps even messy. It may go to the extreme of being daring, embellished, showy, or immodest. It bears repeating that this description, like the ones that preceded it, focuses on the extremes of the dimension in an attempt to make it vivid, even at the risk of caricature, which means that in one sense at least, the text is informal.

PERSONALITY TRAITS

The animated–lethargic dimension of style is closely linked to the temperament of activity level, virtually by definition. Recall that animation consists largely of the elements of movement: displacement, vigor, tempo, and suddenness. The first three of these elements also serve to operationalize activity level, which may explain why energetic people are likely to be labelled as *animated.* Suddenness, which is essentially the latency of responding, is only marginally associated with activity level. Rather, it may be linked with the trait of impulsivity, which was part of the original four temperaments that constituted the EASI (Buss & Plomin, 1975). The impulsivity items are:

1. I tend to be impulsive.
2. I find self-control difficult.

3. I get bored easily.
4. I find it difficult to resist temptation.
5. I tend to hop from interest to interest quickly.

The person who answers these items in the affirmative appears to have trouble inhibiting behavior and is therefore likely to respond quickly. At the other extreme of this trait dimension is a person who thinks twice before acting and so is deliberate in responding. The stylistic accompaniment of the trait is therefore likely to be suddenness.

The expressiveness dimension represents the stylistic aspect of extraversion, which is viewed here being a combination of sociability and unshyness. The trait of shyness would seem to be especially important in expressiveness, for the shy person is likely to inhibit expressive behavior, whereas the unshy person is likely to be spontaneous and unconstrained, allowing expressive behavior to occur as it may.

The expressiveness dimension contains two subdimensions, each of which is linked to a different personality trait. The emphatic–mild dichotomy should covary with dominance–submissiveness. Other things equal, dominant people are likely to pound on the table and talk louder, whereas submissive people usually refrain from making strong gestures and they speak softly. There may be an even closer link between dramatic–bland and the trait of exhibitionism, although the relationship may be unidirectional. Exhibitionists tend to make more provocative gestures, use gestures of larger displacement, and inflect their speech in a stagy manner as part of the attempt to capture the attention of others. Not everyone who is stylistically dramatic is necessarily an exhibitionist, however. Some merely may be extraverts who are behaving extremely sociably and unshyly but not in any attempt to seize the attention of others. Thus, the assumed arrow of causality is from exhibitionism to a dramatic style, not the reverse.

There is no personality trait to match the stylistic dimension of skill, but the tense–relaxed dichotomy included as part of skill is surely connected with the temperament of emotionality. The assumption is that any person with an enduring tendency to become distressed easily and intensely is likely to be tense, whereas someone low in this trait is likely to be relaxed in bodily movements, gestures, and speech.

Formality in style is merely a counterpart of the trait of formality, which is defined by content. Thus, the person who abides by the rules of social behavior also tends to be conventional and rigorous in body posture and gestures, and careful in facial expressions and patterns of speech. At the other end of the dimension, informal people are expected to be, if not unconventional, at least relatively unconcerned about being "correct" in gestures, speech, and grooming.

The relationship of styles to personality traits is summarized in Table 8.2. Although most of the styles are bipolar (animated–lethargic), only one extreme of the dimension is listed (animated). In most instances, there is a match between both ends of both the stylistic and the trait dimensions. Thus, impulsive people are expected to act suddenly and deliberate people, slowly. For the dramatic style, however, the match is only for the high end of exhibitionism; those who are low in exhibitionism may be bland or somewhat dramatic, for exhibitionism is not the only cause of being dramatic.

The dimension of intensity, part of precision, seems not to be linked to any personality trait. Perhaps it should be considered as a stylistic trait dimension devoid of any particular content. In social interaction there are marked individual differences in the intensity of the participants. Some people are direct and focused in their social behavior, sometimes to the discomfort of others in the interaction, whereas other people deliver responses or reactions that are unfocused and ambiguous, and therefore they rarely cause discomfort; there is a risk of boredom, however.

Two aspects of skill should also be regarded as personality traits: graceful–clumsy and eloquent–inarticulate. These are not linked to extraversion, for extraverts are not any more graceful or eloquent than anyone else; talkativeness is not the same as eloquence. Instead, the two dichotomous dimensions may be regarded as distinct personality traits in their own right. Clearly, the individual differences along these two dimensions make an impact on the social behavior of participants in social interaction.

The problem with styles as traits, however, is that they are not easily assessed by self-reports and must usually be assessed by observation. It is true that the elements of movement can be recorded along the strictly physical dimensions of space, time, or force, but the psychological dimen-

TABLE 8.2
Dimensions of Style and Associated Personality Traits

Style	Trait
Animated	Activity
Suddenness	Impulsivity
Expressiveness	Extraversion
Emphatic	Dominance
Dramatic	Exhibitionism
Tense	Emotionality
Formal	Formality

sions of style require judgments to be made. Whether observers are present during the behavior or it is videotaped, the behavior must be coded and evaluated. The effort is considerable, which may be one reason why style tends to be neglected by psychologists.

Another reason may be that style is considered a trivial aspect of social behavior and personality. Although this opinion might be true for some people, it is not true for most of the population. The style of our friends and acquaintances has a strong impact on how we interact with them, and the style of strangers is an important determiner of person perception. As a concrete example, it is instructive to compare the styles of Jimmy Carter and Ronald Reagan. Carter appears to be higher in precision, focus, and formality but lower in expressiveness. Reagan is not only more informal but also more dramatic and eloquent than Carter and certainly less stiff. What is true for these presidents tends to be true for the rest of us: The stylistic aspects of interpersonal behavior deserve attention.

One problem with style is that the line between it and content easily becomes blurred. A shy person, for example, tends to feel awkward or anxious, inhibits normally expected social responses, and tends to be tense, sputtering, and perhaps even inarticulate. This content definition of shy behaviors overlaps the stylistic dimensions of expressiveness, tense–relaxed, and skill. As a result, the personality trait of shyness tends to be measured by self-report, but the everyday behaviors we label *shy* are measured by mainly stylistic aspects of behavior.

The overlap is even greater in activity level, a temperament that appears to be almost entirely stylistic. The problem of keeping style distinct from content is not so different from the problem of overlapping social behaviors and personality traits in general. Our analytic distinctions are designed to enable us to understand and explain behavior, and in this effort we usually cannot say whether our analysis is faulty or the behaviors under study are inextricably linked.

What can be said, however, is that style is an important aspect of personality and that personality traits differ with respect to the relationship between content and style. One kind of trait is wholly stylistic, the best example being activity level. One kind of trait represents a considerable overlap between content and style; examples are formality and exhibitionism. And one kind of trait represents little overlap between content and style, a good example of a content trait being sociability. So long as content and style only overlap and do not completely merge, it seems worthwhile to make the distinction. One consequence of distinguishing between the two is that we can inquire about inconsistencies. Thus, a person who is formal in content but not in style might be a more interesting subject than one who is consistently formal in style and content. Finally, the stylistic aspects of interpersonal behavior are especially susceptible to observation and may therefore provide excellent measures of the social behavior that is especially influenced by personality traits.

NOTES

There is a special problem in reviewing the literature on interpersonal style because currently it is rarely studied. It is true that there is research on cognitive styles, but these concern individual differences in cognitive processes, not in interpersonal behavior. There are authors who use the term *style* in their titles—Norton's *Communication Styles* (1983), for example— but they are referring to individual differences in the content of behavior, not in style. For the past several decades there has been a keen interest in nonverbal behavior in the fields of anthropology, psychology, and communication. An excellent review of the communication approach in this area may be found in Knapp (1978). Observations of nonverbal behavior have provided us with a mine of information about the specific movements and responses that comprise the elements of style, but they are inevitably mixed in with the content of behavior. Thus, a typical researcher might want to examine the differences between a shy smile and a sneer (content), whereas in the present context we would want to analyze individual differences in how a shy smile or a sneer is delivered. The problem, then, is that most of the systematic information about style may be found in research not designed specifically to study it, which is the principal reason why style is not usually separated from content.

Although currently neglected, style was once considered to be an important part of personality. In discussing style, Allport (1961) wrote "Originally style meant a pen or inscribing tool (stylus). It came later to mean handwriting, and then the whole flavor of a written, or any other, work in its entirety. Since man is a fusion of all of his works, the French are wont to say, *Le style est l'homme meme*" (pp. 490–491). Much earlier, Allport (Allport & Vernon, 1933) investigated expressive movement. A factor analysis of observations yielded three factors: large, broad movements versus small, narrow movements (area); movements made outward away from the body versus inward toward the body; and sharp, sudden, movements versus slow, sluggish movements.

Allport regarded style as being part of expressive behavior, and for the past several decades researchers have been studying how emotions are expressed. The modern pioneer in this effort is Ekman (1965), who started out observing the patterning of emotional expression in face and body. In collaboration with Friesen (Ekman & Friesen, 1969, 1974), Ekman set in motion modern research on deception, especially in communicating affect. This effort has been taken up by others and is reviewed briefly in chapter 6.

Style is also involved in the nonverbal aspects of behavior. The pioneer here is the anthropologist Ray Birdwhistell (1970), who laid the groundwork for subsequent research on how the face, body, and voice are used in communication. Birdwhistell originated a graphic code for various movements. A sample of some facial expressions are: single raised or lowered brow, wide-eyed, wink, sidewise look, shifty eyes, flaring nostrils, nose wrinkle, talking out of the side of the mouth, droopy mouth, lip biting, dropped jaw, and ear wiggle. This approach has been adopted by psychologists, of whom Argyle (1975) is a leader. Scherer has specialized in vocal communication with the content of speech excluded. On the basis of preliminary factor analyses, he isolated more than 20 characteristics, of which the following are a sample of vocal qualities: resonant, sonorous, breathy, broken, quavery, ringing, sharp, harsh, rough, and dry. This research and a wealth of other material may be found in his and Ekman's comprehensive handbook on nonverbal behavior (Scherer & Ekman, 1982).

Even casual observation of everyday behavior reveals gender differences in style. Systematic study of such differences typically combines style with content under the heading of *nonverbal behavior,* but such work does offer some information about style. A recent review by Hall (1984) found that men have a more expansive body posture (presumably because of the freedom offered by men's clothes) and that women were more expressive with the head, body, and hands and they touched their faces more often. Although this was an exhaustive review of research on nonverbal behavior in the two sexes, there was evidently no systematic research on gender differences in the *manner* in which men and women move and express themselves. Such research is admittedly difficult because of the qualitative coding required, but the need for it is obvious.

As might be expected, stylistic characteristics are used by all of us to make judgments about personality. Such judgments, based largely on stereotypes (high-pitched voice equals feminine, low-pitched voice equals masculine) are involved in person perception (Addington, 1968). What happens when speech rate is speeded up or slowed down and when pitch is raised or lowered? Both sets of manipulations affect perceptions of male speakers (Apple, Streeter, & Krauss, 1979). Elevating the pitch of speech caused speakers to be perceived as less truthful, potent, emphatic, and composed. Slowing down speech caused speakers to be perceived as less truthful, persuasive, fluent, and active.

In brief, style is no longer studied as such but as part of research on emotion, communication, deception, and person perception. Given the focus of investigators in these various fields, it is not surprising that individual differences have tended to be neglected. They do come up in research on person perception but mainly with respect to the cognitive processes of observers, not with respect to the personalities of those being observed.

Although there has been a little research on the personality trait correlates of particular nonverbal behaviors, the results have not been encouraging. Part of the problem may be that traits are not linked to particular nonverbal behaviors but to dimensions of style. Suppose a person talks fast but otherwise moves slowly; there is no reason to believe that a single response (talking) would be linked with a personality trait (say, extraversion) when all other responses involving rate are in the opposite direction. The point is that nonverbal responses need to be aggregated to form the response classes called *personality traits*.

So long as researchers focus on how emotions are expressed, how deception occurs, and how messages are communicated nonverbally, the personality aspects of style will be neglected. Although previous research on nonverbal behavior sets the stage for discovering how style relates to personality, a new approach is needed if the endeavor is to pay off. Stylistic behavior must be treated in a way that is amenable to such an effort by discovering the stylistic dimensions along which people differ. If such an approach were adopted, it would signal the return of style to personality, and we might find out how interpersonal style relates to social behavior.

Appendix:
Personality Scales

ACTIVITY (BUSS & PLOMIN, 1984)

1. I usually seem to be in a hurry.
2. I like to keep busy all the time.
3. My life is fast paced.
4. I often feel as if I'm bursting with energy.

The energy expended by a person may take the form of a rapid tempo, vigorous responses, or an endurance that tends to outlast others. Items assessing this trait load on a factor separate from the other temperaments (emotionality and sociability). *Temperaments* are defined here as personality traits that are inherited and appear early in life. Evidence for the heritability of activity is summarized by Buss and Plomin (1984). The correlations for identical twins vary from the .50s to the .60s, whereas the correlations for fraternal twins tend to be half these figures or even lower. Individual differences in activity have been reported by many researchers on infants, and this trait is an essential aspect of virtually all approaches to temperament.

The trait of activity may be important in infancy. Active infants may wear out their mothers, who may also regard them as hyperactive and difficult to control. Relatively inactive infants may be regarded as unresponsive, but they are easier to manage and usually cause little difficulty for mothers.

Activity is a crucial aspect of interpersonal style. Variations in tempo and vigor underlie the stylistic dimension called *animated-lethargic,* and tempo is part of the sprightly-ponderous dimension. Indeed, activity is best regarded as a stylistic trait and cannot be defined in terms of any particular content.

AGGRESSIVENESS (BUSS & DURKEE, 1957)

Physical
1. Once in a while I cannot control my urge to harm others.
2. I can think of no good reason for ever hitting someone. (reversed)
3. If somebody hits me first, I let him have it.
4. Whoever insults me or my family is asking for a fight.
5. People who continually pester you are asking for a punch in the nose.
6. I seldom strike back, even if someone hits me first. (reversed)
7. When I really lose my temper, I am capable of slapping someone.
8. I get into fights about as often as the next person.
9. If I have to resort to violence to defend my rights, I will.
10. I have known people who pushed me so far that we came to blows.

Verbal
1. When I disapprove of my friends' behavior, I let them know it.
2. I often find myself disagreeing with people.
3. I can't help getting into arguments when people disagree with me.
4. I demand that people respect my rights.
5. Even when my anger is aroused, I don't use strong language. (reversed)
6. If somebody annoys me, I am apt to tell him what I think of him.
7. When people yell at me, I yell back.
8. When I get mad, I say nasty things.
9. I could not put someone in his place even if he needed it (reversed)
10. I often make threats I don't really mean to carry out.
11. When arguing, I tend to raise my voice.
12. I generally cover up my poor opinion of others. (reversed)
13. I would rather concede a point than get into an argument about it. (reversed)

As may be seen, aggression may be verbal or physical, and we cannot assume that verbally aggressive people are also physically aggressive or the opposite. The two are correlated, however, and appear on an aggressiveness factor that also includes indirect aggression and irritability (Buss & Durkee, 1957). The verbal and physical aggression scales, like the others in the inventory, were arrived at a priori and not through a factor analysis. Thus, the inventory does not meet modern psychometric standards, but the individual scales may be conceptually useful and the inventory has enjoyed wide use. An attempt was made in writing the items to minimize the importance of social desirability, for aggressiveness is a socially undesirable class of behaviors. The items were scaled for social desirability, which was correlated with the probability of endorsing the items. The correlations were .27 for men and .30 for women, which may be as low as can be expected for a hostility inventory.

Aggressiveness is linked to dominance in two ways: It is a major avenue to dominance, and anyone who starts out as mildly aggressive and dominates successfully through fighting is likely to become highly aggressive. Thus, aggression can lead to dominance, or dominance can lead to aggression. Typically, it is instrumental aggression that is linked with domination, for the goal of this kind of aggression is the achieving of any of the common rewards in everyday life. In angry aggression, however, the intent is to hurt or harm regardless of any consequences such as gaining the upper hand. The items in the preceding scales mention anger, which makes these scales a combination of angry and instrumental aggression. It might be worthwhile to devise one scale for instrumental aggression and another for angry aggression. It is precisely this differentiation, which reveals the need for new personality measures that relate to social behavior, that was one of the goals of the present book.

ALTRUISM (RUSHTON, CHRISJOHN, & FEKKIN, 1981)

1. I have helped push a stranger's car out of the snow.
2. I have given directions to a stranger.
3. I have made change for a stranger.
4. I have given money to a charity.
5. I have given money to a stranger who needed it and asked me for it.
6. I have donated goods or clothes to a charity.
7. I have done volunteer work for a charity.
8. I have donated blood.
9. I have helped carry a stranger's belongings (books, parcels, etc.)
10. I have delayed an elevator and held the door open for a stranger.
11. I have allowed someone to go ahead of me in a lineup (Xerox machine, supermarket).
12. I have given a stranger a lift in my car.
13. I have pointed out a clerk's error in a bank (at the supermarket) in undercharging me for an item.
14. I have let a neighbor whom I didn't know too well borrow an item of some value to me (dish, tools, etc.).
15. I have bought charity Christmas cards deliberately because I knew it was a good cause.
16. I have helped a classmate who I did not know well with a homework assignment when my knowledge was greater than his or hers.
17. I have, before being asked, voluntarily looked after a neighbor's pets or children without being paid for it.
18. I have offered to help a handicapped or elderly stranger across the street.
19. I have offered my seat on a bus or train to a stranger who was standing.
20. I have helped an acquaintance to move households.

Unlike most self-report questionnaires, which inquire about general tendencies, this one asks about the frequency of specific acts. Also, the targets of the altruism are strangers or casual acquaintances rather than family or friends. The scale has been found to correlate with other self-report measures of altruism, and a study by Rushton, Chrisjohn, and Fekkin (1981) related this self-report to peer ratings. Several people who knew each subject well were asked to rate the subject for the 20 specific acts and for global altruism. The correlations between peer ratings and self-reports, corrected for attenuation due to internal unreliability, were .56 (peer ratings of specific acts) and .33 (peer ratings of global altruism). The higher correlation is good evidence of the scale's validity as a measure of altruism toward strangers, although its internal reliability is open to question.

It would be just as interesting to have a measure of altruism toward friends or even toward family, but another issue assumes some importance. The items on this scale all involve everyday acts of kindness, politeness, and charity. As such, they represent the low end of a dimension of altruism. The upper end is represented by acts that involve somewhat more self-sacrifice, such as volunteering to replace a subject who is about to receive electric shock (Batson, O'Quin, Fultz, Vanderplas,

& Isen, 1983), giving blood, or donating an organ. It is true that such actions are rarer than the behaviors mentioned in the preceding scale, but self-sacrifice appears more congruent with the definition of altruism than minor acts of helping. Of course the problem may remain whether we can devise a personality measure that includes these rarer acts that occupy the top of the altruism dimension.

ASSERTIVENESS

Selected from a larger scale of dominance (Ray, 1981)
1. Are you the sort of person who always likes to get their own way?
2. Do you tend to boss people around?
3. Do you dislike telling others what to do? (reversed)
4. Do you tend to dominate the conversation?
5. Do you give in to people rather easily? (reversed)
6. Do you like having the last word in an argument or discussion?
7. Are you pretty good at getting your own way in most things?

Selected from a large group of dominance acts (D. Buss, 1981)
1. I demanded that he run an errand.
2. I told her to get off the phone so that I could use it.
3. I interrupted a conversation.
4. I chose to sit at the head of the table.
5. I yelled in order to get my way.
6. I decided which programs we would watch on TV.
7. I told him which item he should purchase.
8. I challenged someone to discuss her position.
9. I forbade her to leave the room.
10. I monopolized the conversation.
11. I walked ahead of everyone else.

These two sets of assertiveness items were selected from a larger pool of dominance items. No one has devised an assertiveness scale previously because dominance was considered to be the appropriate trait, and the means by which dominance is attained remained unanalyzed. Now that the various paths to dominance have been delineated, we can determine whether it is worthwhile to keep them separate. If the approach adopted here is correct, people who endorse assertiveness items will not necessarily endorse aggressiveness, competitiveness, or decisiveness items. These various scales are undoubtedly correlated, else the concept of dominance would have to be discarded as a personality construct, but the correlations should be sufficiently modest for each of the four components to make its own contribution. Assertiveness is expected to be more closely linked to aggressiveness and perhaps to decisiveness than to competitiveness. There may be several clusters of pairs: assertive–aggressive, assertive–decisive, and perhaps even assertive–competitive. And there are likely to be people who are high or low on all four components of dominance.

COMPETITIVENESS

Competitiveness: A factor in the Work and Family Orientation (WOFO) questionnaire (Spence & Helmreich, 1978)
1. I really enjoy working in situations involving skill and competition.
2. When a group I belong to plans an activity, I would rather organize it myself than have someone else organize it and just help out.
3. It is important for me to perform better than others on a task.
4. I feel that winning is very important in both work and games.

The competitiveness factor emerged from a factor analysis of the WOFO. The second item refers less to competition than to leadership, which might account for its being the only item to load on another scale (mastery). Spence and Helmreich (1978) found that men scored slightly higher than women, and the scale correlated modestly with self-esteem and their trait of masculinity. Since its construction, the scale has been used as part of an achievement cluster to study scientific eminence.

Competitiveness factor of the MYTH (Matthews, 1980)
1. When this child plays games, he/she is competitive.
2. This child works quickly and energetically rather than slowly and deliberately.
3. This child is a leader in various activities.
4. He/she seems to perform better when competing against others.
5. When working or playing, he/she tries to do better than other children.
6. It is important for this child to win, rather than have fun in games or schoolwork.
7. The other children look to this child for leadership.
8. This child is competitive.

This form of the scale is meant to be completed by parents or teachers. Notice that the second item taps activity level and that the third and seventh items assess leadership. Although these three items load on the competitiveness factor, the scale would be a purer measure of competitiveness without them. The fact that they do load together may reflect the point made in the dominance chapter that competition and dominance both are ways of achieving dominance.

Competitiveness: New (this book)
1. I get a kick out of matching my ability against other peoples'.
2. I need to be the best in my group.
3. I hate to lose.
4. I am willing to make sacrifices in order to win.
5. It bothers me to meet someone more attractive or talented than I.
6. In sports, the most important thing is winning.
7. I like it when there is a clear winner and loser.
8. I wonder about the motivation of good losers.
9. The only response to losing is to try harder next time.
10. I enjoy being challenged by another person.

The new competitiveness scale focuses on interpersonal competition, in contrast to contests involving groups or struggles in the workplace. It contains a variety of contexts in which competition might occur and strongly emphasizes motivation. Although it currently lacks the necessary psychometric data, the scale would seem to contain only the kinds of items needed for an assessment of competitiveness and no additional items that might spill over into other traits.

DUPLICITY AND CALCULATING

Duplicity—factor of Machiavellianism (Christie & Geis, 1970)
1. There is no excuse for lying to someone else. (reversed)
2. Honesty is the best policy in all cases. (reversed)
3. All in all, it is better to be honest and humble than to be important and dishonest.
4. When you ask someone to do something for you, it is best to give the real reasons for wanting it rather than giving reasons which carry more weight. (reversed)
5. It is wise to flatter important people.
6. The best way to handle people is to tell them what they want to hear.
7. Next to health, wealth is the most important thing in life.
8. One should take action only when sure it is morally right. (reversed)
9. Even today, the way that you make money is more important than how much you make. (reversed)
10. Never tell anyone the real reason you did something unless it is useful to do so.

The duplicity items emerged from a factor analysis of the Machiavellianism scale, which attempts to measure a cynical orientation toward the world, an attitude of doing what is necessary to get ahead, even if it means using trickery and deceit. The Machiavellian scale should not be used as a whole, for it contains several different factors (see Hunter, Gerbing, & Boster, 1982, for documentation). The duplicity subscale, however, might prove useful as a measure of deceit.

Calculating Acts (D. Buss & Craik, 1985)
1. I made a friend in order to obtain a favor.
2. I asked "innocent" questions, intending to use the information against someone.
3. I pretended I was hurt to get someone to do me a favor.
4. I tricked a friend into giving me personal information.
5. I flattered a person in order to get ahead.
6. I pretended to be sick at work, knowing that I would not be there the next day.
7. I made others feel guilty to get what I wanted.

The calculating acts are similar to the duplicity items but involve more trickery and pretense. They were obtained by having subjects select acts from a list that had previously been nominated as representing calculating behavior. Notice that these acts are specific, whereas the duplicity scale contains the more general items typical of personality questionnaires. Neither scale has been used much in research, and it would be interesting to determine their relationship with the Self-Monitoring Scale, which also includes items tapping a willingness to deceive.

The other side of the coin may be regarded as interpersonal trust. There is a well-known questionnaire by that name (Rotter, 1966), but it would not be appropriate here because of its emphasis on trust of unfamiliar and distant others. A measure called the Specific Interpersonal Trust Scale (Johnson-George & Swap, 1982) would seem apt, but the items are specific to a particular person. Respondents are asked to think of a particular person of the same sex whom they especially trust and then answer items of which the following is typical: I would be able to confide in _____ and know that he/she would want to listen. Thus it is not a personality trait that is being assessed here but a disposition toward a particular person. At present, then, it seems best to rely on measures of the opposite tendency of deceiving others or acting in a calculating way.

EMOTIONALITY AND FEARFULNESS

Emotionality
1. I frequently get distressed.
2. I often feel frustrated.
3. Everyday events make me troubled and fretful.
4. I get emotionally upset very easily.

Fearfulness
1. I am easily frightened.
2. I often feel insecure.
3. When I get scared, I panic.
4. I have fewer fears than most people my age. (reversed)

These two traits have been shown to be inherited in studies of twins, and they appear during the first year of life; therefore, they are called *temperaments* (Buss & Plomin, 1984). Emotionality is assumed to be primordial, and fear differentiates from it after several months of life. The difference between the two traits may be seen in the aforementioned items. Emotionality includes distress, frustration, and being troubled or upset; fearfulness includes being frightened, panicky, and insecure. The two traits correlate .63 for men and .52 for women. They derive from earlier work on temperaments (Buss & Plomin, 1975), and in one form or another, they are represented on most lists of temperament and personality traits.

Emotionality is linked to the social reward of sympathy (see chapter 2, this volume) on the assumption that emotional people tend to become distressed more often, which makes sympathy a more powerful reward. Emotionality and fearfulness are assumed to be determinants of attachment, infants tending to develop stranger anxiety more easily if they are high on these traits (see chapter 3, this volume). Fearful people tend not to resist aggression and therefore are expected to be submissive (see chapter 4, this volume). Emotionality should be one determinant of whether people react strongly to another's distress, for the personal distress experience in such a situation is little different from the distress in emotionality (see chapter 5, this volume). Both temperaments enter into fearful shyness (see chapter 7, this volume), and emotionality should be correlated with having a tense interpersonal style (see chapter 8, this volume).

EMOTIONAL EMPATHY AND PERSPECTIVE TAKING
(DAVIS, 1983)

Emotional Empathy
1. I am often quite touched by the things I see happen.
2. I would describe myself as a pretty soft-hearted person.
3. Sometimes I don't feel very sorry for other people when they are having problems. (reversed)
4. When I see someone being treated unfairly, I don't feel very much pity for them. (reversed)
5. When I see someone being taken advantage of, I feel kind of protective toward them.
6. I have tender, concerned feelings for people less fortunate than me.
7. Other people's misfortunes do not usually disturb me a great deal. (reversed)

Perspective Taking
1. I believe that there are two sides to every question and try to look at them both.
2. When I'm upset with someone, I usually try to "put myself in his shoes" for a while.
3. I try to look at everybody's side of disagreement before I make a decision.
4. I sometimes find it difficult to see things from the "other guy's" point of view. (reversed)
5. Before criticizing somebody, I try to imagine how I would feel if I were in their place.
6. If I'm sure I'm right about something, I don't waste much time listening to other people's arguments. (reversed)
7. I try to understand my friends better by imagining how things look from their perspective.

These two scales are part of Davis' questionnaire assessing the personality traits believed to be linked with empathy. The factor analysis that led to the scales was part of Davis' (1979) doctoral dissertation. The items were subsequently revised, and the revised list is presented here. In the published article, *emotional empathy* was renamed *empathic concern,* but the original name is retained here as a more apt description. The emotional empathy scale contains items similar to some of those in Cattell's (1973) tendermindedness scale, but the perspective-taking items seem not to be represented on traditional personality questionnaires. The scales correlate in the .30s for both men and women.

Their correlations with other empathy questionnaires is revealing. Emotional empathy correlates strongly with the scale developed by Mehrabian and Epstein (1972): .63 for men and .56 for women. Perspective taking correlates not quite as strongly with Hogan's (1969) empathy scale: .42 for men and .37 for women. Presumably, Hogan's scale has a cognitive slant, whereas that of Mehrabian and Epstein is tilted toward emotion. Hogan's empathy questionnaire contains a broad mixture of contents in its 62 items. Johnson, Cheek, and Smither (1983) found several factors, which on the surface appear to be unrelated to empathy.

The Mehrabian–Epstein questionnaire contains a variety of subscales that were arrived at a priori: susceptibility to emotional contagion, appreciation of the feelings of unfamiliar others, extreme emotional responsiveness, a tendency to be moved by others' positive or negative experiences, sympathetic tendencies, and a willingness to be in contact with others who have problems. As these subscales suggest, there are probably a few (as yet undiscovered) factors underlying the scale, and for this reason Davis' factorially derived measure should be easier to interpret.

EXHIBITIONISM

In children (Paivio, Baldwin, & Berger, 1961)
1. I like to recite poems in front of other people.
2. Every time I get a chance to do something in front of class I take it.
3. In school, I always raise my hand if I know the answer.
4. Even if I know the answer, I usually do not raise my hand. (reversed)
5. If I wrote a prize-winning poem, I would rather have someone else read it in front of the class. (reversed)
6. If my paper is hung on the bulletin board, I'd rather not have my name on it. (reversed)
7. I like to show things I make to other children.
8. I would like to make something while the whole class watches.
9. I like to show my work to my classmates.
10. I like to sing in front of others.
11. I like to tell a story in front of class.
12. I would like to be on the stage in front of many people.
13. If my paper is hung on the bulletin board, I'd like everyone who sees it to know it's mine. (reversed)

New (this book)
1. I would enjoy being interviewed on television.
2. I can't stand being ignored.
3. There is nothing more rewarding than an appreciative audience.
4. I like to be noticed.
5. I sometimes put on a show to get attention.
6. I am a bit of a show off.
7. I would rather act in a play than write one.
8. I would have no trouble in demonstrating products to people in a department store.
9. If I were giving a lecture, I would prefer a large audience to a small one.
10. I admire John Hancock, who wrote his name larger than anyone who signed the constitution.
11. I sometimes dress just to catch the eye of others.
12. Being conspicuous does not bother me at all.

The children's questionnaire was developed as part of the Children's Audience Sensitivity Questionnaire, which also includes items on audience anxiety and self-consciousness. Scores on the exhibitionism scale were compared with whether children volunteered to perform in a summer camp skit, and the correlations were .31 for girls and .14 for boys. Thus, the scale may possess modest validity for girls but none for boys.

There is an adult questionnaire of exhibitionism (Jackson, 1974), but it appears to assess more than just exhibitionism—extraversion, for example. Although extraversion is expected to be correlated with exhibitionism, there are extraverts who are not exhibitionists, which means that separate measures of each trait are needed.

The new scale assesses a strong need for attention and its complement, the aversiveness of being ignored. Whether the scale has the requisite psychometric properties and is an adequate selection device are matters for subsequent research.

FORMALITY (L. BUSS, 1984)

1. I believe it is important to behave with good manners.
2. I consider myself a formal person.
3. I feel quite at home at formal functions.
4. I have a strong sense of propriety.
5. I tend to behave in a dignified fashion.
6. I believe that physical expressions of intimacy are not proper in public situations.
7. I enjoy being spontaneous and expressive, even when it is not appropriate. (reversed)
8. It does not bother me to express my true feelings at social gatherings. (reversed)
9. Social standards of behavior are too confining for me. (reversed)
10. My manners are better than most people's.

The items on this scale would seem to meet the definition of formality, which includes a strong sense of propriety, preferring situations in which social rules are salient, emphasizing dignity, and having good manners. It was compared with the social behavior of subjects who took part in an all-day assessment, during which they were interviewed and observed by a group of psychologists. The latter ranked the subjects for formality, and the average of these rankings correlated .67 with scores on the self-report measure. There is also evidence of discriminant validity in the low correlations between this scale and other personality questionnaires. Thus, the scale appears to be a promising instrument for the measurement of the trait of formality.

IMPULSIVITY

From the EASI-I (Buss & Plomin, 1975)
1. I tend to be impulsive.
2. I find self-control difficult.
3. I get bored easily.
4. I find it difficult to resist temptation.
5. I tend to hop from interest to interest quickly.

The scale was originally part of a cluster of temperaments, along with emotionality, activity, and sociability, yielding the acronym EASI (Buss & Plomin, 1975). There was a question about its heritability, however, roughly half of the studies yielding positive evidence and the remainder, negative evidence. Furthermore, it is difficult to know precisely when it appears during childhood. For these reasons it subsequently was dropped as a temperament (Buss & Plomin, 1984). It is still useful as a personality trait, though, and it may be a determinant of the stylistic trait of suddenness (see chapter 8, this volume).

IRRITABILITY (BUSS & DURKEE, 1957)

1. I lose my temper easily but get over it quickly.
2. I am always patient with others. (reversed)
3. I am irritated a great deal more than people are aware of.
4. If makes my blood boil to have people make fun of me.
5. If someone doesn't treat me right, I don't let it annoy me. (reversed)
6. Sometimes people bother me just by being around.
7. I often feel like a powder keg ready to explode.
8. I often carry a chip on my shoulder.
9. I can't help being a little rude to people I don't like.
10. I don't let a lot of unimportant things irritate me. (reversed)
11. Lately, I have been kind of grouchy.

Like the other scales of the Buss–Durkee Inventory, the items on this scale were assigned a priori. When a factor analysis was done, it was performed on correlations among the scales, not the items. This scale is part of an aggressiveness factor that also includes physical, indirect, and verbal aggression.

The irritability scale attempts to assess anger, which may remain latent or become manifest in angry aggression. Such aggression does not lead to dominance as efficiently as instrumental aggression, but any successful attack inevitably leads to at least some dominance. The target of an attempt at dominance may also become angry and may counteraggress. The personality trait of irritability must be considered as one determinant of aggression, which can lead to dominance. The other side of the coin may also be true: Being the target of other's dominance behavior can spawn irritability.

LEADERSHIP

Directiveness factor (Lorr & More, 1980)
1. I have no particular desire to be the leader of the group. (reversed)
2. I shy away from situations where I might be asked to take charge. (reversed)
3. I let others lead when I'm on a committee. (reversed)
4. I would avoid a job which required me to supervise other people. (reversed)
5. I work best when I'm the person in charge.
6. I seek positions where I can influence others.
7. I am usually the one who initiated activities in my group.
8. In an emergency I get people organized and take charge.

Decisiveness and Inititiative — selected from a larger group of dominance acts (D. Buss, 1981)
1. I set goals for the group.
2. I volunteered an idea in order to start the group conversation.
3. I took the lead in livening up a dull party.
4. I organized a protest meeting.
5. I took the lead in organizing a project.
6. I took the initiative in planning the party.
7. I settled a dispute among other members of the group.
8. I issued orders that got the group organized.
9. I assigned roles and got the game going.
10. I made decisions without consulting the others involved in them.
11. I took command of the situation after the accident.
12. I made the final decision.

The directiveness items constitute a leadership factor, which combines making decisions and taking the initiative. The specific acts tapping decisiveness and initiative (D. Buss, 1981) were selected from a larger list of dominant acts. Clearly, both scales are related to dominance, but we do not yet know the relationship of the trait of leadership to the other dominance-related traits: aggressiveness, competitiveness, and assertiveness. Until we do, it may be best to keep these four traits separate. If the relationships are found to be sufficiently strong, the scales can always be combined to form a supertrait of dominance.

LONELINESS (RUSSELL, PEPLAU, & CUTRONA, 1980)

1. I feel in tune with the people around me. (reversed)
2. I lack companionship.
3. There is no one I can turn to.
4. I do not feel alone. (reversed)
5. I feel part of a group of friends. (reversed)
6. I have a lot in common with the people around me. (reversed)
7. I am no longer close to anyone.
8. My interests and ideas are not shared by those around me.
9. I am an outgoing person. (reversed)
10. There are people I feel close to. (reversed)
11. I feel left out.
12. My social relationships are superficial.
13. No one really knows me well.
14. I feel isolated from others.
15. I can find companionship when I want to. (reversed)
16. There are people who really understand me. (reversed)
17. I am unhappy at being so withdrawn.
18. People are around me but not with me.
19. There are people I can talk to. (reversed)
20. There are people I can turn to. (reversed)

This revision of an earlier scale has a coefficient alpha of .94, suggesting considerable internal consistency. As might be expected, the scale correlates positively with depression (.51) and anxiety (.36), and negatively with self-esteem (−.49), extraversion (−.46), and affiliation (−.45).

The items appear to tap feelings and moods that may vary with the present social situation, and the score would surely reflect the presence or absence of friendships or a romantic attachment. Thus, insofar as there is a trait of loneliness, it appears to be a tendency that would fluctuate to some extent with the interpersonal environment. The strong correlations with other personality traits suggest that loneliness may derive from a combination of several related traits. Suppose that a multiple correlation were calculated between the loneliness scale and depression, self-esteem, anxiety, and extraversion. If this correlation were sufficiently high, it could be argued that what is called a trait of loneliness is a composite of these other traits.

These considerations aside, loneliness is expected to affect the potency of all the stimulation social rewards and also the affective rewards of sympathy and affection. Lonely people would be especially susceptible to romantic love, and a disappointment in love would undoubtedly increase loneliness.

NEGATIVISM AND RESENTMENT (BUSS & DURKEE, 1957)

Negativism
1. Unless somebody asks me in a nice way, I won't do what they want.
2. When someone makes a rule I don't like, I am tempted to break it.
3. When someone is bossy, I do the opposite of what he asks.
4. When people are bossy, I take my time just to show them.
5. Occasionally when I am mad at someone, I will give him the silent treatment.

Resentment
1. I don't seem to get what's coming to me.
2. Other people always seem to get the breaks.
3. When I look back at what's happened to me, I can't help feeling mildly resentful.
4. Almost every week I see someone I dislike.
5. Although I don't show it, I am sometimes eaten up with jealousy.
6. I don't know any people that I downright hate. (reversed)
7. If I let people see the way I feel, I'd be considered a hard person to get along with.
8. At times I feel I get a raw deal out of life.

These two scales are part of a 30-year-old inventory, which researchers still find useful because it contains a variety of specific scales, although they were assigned a priori and not through factor analysis. These two are grouped here because they are involved with reactions to attempted dominance (see Table 4.1). An aggressive act by another may cause hostility in the resister, especially a person high in the trait of resentment. The trait of resentment might be the result of months or years of being the victim of another's aggression, and it is likely that a person who is initially resentful will react with hostility to being dominated.

Bossiness is likely to elicit passive resistance, especially by someone high in the trait of negativism. A person who is negativistic is likely to respond to the domination of others by being passively resistant, a reaction that is sometimes labelled *passive aggression.*

SELF–CONSCIOUSNESS (FENIGSTEIN ET AL., 1975)

Private Self-Consciousness
1. I reflect about myself a lot.
2. I'm generally attentive to my inner feelings.
3. I'm always trying to figure myself out.
4. I'm constantly examining my motives.
5. I'm alert to changes in my mood.
6. I tend to scrutinize myself.
7. Generally, I'm aware of myself.
8. I'm aware of the way my mind works when I work through a problem.
9. I'm often the subject of my own fantasies.
10. I sometimes have the feeling that I'm off somewhere watching myself.

Public Self-Consciousness
1. I'm concerned about what other people think of me.
2. I usually worry about making a good impression.
3. I'm concerned about the way I present myself.
4. I'm self-conscious about the way I look.
5. I'm usually aware of my appearance.
6. One of the last things I do before leaving the house is look in the mirror.
7. I'm concerned about my style of doing things.

The two self-consciousness scales emerged from a series of factor analyses, with the total number of subjects approximating 2,000, which yielded these two factors and a third, social anxiety (not discussed here).

The scales have been translated into German (Heinemann, 1979), Dutch (Vleeming & Engelse, 1981), and Polish (Zakrzewski, 1985), and factor analyses yielded roughly the same pattern of factors as was found in the original, American version. They have also been translated into Japanese (Tsuji, 1982) and administered to young adolescents. Again, the factorial patterns were fairly consistent, but one public item (when translated) also appeared on the private factor: I'm concerned about how teachers and friends think of me. The placement of this item and other aspects of the analysis are understandable when we consider how strongly the social self is socialized in Japan.

Private and public self-consciousness originally correlated in the low .20s, but subsequent research suggests that the correlation is nearer to .30. Although correlated, the two traits affect behavior differently. Private self-consciousness intensifies angry aggression, but public self-consciousness has no effect (Scheier, 1976). Public self-consciousness makes subjects more sensitive to being ignored, but private self-consciousness has no effect (Fenigstein, 1979). Private self-consciousness is a positive moderator of the relationship between self-reports and behavior, whereas public self-consciousness is a negative moderator (Buss, 1980, p. 59). The two kinds of self-consciousness are linked with different aspects of identity. Cheek and Briggs (1982) separated identity items into personal (example: my intellectual ability) and social (example: my popularity and attractiveness to other people). The identity items inquire about the importance of each aspect, whereas self-consciousness items inquire about awareness. Private self-consciousness correlated .37 with personal identity but nearly 0 with social identity, and public self-consciousness correlated .30 with social identity but nearly 0 with personal identity.

Of the two traits, public self-consciousness is the more important determiner of social behavior. Miller and Cox (1982) photographed women and found a correlation of .32 between how much makeup they used and public self-consciousness. The latter trait also correlated .40 with the belief that makeup makes one's social interactions go more smoothly. Women may be so interested in clothes that personality traits exert no influence, but the situation should be different for men. Public self-consciousness correlates .42 with interest in clothes for men but only .14 for women (Solomon & Schopler, 1982).

Public self-consciousness, by definition, involves a particular awareness of oneself as a social object, which means that those who are high in this trait are likely to view themselves as objects of the attention of others. Three facts are consistent with this expectation: high public self-conscious subjects believe that their exam will be singled out by the teacher, overestimate whether they will be selected for an experimental demonstration, and think that hypothetical social situations are relevant or directed to themselves (Fenigstein, 1984).

SELF-ESTEEM (CHEEK & BUSS, 1981)

1. I have a low opinion of myself. (reversed)
2. I often wish I were someone else. (reversed)
3. Things are all mixed up in my life. (reversed)
4. I'm fairly sure of myself.
5. I am a failure. (reversed)
6. I am basically worthwhile.

The scale contains a small number of general items, in keeping with the nature of self-esteem as a global trait. It correlates .88 with the well-known questionnaire of Rosenberg (1965), which suggests that they are measuring roughly the same trait. Self-esteem correlates negatively with shyness ($-.51$) and positively with extraversion (.38). Although it is not clear what the direction of causality is in these correlations, at least we know that self-esteem is related to important social traits.

Self-esteem has been hypothesized in this book to strengthen the potency of the social rewards of praise and affection (see chapter 2) and to be linked to attachment and romantic love (see chapter 3). It may also be a determiner of the outcome of contests for dominance (see chapter 4), and its empirical relationship to shyness has already been established (see chapter 6).

SELF-MONITORING

Given the importance of the self-presentation approach in the social psychological analysis of interaction, Snyder's (1974) Self-Monitoring Scale seemed to offer an ideal personality instrument, one that would identify those especially likely to use the tactics and strategies of self-presentation. The questionnaire was constructed by assembling items and correlating the endorsement of each item with the total scale, a procedure that rarely leads to a univocal trait. Examination of the items revealed considerable diversity and accordingly, Briggs, Cheek, and Buss (1980) factor analyzed the scale, using two large samples of college students. Three factors were extracted and named on the basis of both the item content and correlations with other personality trait measures. The three factors were replicated by Gabrenya and Arkin (1980) and Riggio and Friedman (1982).

The three factors extracted by Briggs, Cheek, and Buss (1980) are as follows:

Acting factor
1. I would probably make a good actor.
2. I have considered being an entertainer.
3. I have never been good at games like charades or improvisational acting. (reversed)
4. I can make impromptu speeches on topics about which I have almost no information.
5. I can look anyone in the eye and tell a lie with a straight face (if for a right end).

Other-Directed factor
1. In different situations and with different people, I often act like very different persons.
2. In order to get along and be liked, I tend to be what people expect me to be rather than anything else.
3. I'm not always the person I appear to be.
4. I guess I put on a show to impress or entertain people.
5. Even if I am not enjoying myself, I often pretend to be having a good time.
6. I may deceive people by being friendly when I really dislike them.
7. I would not change my opinion (or the way I do things) in order to please someone else or win their favor. (reversed)
8. I feel a bit awkward in company and do not show up as well as I should. (reversed)
9. When I am uncertain how to act in social situations, I look to the behavior of others for cues.
10. My behavior is usually an expression of my true inner feelings, attitudes, and beliefs. (reversed)
11. At parties and social gatherings, I do not attempt to do or say things that others will like. (reversed)

Extraversion factor
1. I feel a bit awkward in company and do not show up as well as I should. (reversed)
2. At a party I let others keep the jokes and stories going. (reversed)
3. In a group of people I am rarely the center of attention. (reversed)
4. I am not particularly good at making other people like me. (reversed)
5. I have never been good at games like charades or improvisational acting. (reversed)
6. I have trouble changing my behavior to suit different people and different situations. (reversed)

The Self-Monitoring Scale as a whole has been related to various aspects of social behavior, but the findings are mixed, probably because of the presence of three different factors. Riggio and Friedman (1982) had subjects attempt to read sentences with different emotional shadings and also to deceive others. In summarizing their findings with the Self-Monitoring Scale (SMS), they wrote: "Self-monitoring, as measured by the SMS, appears to measure two basic dimensions of social skills: The first deals with ability to send emotional displays; SMS Extraversion appears to assess natural, spontaneous expressiveness, while SMS Acting reflects a controlled, posed sending ability. The second dimension deals with social sensitivity and knowledge of social rules and is measured by Other-Directedness" (p. 44).

In another experiment, Riggio and Friedman (1982) tested whether subjects could decode meanings from the vocal characteristics of speech, and they were asked to express empathy in a social interaction. Performance on the decoding task correlated significantly with extraversion and acting but not with other-directedness, whereas the ability to express empathy correlated significantly with other-directness but not the other two scales.

After summarizing the mixed findings with the Self-Monitoring Scale, Lennox and Wolfe (1984) concluded: "The scale's multidimensionality extends beyond the limits of the construct, creating a situation in which its factors compete with one another. . . . Consequently, the total score on Snyder's (1974) scale tends to defy interpretation: it is impossible to determine what the scale as whole might be measuring" (p. 1350). These researchers proceeded to develop a revised scale consisting of two factors, one involving control over one's social behavior and the other, sensitivity to others' behavior.

Ability to Modify Self-Presentation (Lennox & Wolfe, 1984)
1. In social situations, I have the ability to alter my behavior if I feel that something else is called for.
2. I have the ability to control how I come across to people, depending on the impression I want to give them.
3. When I feel that the image I'm portraying isn't working, I can readily change it to something that does.
4. I have trouble changing my behavior to suit different people in different situations. (reversed).

5. I have found that I can adjust my behavior to meet the requirements of any situation I find myself in.
6. Even when it might be to my advantage, I have difficulty putting up a good front. (reversed)
7. Once I know what a situation calls for, it's easy for me to regulate my actions accordingly.

Sensitivity to Expressive Behavior in Others (Lennox & Wolfe, 1984)
1. I am often able to read people's true emotions correctly through their eyes.
2. In conversations, I am sensitive to even the slightest change in the facial expression of the person I'm conversing with.
3. My powers of intuition are quite good when it comes to understanding others' emotions and motives.
4. I can usually tell when others consider a joke to be in bad taste, even though they laugh convincingly.
5. I can usually tell when I've said something inappropriate by reading it in the listener's eyes.
6. If someone else is lying to me, I usually know it once from that person's manner of expression.

SHYNESS (CHEEK & BUSS, 1981)

1. I am socially somewhat awkward.
2. I find it hard to talk to strangers.
3. I feel tense with people I don't know well.
4. When conversing, I worry about saying something dumb.
5. I feel nervous when speaking to someone in authority.
6. I am uncomfortable at parties and other social functions.
7. I feel inhibited in social situations.
8. I have trouble looking someone right in the eye.
9. I am more shy with members of the opposite sex.

The scale was constructed, using factor analysis, to provide a univocal measure of shyness, which is defined as tension, concern, discomfort, and inhibition in social contexts. Other instruments assess shyness together with other social anxieties (speech anxiety, for example) or as part of an extraversion questionnaire that includes sociability items. Sociability and shyness were deliberately kept separate, and their correlation is $-.30$. Shyness also correlates $.50$ with fearfulness and $-.51$ with self-esteem. This scale predicts how people will behave when they meet strangers (Cheek & Buss, 1981).

In this book, shyness is hypothesized to tilt the dimension of attention from others, shy people finding "normal" amounts of attention to be aversive; and they may be rewarded by initiation of social interaction from another person because they are too inhibited to start conversations themselves (see chapter 2). Also suggested is a distinction between early developing, fearful shyness and late developing self-conscious shyness, a dichotomy not reflected in the above items. Writing items that separate the two kinds of shyness may prove difficult, for it is likely that the two are experienced similarly, and we may have to rely on observations to sustain the distinction.

SOCIABILITY (CHEEK & BUSS, 1981)

1. I like to be with people.
2. I welcome the opportunity to mix socially with people.
3. I prefer working with others than alone.
4. I find people more stimulating than anything else.
5. I'd be unhappy if I were prevented from making many friends.

These items reflect the definition of sociability as the tendency to prefer being with others. Sociability is typically assessed in conjunction with shyness or as part of an extraversion questionnaire. The present scale measures sociability and nothing else, as the factor analysis confirmed. Its correlation with shyness is −.30.

This scale contains three of the four items that make up the sociability scale that is part of the temperament questionnaire (Buss & Plomin, 1984). In earlier research, sociability was found to be inherited (Buss & Plomin, 1975), and the trait may be seen during the first year of life. Subsequent research has confirmed these facts (for a review, see Buss and Plomin, 1984). The trait also appears in one form or another in virtually all standard personality questionnaires.

Sociability is hypothesized to affect the valence of all of the stimulation rewards, the assumption being that sociable people especially value social stimulation (see chapter 2, this volume). It may also be related to the events of attachment, sociable infants being more drawn to strangers and more willing to tolerate the aversiveness of unfamiliarity because of a need for the arousal that derives only from interaction (see chapter 3, this volume).

SPEECH ANXIETY (SLIVKEN & BUSS, 1984)

1. I always avoid speaking in public if possible.
2. Although I do OK with friends, I am at a loss for words in front of an audience.
3. I feel extremely self-conscious while I am speaking in front of a group.
4. I feel very relaxed just before I speak in front of a group. (reversed)
5. I tend to make mistakes and do poorly when speaking before a group.
6. I am afraid to express myself in a group.

This scale assesses anxiety and self-consciousness during the speech and worry prior to the speech. It has been used to predict these responses during public speaking: nervous smiling, tension, a lack of expressivity, and a shorter length of speech (Slivken & Buss, 1984). Speech anxiety and shyness are closely linked, although the two differ in their prevalence: Speech anxiety is considerably more common than shyness, probably because most people lack experience in public speaking.

References

Addington, D. W. (1968). The relationship of selected vocal characteristics to personality perception. *Speech Monographs, 35,* 492–503.

Adorno, T. W., Frenkel-Brunswik, E., Levinson, D. J., & Sanford, R. N. (1950). *The authoritarian personality.* New York: Harper.

Ainsworth, M.D.S. (1979). Infant-mother attachment. *American Psychologist, 34,* 932–937.

Ainsworth, M. D. S., Blehar, M. C., Waters, E., & Wall, S. (1978). *Patterns of attachment: A psychological study of the strange situation.* Hillsdale, NJ: Lawrence Erlbaum Associates.

Allport, G. A. (1961). *Pattern and growth in personality.* New York: Holt, Rinehart & Winston.

Allport, G. W., & Vernon, P. E. (1933). *Studies in expressive movement.* New York: Macmillan.

Altman, I. (1975). *The environment and social behavior.* Monterey, CA: Brooks/Cole.

Amsterdam, B. (1972). Mirror self-image reactions before the age of two. *Developmental Psychology, 5,* 297–305.

Apple, W., Streeter, L. A., & Krauss, R. M., (1979). Effects of pitch and speech rate on personal attributions. *Journal of Personality and Social Psychology, 37,* 715–727.

Argyle, M. (1975). *Bodily communication.* London: Methven.

Aronoff, J., & Wilson, J. P. (1985). *Personality in the social process.* Hillsdale, NJ: Lawrence Erlbaum Associates.

Batson, C. D. (1984). *A theory of altruistic motivation.* Unpublished manuscript, University of Kansas.

Batson, C. D., O'Quin, K., Fultz, J., Vanderplas, M., & Isen, A. M. (1983). Influence of self-reported distress and empathy on egoistic versus altruistic motivation to help. *Journal of Personality and Social Psychology, 45,* 706–718.

Baumeister, R. F. (1982). A self-presentational view of social phenomena. *Psychological Bulletin, 91,* 3–26.

Becker, E. (1975). The self as a locus of linguistic causality. In D. Brissett & C. Edgley (Eds.), *Life as theater* (pp. 58–67). Chicago: Aldine.

Becker, W. C., & Krug, R. S. (1964). A circumplex model for social behavior in children. *Child*

Development, 35, 371–396.

Belsky, J., Rovine, M., & Taylor, D. G. (1984). The Pennsylvania Infant and Family Development Project, III. The origins of individual differences in infant & mother attachment: Maternal and infant contributions. *Child Development, 55,* 718–728.

Benjamin, L. S. (1974). Structural analysis of social behavior. *Psychological Review, 81,* 392–425.

Birdwhistell, R. L. (1970). *Kinesics and context.* Philadelphia: University of Pennsylvania Press.

Bowlby, J. (1967). Foreword. In M. D. S. Ainsworth. *Infancy in Uganda.* Baltimore: Johns Hopkins Press.

Bowlby, J. (1969). *Attachment and loss.* Vol 1. *Attachment.* London: Hogarth.

Brehm, J. W. (1966). *A theory of psychological reactance.* New York: Academic Press.

Briggs, S. R., Cheek, J. M., & Buss, A. H. (1980). An analysis of the self-monitoring scale. *Journal of Personality and Social Psychology, 38,* 679–686.

Brodt, S. E., & Zimbardo, P. G. (1981). Modifying shyness-related social behavior through symptom misattribution. *Journal of Personality and Social Psychology, 41,* 437–449.

Buss, A. H. (1961). *The psychology of aggression.* New York: Wiley.

Buss, A. H. (1966). The effect of harm on subsequent aggression. *Journal of Experimental Research in Personality,* 1, 249–255.

Buss, A. H. (1980). *Self-consciousness and social anxiety.* San Francisco: Freeman.

Buss, A. H. (1985). Two kinds of shyness. In R. Schwarzer (Ed.), *Self-related cognitions* in anxiety and motivation (pp. 65–75). Hillsdale, NJ: Lawrence Erlbaum Associates.

Buss, A. H., & Briggs, S. R. (1984). Drama and the self in social interaction. *Journal of Personality and Social Psychology,* 47, 1310–1324.

Buss, A. H., & Durkee, A. (1957). An inventory for assessing different kinds of hostility. *Journal of Consulting Psychology, 21,* 343–349.

Buss, A. H., Iscoe, I., & Buss, E. (1979). The development of embarrassment. *Journal of Psychology, 103,* 227–230.

Buss, A. H., & Plomin, R. (1975). *A temperament theory of personality development.* New York: Wiley-Interscience.

Buss, A. H., & Plomin, R. (1984). *Temperament: Early developing personality traits.* Hillsdale, NJ: Lawrence Erlbaum Associates.

Buss, D. M. (1981). *The act frequency analysis of interpersonal dispositions.* Unpublished doctoral dissertation, University of California, Berkeley.

Buss, D. M., & Craik, K. H. (1983). The act frequency approach to personality. *Psychological Review,* 90, 105–126.

Buss, D. M., & Craik, K. H. (1985). Why *not* measure that trait? Alternative criteria for identifying important dispositions. *Journal of Personality and Social Psychology, 48,* 934–946.

Buss, L. (1980). *Does overpraise cause embarrassment?* Unpublished manuscript, University of California, Berkeley.

Buss, L. (1984). *A personality measure of formality.* Unpublished research, University of California, Berkeley.

Byrne, D. (1971). *The attraction paradigm.* New York: Academic Press.

Cairns, R. B. (1979). *Social development.* San Francisco: Freeman.

Campbell, D. T. (1975). On the conflicts between biological and social evolution and between psychology and moral tradition. *American Psychologist, 30,* 1103–1126.

Carey, W. B. (1970). A simplified method for measuring infant temperament. *Journal of Pediatrics, 77,* 188–194.

Carey, W. B., & McDevitt, S. C. (1978). Revision of the infant temperament questionnaire. *Pediatrics, 61,* 735–739.

Carson, R. C. (1969). *Interaction concepts of personality.* Chicago: Aldine.

Carver, C. S., & Scheier, M. F. (1981). *Attention and self-regulation: A control theory approach to human behavior.* New York: Springer Verlag.

Cattell, R. B. (1973). *Personality and mood by questionnaire.* San Francisco: Jossey-Bass.

Cheek, J. M., & Briggs, S. R. (1982). Self-consciousness and aspects of identity. *Journal of Research in Personality, 16,* 401-408.

Cheek, J. M., & Busch, C. M. (1981). The influence of shyness on loneliness in a new situation. *Personality and Social Psychology Bulletin, 7,* 572-577.

Cheek, J. M., & Buss, A. H. (1981). Shyness and sociability. *Journal of Personality and Social Psychology, 41,* 330-339.

Chlopan, B. E., McCain, M. L., Carbonell, J. L., & Hagen, R. L. (1985). Empathy: Review of available measures. *Journal of Personality and Social Psychology, 48,* 635-653.

Christie, R., & Geis, F. L. (Eds.). (1970). *Studies in machiavellianism.* New York: Academic Press.

Clark, M. S., & Mills, J. (1979). Interpersonal attraction in exchange and communal relationships. *Journal of Personality and Social Psychology, 37,* 12-24.

Conte, H. R., & Plutchik, R. (1981). A circumplex model for interpersonal personality traits. *Journal of Personality and Social Psychology, 40,* 701-711.

Crockenberg, S. (1981). Infant irritability, mother responsiveness, and social support influences on the security of infant-mother attachment. *Child Development, 52,* 857-865.

Daly, J. A., & McCroskey, J. C. (Eds.). (1984). *Avoiding communication.* Beverly Hills, CA: Sage.

Darley, J. M., & Fazio, R. H. (1980). Expectancy confirmation processes arising in the social interaction sequence. *American Psychologist,* 867-881.

Davis, M. H. (1979). *Individual differences in empathy: A multidimensional approach.* Unpublished doctoral dissertation, University of Texas.

Davis, M. H. (1983). Measuring individual differences in empathy: Evidence for a multidimensional approach. *Journal of Personality and Social Psychology, 44,* 113-126.

DePaulo, B. M., Stone, J. I., & Lassiter, G. D. (1985a). Deceiving and detecting deceit. In B. R. Schlenker (Ed.), *The self and social life* (pp. 323-370). New York: McGraw-Hill.

DePaulo, B. M., Stone, J. I., & Lassiter, G. D. (1985b). Telling ingratiating lies: Effects of target sex and target attractiveness on verbal and nonverbal deceptive success. *Journal of Personality and Social Psychology, 48,* 1191-1203.

Derber, C. (1979). *The pursuit of attention: Power and individualism in everyday life.* Boston, MA: G. K. Hall.

Driscoll, R., Davis, K. E., & Lipetz, M. E. (1972). Parental influence and romantic love: The Romeo and Juliet effect. *Journal of Personality and Social Psychology, 24,* 1-10.

Easterbrooks, M. A., & Lamb, M. E. (1979). The relationship between quality of mother-infant attachment and infant competence in initial encounters with peers. *Child Development, 50,* 380-387.

Egeland, B., & Farber, E. A. (1984). Infant-mother attachment: Factors related to its development and changes over time. *Child Development, 55,* 753-771.

Eibl-Eibesfeldt, I. (1971). *Love and hate.* London: Methuen.

Ekman, P. (1965). The differential communication of affect by head and body cues. *Journal of Personality and Social Psychology, 2,* 726-735.

Ekman, P., & Friesen, W. V. (1969). Nonverbal leakage and clues to deception. *Psychiatry, 32,* 88-106.

Ekman, P., & Friesen, W. V. (1974). Detecting deception from the body or face. *Journal of Personality and Social Psychology, 29,* 288-298.

Erkut, S., Jaquette, D. S., & Staub, E. (1981). Moral judgment-situation interaction as a basis for predicting prosocial behavior. *Journal of Personality, 49,* 1-14.

Eysenck, H. J. (1970). *The structure of human personality.* (rev. ed.) London: Methuen.

Fenigstein, A. (1979). Self-consciousness, self-attention, and social interaction. *Journal of Personality and Social Psychology, 37,* 75–86.

Fenigstein, A. (1984). Self-consciousness and the overperception of self as a target. *Journal of Personality and Social Psychology, 47,* 860–870.

Fenigstein, A., Scheier, M. F., & Buss, A. H. (1975). Private and public self-consciousness: Assessment and theory. *Journal of Consulting and Clinical Psychology, 43,* 522–527.

Foa, U. G., & Foa, E. B. (1974). *Societal structures of the mind.* Springfield, IL: Charles C. Thomas.

Fodor, E. M. (1984). The power motive and reactivity to power stresses. *Journal of Personality and Social Psychology, 47,* 853–859.

Fodor, E. M., & Farrow, D. L. (1979). The power motive as an influence on the use of power. *Journal of Personality and Social Psychology, 37,* 2091–2097.

Freedman, J. L. (1975). *Crowding and behavior.* San Francisco: Freeman.

French, J.R.P. Jr., & Raven, B. (1959). The bases of social power. In D. Cartwright (Ed.), *Studies in social power* (pp. 150–167). Ann Arbor, MI: Research Center for Group Dynamics.

Froming, W. J., Walker, G. R., & Lopyan, K. J. (1982). Public and private self-awareness: When personal attitudes conflict with societal expectations. *Journal of Experimental Social Psychology, 18,* 476–487.

Fromm, E. (1941). *Escape from freedom.* New York: Holt, Rinehart & Winston.

Gabrenya, W. K., & Arkin, R. M. (1980). Self-monitoring scale: Factor structure and correlates. *Personality and Social Psychology Bulletin, 6,* 13–22.

Gallup, G. G., Jr. (1970). Chimpanzees: Self-recognition. *Science, 167,* 86–87.

Gellert, E. (1961). Stability and fluctuation in the power relationships of young children. *Journal of Abnormal and Social Psychology, 62,* 8–15.

Goffman, E. (1959). *The presentation of self in everyday life.* Garden City, NY: Doubleday.

Goffman, E. (1961). *Asylums.* Garden City, NY: Anchor Books.

Goffman, E. (1967). *Interaction rituals.* Garden City, NY: Doubleday.

Hall, E. T. (1966). *The hidden dimension.* Garden City, NY: Doubleday.

Hall, J. A. (1984). *Nonverbal sex differences.* Baltimore: Johns Hopkins University Press.

Hamilton, W. D. (1964). The genetical evolution of social behavior. *Journal of Theoretical Biology, 7,* 1–52.

Harlow, H. F., & Harlow, M. (1962). Social deprivation in monkeys. *Scientific American, 207,* 136–146.

Harris, D. B. (1957). A scale for measuring attitudes of social responsibility in children. *Journal of Abnormal and Social Psychology, 55,* 322–326.

Hays, R. B. (1985). A longitudinal study of friendship development. *Journal of Personality and Social Psychology, 48,* 909–924.

Heinemann, U. (1979). The assessment of private and public self-consciousness: A German replication. *European Journal of Social Psychology, 9,* 331–337.

Hendrick, C., & Brown, S. R. (1971). Introversion, extraversion, and interpersonal attraction. *Journal of Personality and Social Psychology, 20,* 31–36.

Hetherington, M. E., & Brackbill, Y. (1963). Etiology and covariation of obstinacy, orderliness, and parsimony in young children. *Child Development, 34,* 919–943.

Hoffman, M. L. (1977). Sex differences in empathy and related behaviors. *Psychological Bulletin, 84,* 712–722.

Hoffman, M. L. (1981). Is altruism part of human nature? *Journal of Personality and Social Psychology, 40,* 121–137.

Hogan, R. (1969). Development of an empathy scale. *Journal of Consulting and Clinical Psychology, 33,* 307–316.

Hunter, J. E., Gerbing, D. W., & Boster, F. J. (1982). Machiavellian beliefs and personality:

Construct invalidity of the Machiavellianism dimension. *Journal of Personality and Social Psychology, 43,* 1293-1305.

Jackson, D. N. (1974). *Personality research form manual* (rev. ed.) Port Huron, MI: Research Psychologists Press.

Jackson, D. N., Ahmed, S. A., & Heapy, N. A. (1976). Is achievement a unitary construct? *Journal of Research in Personality, 10,* 1-21.

Johnson, J. A., Cheek, J. M., & Smither, R. (1983). The structure of empathy. *Journal of Personality and Social Psychology, 45,* 1299-1312.

Johnson-George, C., & Swap, W. C. (1982). Measurement of specific interpersonal trust: Construction and validation of a scale to assess trust in a specific other. *Journal of Personality and Social Psychology, 43,* 1306-1317.

Jones, E. E. (1964). *Ingratiation. A social psychological analysis.* New York: Appleton-Century-Crofts.

Jones, W. H., Cheek, J. M., & Briggs, S. R. (Eds.). (1985). *A sourcebook of shyness: Research and treatment.* New York: Plenum.

Kahneman, D., & Tversky, A. (1984). Choices, values and frames. *American Psychologist, 39,* 341-350.

Kelley, H. H. (1983). The situational origin of human tendencies: A further reason for the formal analysis of structures. *Personality and Social Psychology Bulletin, 9,* 8-30.

Kernis, M. H., & Reis, H. T. (1984). Self-consciousness, self-awareness, and justice in reward allocation. *Journal of Personality, 52,* 58-70.

Kiesler, D. J. (1983). The 1982 interpersonal circle: A taxonomy for complementarity in human transactions. *Psychological Review, 90,* 185-214.

Knapp, M. L. (1978). *Nonverbal communication in human interaction.* (2nd Ed.) New York: Holt, Rinehart, & Winston.

Kohlberg, L. (1969). Stage and sequence: The cognitive-developmental approach to socialization. In D. A. Goslin (Ed.), *Handbook of socialization theory and research* (pp. 347-380). Chicago: Rand McNally.

Korner, A., & Grobstein, R. (1966). Visual alertness as related to soothing in neonates: Implications for maternal stimulation and early deprivation. *Child Development, 37,* 867-876.

Lamb, M. E. (1976). *The role of the father in child development.* New York: Wiley.

Lamb, M. E. (1979). Parental influences and the father's role. *American Psychologist, 34,* 938-943.

Lasswell, H. D., & Kaplan, A. (1950). *Power and society.* New Haven, CT: Yale University Press.

Leary, M. R., & Schlenker, B. R. (1981). The social psychology of shyness: A self-presentation model. In J. T. Tedeschi (Ed.), *Impression management theory and social psychological research* (pp. 335-358). New York: Academic Press.

Leary, T. (1957). *Interpersonal diagnosis of personality.* New York: Ronald.

Lennox, R. D., & Wolfe, R. N. (1984). Revision of the self-monitoring scale. *Journal of Personality and Social Psychology, 46,* 1349-1364.

Loehlin, J. C., & Nichols, R. C. (1976). *Heredity, environment and personality.* Austin: University of Texas Press.

Lorenz, K. (1966). *On aggression.* London: Methuen.

Lorr, M., & McNair, D. M. (1963). An interpersonal behavior circle. *Journal of Abnormal and Social Psychology, 67,* 68-75.

Lorr, M., & McNair, D. M. (1965). Expansion of the interpersonal behavior circle. *Journal of Personality and Social Psychology, 2,* 823-830.

Lorr, M., & More, W. W. (1980). Four dimensions of assertiveness. *Multivariate Behavioral Research, 15,* 127-138.

Lorr, M., & Youniss, R. P. (1973). An inventory of interpersonal style. *Journal of Personality Assessment, 37,* 165-173.

Lott, A. J., & Lott, B. E. (1974). The role of reward in the formation of positive interpersonal attitudes. In T. L. Huston (Ed.), *Foundations of interpersonal attraction* (pp. 171-192). New York: Academic Press.

Maccoby, E. E., & Jacklin, C. N. (1974). *The psychology of sex differences.* Stanford, CA: Stanford University Press.

Mason, W. A. (1968). Early social deprivation in nonhuman primates: Implications for human behavior. In D. C. Glass (Ed.), *Biology and behavior: Environmental influences* (pp. 70-101). New York: Rockefeller University Press.

Mason, W. A. (1970). Motivational factors in psychosocial development. In U. J. Arnold & M. M. Page (Eds.), *Nebraska symposium on motivation* (pp. 35-67). Lincoln: University of Nebraska Press.

Matthews, K. A. (1980). Measurement of type A behavior in children: Assessment of children's competitiveness, impatience-anger, and aggression. *Child Development, 51,* 466-475.

Matthews, K. A. (1982). Psychological perspectives on the type A behavior pattern. *Psychological Bulletin, 91,* 293-323.

Matthews, K. A., Krantz, D. S., Dembroski, T. M., & MacDougall, J. M. (1982). Unique and common variance in structured interview and Jenkins Activity Survey measures of type A behavior pattern. *Journal of Personality and Social Psychology, 42,* 303-313.

McClelland, D. C. (1975). *Power: The inner experience.* New York: Irvington.

Megargee, E. I. (1969). The influence of sex roles in the manifestation of leadership. *Journal of Applied Psychology, 53,* 377-382.

Mehrabian, A., & Epstein, N. (1972). A measure of emotional empathy. *Journal of Personality, 40,* 525-543.

Mill, J. (1984). High and low self-monitoring individuals: Their decoding skills and empathic expression. *Journal of Personality, 52,* 372-388.

Miller, L. C., & Cox, C. L. (1982). For appearances' sake: Public self-consciousness and makeup use. *Personality and Social Psychology Bulletin, 8,* 748-751.

Mulac, A., & Sherman, A. R. (1974). Relationships among four parameters of speaker evaluation: Speech skill, source credibility, subjective speech anxiety, and behavioral speech anxiety. *Speech Monographs, 42,* 302-310.

Murray, H. A. (1938). *Explorations in personality.* New York: Oxford University Press.

Norton, R. (1983). *Communicator style.* Beverly Hills, CA: Sage.

Paivio, A., Baldwin, A. L., & Berger, S. (1961). Measurement of children's sensitivity to audiences. *Child Development, 32,* 721-730.

Pastor, D. L. (1981). The quality of mother-infant attachment and its relationship to toddlers' initial sociability with peers. *Developmental Psychology, 17,* 326-335.

Piaget, J. (1932). *The moral judgment of the child.* London: Kegan, Paul.

Pilkonis, P. A. (1977). The behavioral consequences of shyness. *Journal of Personality, 45,* 596-611.

Ray, J. J. (1981). Authoritarianism, dominance, and assertiveness. *Journal of Personality Assessment. 45,* 390-397.

Richmond, V. P. (Ed.). (1983). Communication apprehension. *Communication, 22,* 1-223.

Riggio, R. E., & Friedman, H.S. (1982). The interrelationships of self-monitoring factors, personality traits, and nonverbal social skills. *Journal of Nonverbal Behavior, 7,* 33-45.

Rosenberg, M. (1965). *Society and the adolescent self-image.* Princeton, NJ: Princeton University Press.

Rotter, J. B. (1966). Generalized expectancies for internal versus external control of reinforcement. *Psychological Monographs, 80* (Whole No. 609)

Rubin, Z. (1970). Measurement of romantic love. *Journal of Personality and Social Psychology, 16*, 265–273.

Rushton, J. P. (1980). *Altruism, socialization, and society*. Englewood Cliffs, NJ: Prentice-Hall.

Rushton, J. P., Chrisjohn, R. D., & Fekken, G.C. (1981). The altruistic personality and the self-report altruism scale. *Personality and Individual Differences, 2*, 293–302.

Rushton, J. P., Russell, J.H., & Wells, P. A. (1984). Genetic similarity theory: Beyond kin selection. *Behavior Genetics, 14*, 179–193.

Russell, D., Cutrona, C. E., Rose, J., & Yurko, K. (1984). Social and emotional loneliness: An examination of Weiss's typology of loneliness. *Journal of Personality and Social Psychology, 46*, 1313–1321.

Russell, D., Peplau, L. A., & Cutrona, C. E. (1980). The revised UCLA loneliness scale: Concurrent and discriminant validity evidence. *Journal of Personality and Social Psychology, 39*, 472–480.

Rutter, M. (1979). Maternal deprivation, 1972–1978: New findings, new concepts, new approaches. *Child Development, 50*, 283–305.

Savin-Williams, R. C. (1976). An ethological study of dominance formation and maintenance in a group of human adolescents. *Child Development, 47*, 972–979.

Savin-Williams, R. C. (1979). Dominance hierarchies in groups of early adolescents. *Child Development, 50*, 923–935.

Scarr, S., & McCartney, K. (1983). How people make their own environments: A theory of genotype-environment correlations. *Child Development, 54*, 424–435.

Scheier, M. F. (1976). Self-awareness, self-consciousness, and angry aggression. *Journal of Personality, 44*, 627–644.

Scherer, K. R., & Ekman, P. (Eds.). (1982). *Handbook of methods in nonverbal behavior research*. New York: Cambridge University Press.

Schlenker, B. R. (1980). *Impression management: The self-concept, social identity, and interpersonal relations*. Monterey, CA: Brooks/Cole.

Schlenker, B. R., & Leary, M. R. (1982). Social anxiety and self-presentation: A conceptualization and model. *Psychological Bulletin, 92*, 641–669.

Schulman, A. H., & Kaplowitz, C. (1977). Mirror-image response during the first two years of life. *Developmental Psychobiology, 10*, 133–142.

Schwartz, S. H. (1975). The justice of need and the activation of humanitarian norms. *Journal of Social Issues, 31*, 111–136.

Seligman, C., Fazio, R. H., & Zanna, M. P. (1980). Effects of salience on extrinsic rewards on liking and loving. *Journal of Personality and Social Psychology, 38*, 453–460.

Siegman, A. W., & Reynolds, M. A. (1983). Self-monitoring and speech in feigned and unfeigned lying. *Journal of Personality and Social Psychology, 45*, 1325–1333.

Simner, M. L. (1971). Newborn's response to the cry of another infant. *Developmental Psychology, 5*, 136–150.

Singerman, K. J., Borkovec, T. D., & Baron, R. S. (1976). Failure of a "misattribution therapy" manipulation with a clinically relevant target behavior. *Behavior Therapy, 7*, 306–313.

Slivken, K. E., & Buss, A. H. (1984). Misattribution and speech anxiety. *Journal of Personality and Social Psychology, 47*, 396–402.

Snodgrass, S. E., & Rosenthal, R. (1984). Females in charge: Effects of sex of subordinate and romantic attachment status upon self-ratings of dominance. *Journal of Personality, 52*, 355–371.

Snyder, M. (1974). The self-monitoring of expressive behavior. *Journal of Personality and Social Psychology, 30*, 526–537.

Snyder, M. (1979). Self-monitoring processes. In L. Berkowitz (Ed.), *Advances in experimental social psychology* (Vol. 12, pp. 86–128). New York: Academic Press.

Snyder, M. (1981). Impression management: The self in social interaction. In L. S. Wrightsman

& K. Deaux, *Social psychology in the eighties* (3rd Ed., pp. 90–123). Monterey, CA: Brooks/Cole.

Solomon, M. R., & Schopler, J. (1982). Self-consciousness and clothing. *Personality and Social Psychology Bulletin, 8,* 508–514.

Spence, J. T., & Helmreich, R. L. (1978). *Masculinity and femininity: Their psychological dimensions, correlates and antecedents.* Austin: University of Texas Press.

Sroufe, L. A. (1985). Attachment classification from the perspective of infant-caregiver relationships and infant temperament. *Child Development, 56,* 1–14.

Sroufe, L. A., Fox, N. E., & Pancake, V. R. (1983). Attachment and dependency in developmental perspective. *Child Development, 54,* 1615–1627.

Staub, E. (1978). *Positive social behavior and morality.* Vol. 1. New York: Academic Press.

Staub, E. (1979). *Positive social behavior and morality.* Vol. 2. New York: Academic Press.

Sternberg, R. J., & Grajek, S. (1984). The nature of love. *Journal of Personality and Social Psychology, 47,* 312–329.

Strom, J. C., & Buck, R. W. (1979). Staring and participants' sex: Physiological and subjective reactions. *Personality and Social Psychology Bulletin, 5,* 114–117.

Sullivan, H. S. (1953). *The interpersonal theory of psychiatry.* New York: Norton.

Tedeschi, J. T., & Norman, N. (1985). Social power, self-presentation, and the self. In B. R. Schlenker (Ed.), *The self and social life* (pp. 293–322). New York: McGraw-Hill.

Tedeschi, J. T., Smith, R. B., & Brown, R. C. (1974). A reinterpretation of research on aggression. *Psychological Bulletin, 81,* 540–562.

Teglasi, H., & Hoffman, M. A. (1982). Causal attributions of shy subjects. *Journal of Personality, 16,* 376–385.

Tennov, D. (1979). *Love and limerence.* New York: Stein & Day.

Thibaut, J. W., & Kelley, H. H. (1959). *The social psychology of groups.* New York: Wiley.

Thomas, E. J., & Biddle, B. J. (1966). The nature and history of role theory. In B. J. Biddle & E. J. Thomas (Eds.), *Role theory: Concepts and research* (pp. 3–19). New York: Wiley.

Thompson, R. A., & Lamb, M. E. (1983). Security of attachment and stranger sociability in infancy. *Developmental Psychology, 19,* 184–191.

Tobey, E. L., & Tunnell, G. (1981). Predicting our impressions on others: Effects of public self-consciousness and acting, a self-monitoring subscale. *Personality and Social Psychology Bulletin, 7,* 661–669.

Trivers, R. L. (1971). The evolution of reciprocal altruism. *The Quarterly Review of Biology, 46,* 35–57.

Tsuji, H. (1982). *Self-consciousness scale for Japanese children.* Unpublished research, Konen Women's University, Kobe, Japan.

Turner, J. L., Foa, E. B., & Foa, U. G. (1971). Interpersonal reinforcers: Classification, interrelationship and some differential properties. *Journal of Personality and Social Psychology, 19,* 168–180.

Turner, R. N. (1976). The real self: From institution to impulse. *American Journal of Sociology, 81,* 989–1016.

Uleman, J. S. (1972). The need for influence: Development and validation of a measure, and comparison with the need for power. *Genetic Psychology Monographs, 85,* 157–214.

Veroff, J. (1957). Development and validation of a projective measure of power motivation. *Journal of Abnormal and Social Psychology, 54,* 1–8.

Veroff, J. (1982). Assertive motivations: Achievement vs. power. In A. J. Stewart (Ed.), *Motivation and society* (pp. 99–132). San Francisco: Jossey-Bass.

Veroff, J., & Veroff, J. B. (1980). *Social incentives: A life-span developmental approach.* San Francisco: Academic Press.

Vleeming, R. G., & Engelse, J. A. (1981). Assessment of private and public self-consciousness: A Dutch replication. *Journal of Personality Assessment, 45,* 385–389.

Walster, E., Walster, G. W., & Berscheid, E. (1978). *Equity: Theory and research.* Boston: Allyn & Bacon.

Watson, D., & Friend, R. (1969). Measurement of social-evaluative anxiety. *Journal of Consulting and Clinical Psychology, 33,* 448–557.

Weiss, R. S. (1973). *Loneliness: The experience of emotional and social isolation.* Cambridge, MA: MIT press.

Weiss, R. S. (1974). The provisions of social relationships. In Z. Rubin (Ed.), *Doing unto others* (pp. 17–26). Englewood Cliffs, NJ: Prentice-Hall.

Wiesenfeld, A. R., Whitman, P. B., & Malatesta, C. Z. (1984). Individual differences among adult women in sensitivity to infants: Evidence for support of an empathy concept. *Journal of Personality and Social Psychology, 46,* 118–124.

Wiggins, J. S. (1979). A psychological taxonomy of trait-descriptive terms: The interpersonal domain. *Journal of Personality and Social Psychology, 37,* 395–412.

Winter, D. G. (1973). *The power motive.* New York: Free Press.

Wrong, D. H. (1979). *Power.* New York: Harper & Row.

Zajonc, R. B. (1965). Social facilitation. *Science, 149,* 269–274.

Zackrgewski, J. (1985). Personal communication, Polish Academy of Sciences, Warsaw, Poland.

Zuckerman, M. (1979). *Sensation seeking: Beyond the optimal level of arousal.* Hillsdale, NJ: Lawrence Erlbaum Associates.

Author Index

Subject Index

F